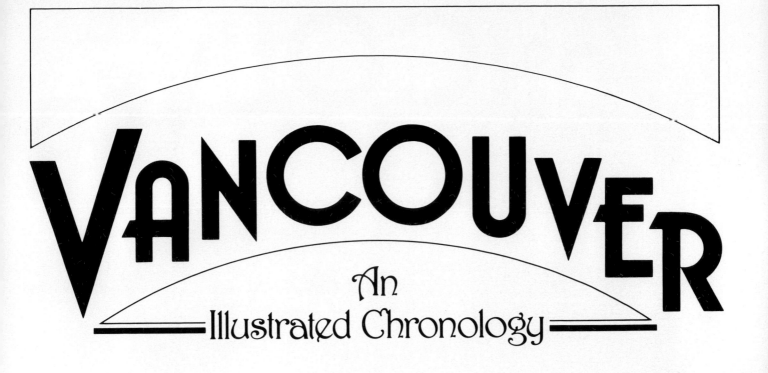

VANCOUVER

An Illustrated Chronology

VANCOUVER

An
Illustrated Chronology

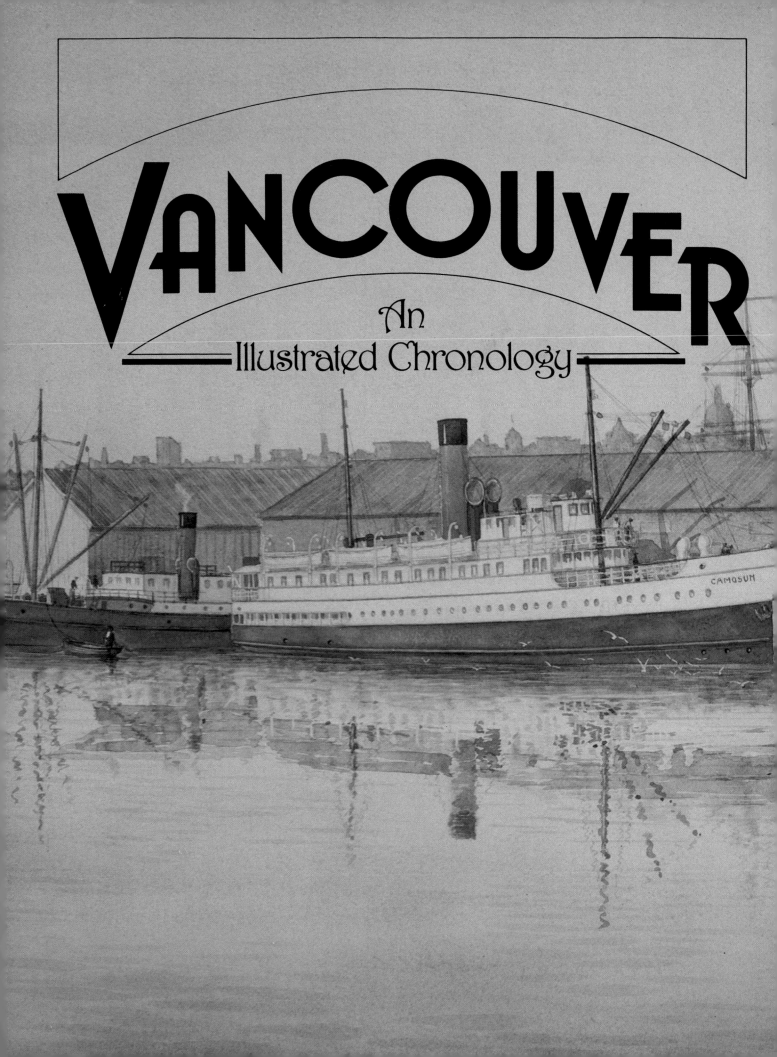

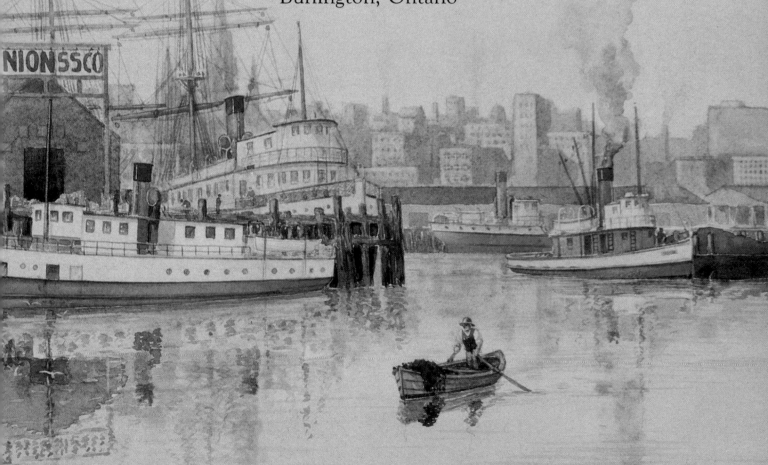

By Chuck Davis and Shirley Mooney
Photo Research by Henri Robideau
"Partners in Progress" by Moyra A. Pepper

Produced in cooperation with The Vancouver Board of Trade
Windsor Publications, Ltd.
Burlington, Ontario

NION SS CO

Windsor Publications—History Books Division
Publisher: John M. Phillips
Editorial Director: Teri Davis Greenberg
Design Director: Alexander D'Anca

Staff for *Vancouver: An Illustrated Chronology*
Senior Editor: Julie Jaskol
Director, Corporate Biographies: Karen Story
Assistant Director, Corporate Biographies: Phyllis Gray
Editor, Corporate Biographies: Judy Hunter
Sales Representative, Corporate Biographies: Beverly Cornell
Editorial Assistants: Kathy M. Brown, Laura Cordova, Marcie Goldstein,
    Marilyn Horn, Pat Pittman, Sharon L. Volz
Designer and Layout Artist: Thom Dower

Library of Congress Cataloging-in-Publication Data

Davis, Chuck, 1935-
    Vancouver : an illustrated chronology.

    "Produced in cooperation with the Vancouver Board
of Trade."
    Includes index.
    1. Vancouver (B.C.)—History—Chronology. 2. Vancouver
(B.C.)—Description. I. Mooney, Shirley. II. Title.
F1089.5.V22D39   1986   971.1'33   86-9270
ISBN 0-89781-176-3

Preceding pages: This watercolor of the Vancouver waterfront and Union Steamship docks was painted in 1907 by S.P. Judge, one of the founders of the Vancouver School of Art. Courtesy, Vancouver Grain Exchange

Facing page: Rain falls on Hastings Street at the turn of the century. For Vancouverites rain is a way of life—they happily accept the more than sixty inches a year of the stuff, cheerfully commenting, "We don't tan—we rust!" Courtesy, Vancouver Public Library (VPL)

Page six: The *Beaver*, a Hudson's Bay Company ship, was the first steamship on the Northwest Coast in 1836. This watercolor by W. Farris shows the ship wrecked off Prospect Point in Stanley Park. Courtesy, City of Vancouver Archives

CONTENTS

PROLOGUE

Imagine yourself in a balloon floating gently high above Vancouver, seeing the entire city in a glance. To the north you see the ship-crowded waters of Burrard Inlet, and beyond the inlet are the suburban cities of the North Shore and the dark green mountains of the Coast Range. To the south more suburbs spread across the broad delta of the Fraser River. To the west is Georgia Strait with its scattering of small islands. Past them is Vancouver Island's long shape of hills misted against the horizon. To the east are Burnaby, Port Moody, the Coquitlams, New Westminster, and a gradual smoothing of the land as the Fraser Valley begins. More than a million people live down there under your balloon.

From one small corner of this spectacularly beautiful peninsula a cluster of high office towers crowds upward: Harbor Centre, the black slab of the Toronto-Dominion Tower, the four Bentall buildings, the famous green copper roof of the Hotel Vancouver, the MacMillan-Bloedel Building with its deeply indented windows, the five beating sails of Canada Place and its glossy Pan Pacific Hotel and World Trade Centre, golden Park Place, the IBM Tower, Royal Centre, and a hundred more. At their bases, the streets swarm with people, with cars and trucks, with buses and motorcycles. Traffic signals flick, store windows glow with light, construction cranes swing in broad arcs, people climb into taxis and clamber out of buses, street crews chop at the pavement.

Just beyond this frenetic activity lies the quiet expanse of deep green trees and broad lawns of thousand-acre Stanley Park. Perhaps you can see a cricket game being played on the Brockton Point pitch. The West End's apartment blocks crowd up against the park, people moving behind their thousands of windows, looking south and west across English Bay to the very tip of the city's west side and the big rolling campus of the University of British Columbia.

Below you thousands of buildings of every size sprawl over the city's 114 square kilometres: houses, apartment blocks, schools, super-markets, churches, post offices, banks, computer shops, beauty parlors, libraries, gas stations, office blocks, grocery stores, restaurants, and hotels . . . .

And, everywhere, noise: cars and trucks race, horns blow, brakes screech, sirens wail, telephones ring, ships sound their horns, seaplanes lift with a roar from the inlet, factory machinery thumps, trains shunt on the waterfront, time whistles shriek, construction equipment rumbles, men yell, children laugh, and dogs bark . . . .

Stop.

Stay in that imaginary balloon high above the city, but now go back in your imagination to, let's say, July 5, 1791.

Much of what you see has not changed. The waters of Burrard Inlet are there . . . so are the dark green mountains of the Coast Range

... the broad delta of the Fraser River ... island-dotted Georgia Strait ... and a gradual smoothing into the Fraser Valley.

But below you now, instead of a city, spreads a dark rolling forest of tall trees. It is awesomely, frighteningly *quiet*. Wisps of smoke drift up from small fires in a scattering of Indian villages along the many shorelines, a branch snaps somewhere in the woods under the heavy foot of a bear, there is a small splash as a fish breaks the still waters of the inlet, and more quiet splashes from the paddles of a small flotilla of canoes.

The men in these canoes are paddling westward into the waters off what we now call Point Grey, staring in wild surmise at a small ship (gigantic to them!) that has just come into view. Great white blankets billow above the ship. The men in the canoes can see other men now, oddly dressed, moving around on the strange new vessel, pointing at the approaching canoes, shouting greetings.

The people of two different worlds are meeting for the first time.

And our chronology has begun.

This panoramic view of the city of Vancouver was drawn in 1898. Courtesy, City of Vancouver Archives

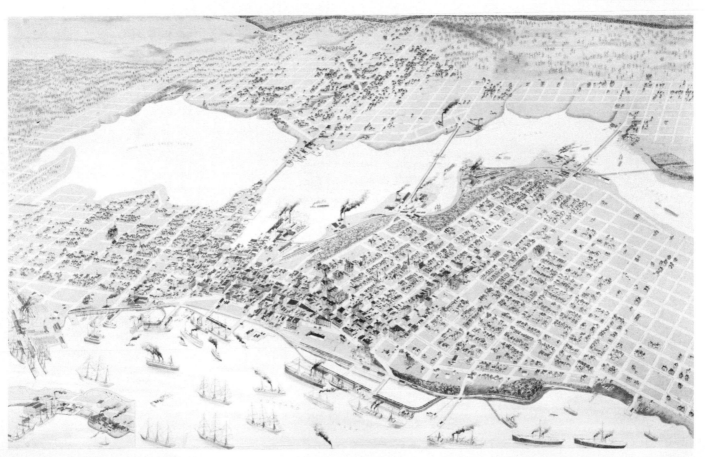

PART I

BEGINNINGS TO INCORPORATION

JULY 5, 1791 Spanish explorer Don Jose Maria Narvaez anchors west of Point Grey in command of the thirty-six-foot schooner *Santa Saturnina*. Narvaez, the first European to set eyes on the future site of Vancouver, makes an error-filled chart of the area.

JUNE 13, 1792 British explorer George Vancouver, his two ships anchored in the Gulf of Georgia, begins exploring local waters in two small skiffs. He lands on and names Point Grey (after a Navy friend, George Grey), then enters Burrard Inlet (named for Harry Burrard, another Navy friend).

JUNE 22, 1792 Vancouver is startled to meet two Spanish ships, commanded by explorers Dionisio Galiano and Cayetano Valdes, on English Bay. Vancouver and Galiano hit it off well and trade information and charts. On June 22 Vancouver turns thirty-five.

JUNE 25, 1792 Accompanied by the Spanish ships, Vancouver sails north for further exploration, leaving behind forever the site of the city that will be named for him. He takes note as he leaves of "a very great number of whales."

JULY 2, 1808 Simon Fraser of the Northwest Company, looking for new trade routes for furs, arrives at Musqueam at the mouth of the Fraser River. He and his men are chased off by angry Musqueam tribesmen and retreat up the river in their canoes.

1827 The Hudson's Bay Company, which now has complete control of trade west of the Rockies, establishes a trading post on the Fraser thirty miles from its mouth. They name it Fort Langley after a shareholder, and begin to trade with the local Indians.

JUNE 15, 1846 The 49th parallel is decided on as the U.S.-British border west of the Rockies, with a jog south around Vancouver Island. (The same parallel is already the border east of the Rockies.) The island is made a Crown colony under Governor James Douglas, with its capital at Fort Victoria.

1858 With the discovery earlier of gold on the Fraser, Governor Douglas establishes Crown control over the mainland. On April 25 some 450 wild-eyed prospectors arrive by ship from San Francisco— the first of a flood of 25,000.

AUGUST 2, 1858 The British parliament passes an act establishing the colony of British Columbia. Like Vancouver Island, it will be administered by James Douglas.

NOVEMBER 25, 1858 Colonel Richard Moody arrives from England with an advance party of twenty-five "sappers," or soldiers

Preceding pages: Deadman's Island was so called because it was an Indian burial ground. It later became the site of a whale-rendering plant and today is the site of HMCS Discovery. Courtesy, City of Vancouver Archives

charged with the construction of fortifications. Moody and his troops have been sent to show military force, but he will also be in charge of the colony's public works and will have an important affect on the physical development of Greater Vancouver with his construction of roads and selection of military reserves.

FEBRUARY 14, 1859 On Moody's advice, Douglas builds a new capital, Queensborough, on the north side of the Fraser downstream from Fort Langley. Moody has been dismayed by Fort Langley's position on the south side of the river, with its "back" to the Americans.

JUNE 13, 1859 Report is made of the discovery of coal on the south shore of Burrard Inlet by HMS *Plumper,* under Captain G.H. Richards. The coal is of good quality, but the seam is later discovered to be small.

JULY 20, 1859 Queensborough's name is changed to New Westminster by Queen Victoria. The city will be incorporated July 16, 1860.

ALSO IN 1859 Colonel Moody has a trail due north to Burrard Inlet from New Westminster built by private contractors. (We know it today as North Road, the first road on the peninsula.) It is to provide access to an ice-free harbor if the Fraser should freeze.

ALSO IN 1860 Smitten by Miss Lulu Sweet, a dancer in a touring show performed for the troops in New Westminster, Colonel Moody names Lulu Island in her honor.

1860 OR 1861 A government reserve for a townsite on the south shore of Burrard Inlet is created. This will later become known as Hastings Townsite.

WINTER OF 1861/1862 Moody's foresight in building North Road is rewarded; the Fraser freezes for three months and the road is used to haul freight on sleds from ships that have sailed into ice-free Burrard Inlet.

SEPTEMBER 26, 1862 The McCleery family becomes the first settlers in what is today's Vancouver when they occupy land on the north bank of the Fraser on what is now McCleery Golf Course.

OCTOBER 1862 A chunk of Burrard Inlet coal is seen in a New Westminster shop window by John Morton. Morton comes from a family of Yorkshire potters, and knows that where there is coal there is often clay—and from clay can be made bricks. He talks to the shop owner and learns that the coal was brought in by an Indian.

OCTOBER 1862 Morton, with his Indian coal-discoverer to guide him, visits the seam. They walk to Hastings Townsite, then west to Coal Harbor, packing between them a heavy box of provisions and blankets. The coal seam is a modest one and contains no clay. But Morton decides to pre-empt the land, anyway, and try farming. He and fellow immigrants Samuel Brighouse and William Hailstone file a claim of the area on November 3. Their 500 acres (Lot 185) cost 114 pounds, 11 shillings, 8 pence—about $550, or $1.01 an acre. Morton, Brighouse, and Hailstone settle near the north foot of today's Burrard Street, build a cabin, and start to raise cows. Wits in New Westminster, amused at the high price paid for such a remote piece of property, brand the men the "Three Greenhorns." Their claim is today's apartment-crammed West End.

WINTER 1862 T.W. Graham and Company of New Westminster pre-empts 480 acres of timber on the north shore of Burrard Inlet in an area later known as Moodyville. This is the beginning of a thriving lumber industry in the inlet.

FEBRUARY 1863 George Turner of the Royal Engineers makes a survey of Burrard Inlet, and begins to lay out lots. The area showing

Granville, later Vancouver, is depicted here in 1883 by Lauchlan Hamilton, a CPR surveyor. Courtesy, City of Vancouver Archives

14

today's West End is marked "Heavily timbered land very swampy in places."

MARCH 1863 Morton, Brighouse, and Hailstone have by now built themselves a cabin. It stands near the foot of present-day Burrard Street.

APRIL 1863 John Robson, editor of the *British Columbian* in New Westminster, hearing of cod fishing in Burrard Inlet, urges expansion of the trade. He also pushes for a road from New Westminster to the inlet near the First Narrows, citing a wealth of timber and a fine harbor.

END OF JUNE 1863 T.W. Graham's water-powered sawmill, the Pioneer Mills (the first industrial plant of any kind on Burrard Inlet) begins operations. Capacity is 40,000 feet in twenty-four hours, and logs are hauled in by oxen along skid roads.

AUGUST 1863 The first cargo (25,000 feet of three-inch plank) is shipped to New Westminster by Pioneer Mills aboard the *Flying Dutchman.* Aboard the vessel when it arrives at the inlet is a party

The University of British Columbia Museum of Anthropology houses one of the best collections of Northwest Coast Indian art in the world. The museum also serves as a centre for contemporary Native artists who often assist the anthropologists in identifying cultural artifacts. Photo by Henri Robideau

William Hailstone, Sam Brighouse, and John Morton (left to right) were known as "The Three Greenhorns." These three Englishmen pre-empted land in 1867 that became the entire West End of Vancouver. (VPL)

of New Westminster businessmen wanting to see Burrard Inlet. They also want to see HMS *Sutlej,* docked in the harbor. The *Sutlej,* under Admiral Kingcombe, is visiting apparently for the purpose of examining the inlet's suitability as a naval base.

OCTOBER 1863 The Columbia detachment of the Royal Engineers is disbanded. Colonel Moody returns to England with twenty-five or thirty of the force. The rest elect to stay in British Columbia, each allowed 150 acres of unoccupied land at no cost.

EARLY DECEMBER 1863 Pioneer Mills is unsuccessful, closes, and advertises an auction of the entire operation. It includes about a million feet of cut timber lying in the nearby woods. On December 16 John Oscar Smith, a grocer, buys the mill for $8,000 and changes its name to Burrard Inlet Mills. The only other bidder is Sewell "Sew" Moody, a seasoned New Westminster lumberman.

ALSO IN 1863 John Morton and William Hailstone, two of the Three Greenhorns, leave for the Cariboo to seek gold. Samuel Brighouse stays in the cabin to satisfy residence requirements of the pre-emption. Later, Hailstone will move to California. Morton will die in Vancouver April 18, 1912, aged seventy years and two days, living in a house on Pendrell Street, its lot a tiny portion of the land that once belonged to him. His will leaves nearly $770,000. Brighouse will prosper, as well.

APRIL 21, 1864 Frederick Seymour is appointed governor of the colony of British Columbia upon Governor Douglas' retirement.

NOVEMBER 9, 1864 John Oscar Smith ships 277,500 feet of lumber from Burrard Inlet Mills to Adelaide aboard the *Ellen Lewis*. This is the earliest export of lumber from the inlet to a foreign port.

DECEMBER 1864 Twelve months after he begins Burrard Inlet Mills, Smith fails. The mill and 480 acres of timber are sold to the patient Sewell Moody.

EARLY 1865 This is the year in which the lumber industry on the inlet really begins to grow. In the early part of the year Edward Stamp (who had first visited this part of the world back in 1858) arrives with New Brunswick logger Jeremiah "Jerry" Rogers to look over the south shore for a suitable sawmill site.

FEBRUARY 1865 Sewell Moody improves operations at his mill and starts a sales agency in New Westminster. He begins to build the first substantial lumber export business on the mainland, and will ship to California, Hawaii, Peru, China, Australia, New Zealand, and Great Britain.

SPRING 1865 It is noticed that the usual spring rush of miners from California fails to materialize. The gold rush has petered out.

APRIL 1865 Edward Stamp incorporates the British Columbia and Vancouver Island Spar, Lumber and Sawmill Company in England with a capital of 100,000 British pounds to buy timber limits and build a sawmill on Burrard Inlet.

JUNE 1865 Moody ships to New Westminster a load of "sticks" seventy feet long and twenty inches square without a knot in them. They will be used for the bell tower of the Trinity Church.

JUNE 28, 1865 Edward Stamp begins to clear land for a mill near Brockton Point, but tide rips at the First Narrows make the site unsuitable.

JULY 1865 Edward Stamp begins to build the British Columbia and Vancouver Island Spar, Lumber and Sawmill Company near the foot of present-day Dunlevy Street. He will also build a store this year. This building still exists, the oldest in Vancouver, but is moved in 1930 to a new location at the north foot of Alma Street. The Native Daughters of Vancouver operate it as a small museum.

JULY 1865 Stamp also contracts to have a steam tug built. The *Isobel* in Victoria will tow ships into and out of the inlet. (Sewell

Moody has been getting along without a steamer; his ships either sail in or are towed in by Victoria tugboats.)

JULY 30, 1865 The first religious service on Burrard Inlet is conducted by the Reverend Ebenezer Robson, a Methodist, at Moodyville. He preaches to fifteen men from the mill and the ship *Metropolis.*

AUGUST 1865 Oliver Hocking and Fred Houston open the Brighton Hotel, with "beautiful grounds and picturesque walks" at the north end of Douglas Road, about where the north foot of Windermere Street is today. They build a floating wharf, and welcome vacationers from New Westminster.

NOVEMBER 4, 1865 Stamp begins to ship spars out on chartered vessels. The *Aquila* sails for Ireland on this date with 251 spars cut

English photographer Frederick Dally came to British Columbia in 1862 because of the Cariboo gold rush. On one of his many trips from Victoria to Barkerville he photographed this Indian settlement, circa 1866, which was located on Lost Lagoon at the foot of what is now Robson Street. This may well be the first photograph taken of what would one day be the city of Vancouver. (VPL)

by Jerry Rogers on English Bay near Kitsilano. There is an assortment of other British Columbia products aboard: hides, wool, codfish, salmon, and cranberries.

DECEMBER 20, 1865 The *Kent* arrives at Burrard Inlet from Glasgow with a shipment of machinery for Stamp's Mill. It has not brought all the required machinery, because of an error by the manufacturer, and Stamp is delayed in beginning operations.

ALSO IN 1865 Esquimalt, on Vancouver Island, becomes a station of the Royal Navy.

MARCH 1, 1866 Oliver Hocking is made deputy collector of customs at Burrard Inlet. It will now be possible for ships to leave Burrard Inlet without their captains having to walk through the woods to New Westminster to fill out the necessary papers.

AUGUST 6, 1866 The Crown colonies of Vancouver Island and British Columbia are united, and will henceforth be known as British Columbia.

MARCH 28, 1867 The British North America Act (in effect, Canada's constitution) becomes law.

JUNE 18, 1867 Edward Stamp finally begins cutting wood at his mill, two years behind schedule. It will be called Stamp's Mill by everyone, after its manager. The water for its operation is brought in by a three-mile-long flume from Trout Lake. A marker at the north foot of Dunlevy Street today shows where the mill was. Stamp will sue the machinery maker for the delay in getting all the required parts, and will win.

JULY 1, 1867 Confederation. Canada is created, and John A. Macdonald becomes the first prime minister. British Columbia will join Confederation four years later.

SEPTEMBER 30, 1867 John "Gassy Jack" Deighton, thirty-six, a talkative Yorkshireman who has been a river pilot on the Fraser, arrives at Burrard Inlet with "his wife, $6 in cash, a few sticks of furniture, a yellow dog and a barrel of whiskey." With the help of thirsty sawmill workers (the nearest drink was a fifteen-mile walk to New Westminster), he builds a saloon in twenty-four hours. Gastown begins. Historian Alan Morley writes: "Jack set up his saloon just near enough to the mill to cater to its crew, and just far enough away to be beyond the company's control." It stood where Water and Carrall streets meet today. "I can assure you it was a lonesome place when I came here first," Deighton writes his brother Tom in England. "Surrounded by Indians. I dare not look outdoors after dark. There was a friend of mine, about a mile distant, found with his head cut in two."

ALSO IN 1867 Jerry Rogers begins to log in today's Kitsilano area. His operation is at Jerry's Cove, which becomes known as Jericho.

MARCH 1868 The wharf at Stamp's Mill collapses, and 300,000 feet of sawn lumber floats away on the tide.

MAY 25, 1868 The capital of British Columbia is changed from New Westminster to Victoria.

END OF JUNE 1868 In a little more than a year Stamp's Mill has shipped out 4.1 million feet of lumber and 100,000 shingles. Moody's mill has been almost equally productive, and the quality and size of Burrard Inlet timber has become world famous.

NOVEMBER 1868 Hastings Townsite is created from what has been informally known as New Brighton. It is named for Rear-Admiral Hastings, in command of the Pacific Squadron (based at Esquimalt).

ALSO IN 1868 "Portuguese Joe" (Joseph Silvia Simmons), a Delta cattle drover, opens Gastown's first store, a grocery. Located on what is now the southeast corner of Abbott and Water streets, it contains a saloon. Indians bring clams, eggs, vegetables, and fish there to trade.

ALSO IN 1868 R.H. Alexander opens a post office in the store at Stamp's Mill. Canadian stamps will begin to be sold. Heretofore, American stamps had been used.

ALSO IN 1868 George Black arrives, Gastown's first butcher. Nicknamed the "Laird of Granville," he builds a house, shop, and abbatoir projecting out over the water on piles. He slaughters local cattle and hogs and sells meat to visiting ships. His hogs roam the beach, feeding on garbage and clams.

EARLY JANUARY 1869 Edward Stamp—unable to make a financial success of the mill he has managed, despite its great output—leaves Burrard Inlet and returns to England. He owes $6,000 in back wages to Jerry Rogers. The company and its assets are sold in May for $20,000 to Dickson, DeWolf and Company of San Francisco. Stamp is succeeded as manager by Captain James Raymur. Raymur is also armed with the authority of resident magistrate. Described as a "polished gentleman," he looks at the squalor surrounding the mill and says, "What is the meaning of this aggregation of filth?" Saying "I will not permit a running sore to fasten itself upon an industry entrusted to my care!" Raymur will clean things up in and around the mill and rename it Hastings Mill, a name it will bear for more than sixty years.

JANUARY 19 OR 23, 1869 The New London Mechanics Institute is founded at Hastings Mill as a meeting and reading room. It will be renamed Hastings Literary Institute in March, and is counted by some as the city's first library.

MARCH 1869 Hocking and Houston sell their hotel at New Brighton to Maximilien Michaud who has walked to the Pacific Coast from eastern Canada. "Maxie" Michaud will rename it the Hastings Hotel and turn it into a favorite watering hole for vacationing New Westminsterites.

APRIL 11, 1869 The first message goes out over the newly completed telegraph line from Moody's Mill on the North Shore to

Hastings Townsite to New Westminster. The line, which includes a submarine cable across the inlet, has been paid for by Moody.

MAY 1869 The area informally known as New Brighton is formally named Hastings Townsite, and lots are sold.

MAY 31, 1869 Stamp's Mill is sold by its English founders to a San Francisco group.

JUNE 29, 1869 The colonial government grants licences to Gassy Jack Deighton and Ebenezer Brown to operate saloons at Burrard Inlet. Deighton has been operating his for nearly two years.

ALSO IN 1869 Rear-Admiral Hastings ends his tour of duty, but his name will live on in Hastings Townsite, Hastings Street, and other place names. R.H. Alexander begins working at Stamp's Mill. His family will follow next year, and his son Henry will become the first white child born within the present city of Vancouver. Government surveyors are busily mapping Burrard Inlet.

MARCH 1, 1870 The Granville Townsite survey is registered. It includes the area between modern Carrall, Hastings, and Cambie streets and extends to the waterfront. Within this area are three saloons, one hotel, and two stores.

Students pose in front of Vancouver's first school, situated on the Hastings Sawmill lands and opened in 1873. Courtesy, City of Vancouver Archives

MARCH 10, 1870 Granville Townsite is named. Lots will be sold April 11. Virtually everyone continues to call it Gastown. (There are varying theories for the name, but today most people believe Gastown was named for "Gassy Jack" Deighton.) For the next fifteen years, Gastown will remain little more than a clearing on the edge of Burrard Inlet.

ALSO IN 1870 Gassy Jack builds a larger hotel, the Deighton House. It is not as successful as his saloon has been.

ALSO IN 1870 The British Columbia and Vancouver Island Spar, Lumber and Sawmill Company becomes Hastings Mill. Gastown gets a jail.

JULY 20, 1871 British Columbia joins Confederation, and so becomes a part of Canada. One of the stipulations it has made is that the railway be extended to link the province with the rest of the country. Burrard Inlet celebrates with a day of races and sports, and Gassy Jack raises a Canadian flag over his saloon.

ALSO IN 1871 Gassy Jack's second wife (whom he married when she was twelve) bears him a son, Richard. The child will be sickly and backward and will be wryly known as the "Earl of Granville." Jonathan Miller is appointed provincial government agent in Granville.

OCTOBER 2, 1872 The first bridge is opened over False Creek. The creek at this time extends much farther east, and the bridge is where Main Street is today. It leads to a trail down to the Fraser River.

ALSO IN 1872 Granville gets a post office, and the use of Canadian stamps becomes more general.

Vancouver started life as the seedy sawmill town of Granville—affectionately known as Gastown to the many mill hands who came to get gassed in its smoke-filled saloons. The nearby Hastings Sawmill was the reason for Granville's existence from its beginnings in 1870 until the coming of the Canadian Pacific Railway in 1886. (VPL)

ALSO IN 1872 John Jessop, superintendent of education, suggests endowment lands be set aside for a university.

FEBRUARY 12, 1873 Granville gets its first school.

SUMMER 1873 Gassy Jack brings his brother Tom, forty, from England to run his hotel. Tom's wife Emma takes an immediate dislike to her brother-in-law and his wife and son.

DECEMBER 23, 1873 Sewell Moody's steam-powered mill burns down. A New Brunswick lumberman, John Hendry, twenty, is hired to superintend its reconstruction.

END OF 1873 Gastown's population is sixty-five.

ALSO IN 1873 Daily steamboat service from Granville to New Westminster begins. The first baby is born in Hastings Townsite to Mr. and Mrs. Richard Alexander. The baby's name is Henry. Henry, the first white child born within the limits of the present city of Vancouver, will grow up to be a magistrate.

APRIL 1874 Gassy Jack Deighton advertises in New Westminster papers "the new Deighton House . . . [with] comfortable parlours and commodious single and double bedrooms." It's managed by his brother Tom and Tom's wife, Emma. Jack returns to the river, becoming master of the new steamer *Onward.*

SEPTEMBER 1874 Gassy Jack, now seriously ill, has a run-in with his brother's wife Emma. "She hated the little Earl of Granville, you know, and she spread the rumor that I didn't have the tackle to father him, and that his mother Madeline had laid with someone else to get pregnant. Didn't take long for that to get back to me, of course;

Granville circa 1883 was the single-street town that was to become the third largest city in Canada. (VPL)

so didn't I just raise hell with her!" Jack takes back control of his hotel. Tom and Emma move to Victoria.

ALSO IN 1874 Joseph Mannion arrives and opens the Granville Hotel. Educated and well-to-do, he will become known as the "mayor" of Granville. A daily steamboat service is established to New Westminster, and a skid road is built from around the present Victory Square down to the inlet. Today it's Cambie Street north of Hastings.

MAY 29, 1875 Gassy Jack lies dying in New Westminster, as a dog barks incessantly outside his window. "Look after the boy," he tells his wife. Then, growling "Damn the dog! I wish he'd shut up," he dies.

ALSO IN 1875 The SS *Pacific,* en route from Victoria to San Francisco, is rammed and sinks with heavy loss of life. Among the victims is Sewell Moody.

JULY 1876 The road between Granville and Hastings is completed.

ALSO IN 1876 A road is begun to connect Granville to Hastings. It will be completed in 1877. We know it today as Hastings Street.

ALSO IN 1876 Morton, Brighouse, and Hailstone divide the "Brickmakers' Claim" amongst themselves. Brighouse takes the eastern third abutting on Burrard Street, Morton that adjoining Stanley Park, and Hailstone takes the middle piece.

DECEMBER 1877 Prime Minister Mackenzie announces adoption of the Fraser Valley route to get the Canadian Pacific Railway (CPR) to tidal water.

JUNE 29, 1878 The *Moodyville Tickler* appears, the first newspaper on Burrard Inlet. Produced by William Colbeck, a mill employee, the *Tickler* deals in jokes and local gossip, and has a short life. It's also expensive: fifty cents.

ALSO IN 1879 The Macdonald government decides on Burrard Inlet as the terminus of the CPR. There is an explosion of land speculation in Port Moody at the head of the inlet.

MAY 14, 1880 Construction of the British Columbia section of the CPR begins at Yale in the Fraser Canyon.

FEBRUARY 1, 1881 A son, Joseph, is born in New Westminster to John and Jane Morton, with his sister Lizzie (born in England in 1879) the only children born to any of the Three Greenhorns. Mrs. Morton dies two days after Joseph is born. Joseph himself will die

Some of the world's largest fir and cedar trees were hacked down to make way for the new city. This prime specimen was used as a real estate office for these tinhorns. (VPL)

in the Asylum for the Insane March 2, 1933, obsessed with his exclusion from his father's will and the belief that someone had manipulated the will after his father's death.

FEBRUARY 16, 1881 A huge land grant of 10,120 hectares (25,000 acres) is given the CPR. It includes most of today's downtown.

ALSO IN 1881 The CPR sends an engineer, John Ross, to Burrard Inlet to survey for a port site. His report, completed in 1882, will recommend strongly against Port Moody because of the shallowness of the water there. He recommends Granville instead. The railway and the government will agree, but will not make their decision known immediately.

ALSO IN 1881 A census of Granville/Hastings (they are beginning to be considered as one) shows two shoemakers, forty-four loggers, one policeman, thirty-one millworkers, four butchers, one schoolteacher, two ministers, and one wine merchant. An additional 100 laborers perform various jobs from saddle-making to construction work. The census does not count wives, children, Chinese, Indians, or prostitutes.

JULY 1882 Captain James Raymur dies, and Richard Alexander becomes manager of Hastings Mill.

ALSO IN 1883 CPR surveyor Lauchlan Hamilton arrives in Vancouver.

MARCH 15, 1883 A shipment of steel for the CPR arrives at Port Moody. More will come in June. In October a locomotive bought from the Panama Railway is landed there. The people of Port Moody still believe their town will be the terminus of the railway, and display an amused contempt for the aspirations of "Gastown."

DECEMBER 12, 1883 The first local telephone call is made, between Port Moody and New Westminster.

JANUARY 23, 1884 The first through train runs from Port Moody to Yale.

JUNE 14, 1884 William Van Horne, general manager of the CPR, begins negotiations with Premier Smithe for extension of the railway's line to Granville, with a right of way to Kitsilano along the southern shore of False Creek. In return, Van Horne will ask for half the present peninsula on which Vancouver stands today.

AUGUST 6, 1884 Van Horne arrives at Burrard Inlet. On September 16 he will ask the railway's directors to choose Granville as the terminus of the railway, not Port Moody. He also decides Granville's name must be changed to better locate it on the world map. He keeps his decisions a secret, except from Lauchlan Hamilton, to whom—according to archivist Major Matthews—he says, "Hamilton! This is destined to be a great city in Canada. We must see that it has a name that will designate its place on the map in Canada. Vancouver it shall be, if I have the ultimate decision." He did.

SEPTEMBER 1884 A pamphlet called *West Shore,* published in Portland, Oregon, says, "It is only once in a lifetime that the public has such a chance as the present, and we would recommend those who have money to invest to investigate the merits of Vancouver on Coal Harbor before making investments."

OCTOBER 6, 1884 The negotiations between the CPR and the provincial government conclude; the railway will get 6,000 acres of land. The grant includes almost the entire waterfront from Gore Avenue to Stanley Park, and will make the railway the city's biggest landlord for a century. Five days later, the Port Moody *Gazette* writes, "It is well known at Lloyd's that Port Moody is safe in every respect, but that in stormy weather, none of the other places is safe for ships. How anyone in his senses could believe the extension would be made, or if made, could be of any use, appears very droll to us."

NOVEMBER 7, 1885 The CPR drives its last spike at Craigellachie in the Rocky Mountains. A few days later a transcontinental freight train arrives at Port Moody.

ALSO IN 1885 Lauchlan Hamilton begins to survey downtown Vancouver. The placement of the streets today is pretty much as he determined it.

JANUARY 15, 1886 Vancouver's first newspaper appears. The *Herald* will have a short life, dying October 12, 1887.

END OF FEBRUARY 1886 Granville continues its rapid growth. Lauchlan Hamilton records that at this time there are barely 100 habitable buildings. By the middle of May there will be at least 600. Some 500 buildings have gone up in 75 days.

APRIL 6, 1886 An act to incorporate the city of Vancouver is given royal assent by Lieutenant-Governor Cornwall. The new city has begun.

Vancouver started as a sawmill, and lumbering has always been an important part of the city's development. (VPL)

PART II

Preceding pages: Three days after the Great Fire Vancouver's first city council and officials were meeting in a tent at the foot of Carrall Street to plan the reconstruction of a devastated city. (VPL)

Left: Malcolm A. MacLean, a real estate dealer, was Vancouver's first mayor. He was elected in 1886, defeating R.H. Alexander by seventeen votes. (VPL)

APRIL 27, 1886 Margaret Florence McNeil is born, the first white child born in the city after incorporation.

MAY 1886 The population of Vancouver is said to be about 1,000. The population of New Westminster is 3,000, of Victoria about 10,000.

MAY 3, 1886 The first election is held in Vancouver. It's as honest as most elections in pioneer towns, which is to say not very. Both sides are guilty of shady practices. Malcolm MacLean wins over Hastings Mill manager R.H. Alexander as mayor by 242 to 225. Indians, Orientals, lunatics, and women are not allowed to vote. Only those who are white male landowners may vote, but many cast ballots who own no land. The election costs $83.75.

MAY 10, 1886 The first council meeting is held in Jonathan Miller's living room and the first resolution passed is an appeal to Ottawa to grant the military reserve on the west to the new city as a park. Approval comes in due course, and Stanley Park is born.

MAY 15, 1886 CPR surveyor and Vancouver alderman Lauchlan Hamilton begins surveying what will become Granville Street south of Nelson.

MAY 28 OR JUNE 2, 1886 Vancouver's first fire department,

Volunteer Hose Company Number One, is formed under Chief F. Peagriff. An engine is ordered, but it will be some time before it arrives from Ontario.

JUNE 13, 1886 A fire, began to burn slash near the ramshackle collection of wooden buildings that is the city of Vancouver, suddenly flares out of control. Buildings begin to catch fire, and soon the whole town is ablaze. The fire is over within an hour, and although the death toll will never be known, an estimate of about twenty is made. The town begins to rebuild almost while the ashes are still warm.

JULY 4, 1886 Engine 371 pulls into Port Moody, the first train to reach coastal waters in western Canada.

AUGUST 1, 1886 Vancouver's first fire engine, a Ronald, arrives. Horses to pull it are not available.

AUGUST 12, 1886 Spratt's Refinery burns. The fire department, lacking horses, can't get to the scene with the new engine, and Spratt's is destroyed.

SEPTEMBER 1, 1886 The city's first bank, the English-owned Bank of British Columbia, which has no connection with today's bank,

The first resolution of the first Vancouver City Council was to ask the federal government for a park site on what was then known as the First Narrows Military Reserve. The request was granted and the park opened September 27, 1888, named after Lord Stanley, the governor general of Canada. (VPL)

opens in a building on the site of the present CPR station. In 1901 the bank will be absorbed by the Bank of Commerce.

BY THE END OF 1886 The little city of Vancouver boasts fourteen offices, twenty-three hotels, fifty-one stores, nine saloons, one church, one roller skating rink, and more than 8,000 people.

FEBRUARY 24 OR 28, 1887 There are anti-Chinese riots in Vancouver. Chinese camps on False Creek and Coal Harbor are burned. In ensuing riots Vancouver's charter is suspended and the city is put under the custody of the provincial police.

MAY 1887 Vancouver's first union is created with the formation of Local 226 of the International Typographical Union. The local holds an immediate strike for an increase in their pay of eighteen dollars a week.

The first Hotel Vancouver stood on the southwest corner of Georgia and Granville streets in 1888 and had a commanding view of the budding young city. William Van Horne, general manager of the CPR, commented upon seeing the finished building that it looked more like a hospital than a hotel. (VPL)

MAY 16, 1887 The first Hotel Vancouver opens, a week before the first through passenger train from Montreal arrives. Its location at Georgia and Granville is ridiculed by some for being too far from the centre of town. William Van Horne, general manager of the CPR (which owns the hotel) says to architect T.C. Sorley, "So you're the damned fool who spoilt the building with all those little windows." The hotel's fabulous views and luxurious style, however, ensure its success, and other businesses—such as the Hudson's Bay Company—build nearby.

MAY 23, 1887 The first CPR passenger train arrives in Vancouver. The train is greeted by Henry Abbott, general superintendent of the CPR, Mayor MacLean, a band, and the volunteer fire brigade. Legend has it that the first passenger to step down off the train is Jonathan Rogers, twenty-two, who will stay on to become a very successful developer and builder. He begins as a painter, and works on the new Hotel Vancouver. With the arrival of the railway, Vancouver's growth begins in earnest.

JUNE 13, 1887 The CPR-chartered *Abyssinia,* the first passenger ship to come to Vancouver, arrives from Yokohama. There are twenty-two first-class and eighty Chinese steerage passengers, as well

The Sunnyside Hotel on Water Street was decked out for Queen Victoria's Golden Jubilee and the arrival of the first CPR train in 1887. The first Sunnyside Hotel burned in the 1886 fire and this one was built to replace it. (VPL)

as a cargo of mail, tea, and silk headed for London. An enthusiastic crowd greets the boat and the Vancouver tradition of "going down to watch the boat come in" is launched. The *Abyssinia*'s arrival marks the start of the Trans-Pacific service, which plays a significant role in the city's growth.

AUGUST 8, 1887 The first electric streetlights are turned on in Vancouver. There are 53 streetlights and 300 private lights. The steam-run power plant doesn't generate much power; the lights on Granville Street barely illuminate.

SEPTEMBER 2, 1887 Police raid Chinese homes looking for white slavers.

SEPTEMBER 7, 1887 The Asiatic Exclusion League demonstrates against the arrival of the SS *Monteagle.* They erect a sign reading "900 Hindus, 1,100 Chinamen, and a bunch of Japs." From 1878 to 1913 more than two dozen anti-Chinese statutes will be passed in B.C.

SEPTEMBER 22, 1887 The Vancouver Board of Trade is formed.

Facing page: In 1888 an outing to Jericho Beach was a major excursion. That portion of Point Grey was practically uncharted wilderness accessible only by water. (VPL)

Below: Every time a passenger ship berthed in Vancouver, it seemed like half the town turned out to greet it, as appears to be the case here with the arrival of the CPR steamer *Empress of India* on April 28, 1891. (VPL)

There are thirty charter members, who have each paid twenty dollars to join. The new board wastes no time in making its presence felt, and sends off eleven proposals to the provincial secretary; they include requests for a resident judge, a courthouse, a land registry office, school improvement, a new bridge over the North Arm of the Fraser, a new post office . . . .

DECEMBER 14, 1887 The city opens its first free public library, at 136 Cordova, operated by a citizens' board headed by the Reverend H.G.F. Clinton, rector of St. James Church. The library is stocked with books from the Hastings and Moodyville mills. Some sixty-three subscribing members pay fifty cents a month.

ALSO IN 1887 The Salvation Army begins in Vancouver with four ladies known as the "Hallelujah Lassies."

JANUARY 1888 Construction begins on the CPR Roundhouse at the east foot of Drake Street in "Yaletown," so named because the CPR shops have been moved to Vancouver from Yale, B.C. The first local of the Brotherhood of Railway Engineers is established by craftsmen working on the roundhouse.

FEBRUARY 2, 1888 A by-law banning women from the Vancouver Reading Room is rescinded. Ladies may now attend upon payment of the usual fees.

JULY 26, 1888 The SS *Beaver* sinks off Brockton Point.

SEPTEMBER 1888 Vancouver's population is now 8,000.

SEPTEMBER 27, 1888 Stanley Park is officially opened by Mayor David Oppenheimer. The usual band, fire brigade volunteers, officials, and dignitaries are on hand.

SEPTEMBER 28, 1888 A city hospital is opened at Beatty and

Cambie. Jointly financed by the province and the city, the new facility has thirty-five beds and replaces a CPR hospital established in 1886.

SEPTEMBER 29, 1888 The *World,* a daily newspaper, is founded by J.C. McLagan. It supports the Liberal Party.

NOVEMBER 12, 1888 Dawson Elementary School opens with a principal, two teachers, and 129 pupils. False Creek School in Mount Pleasant is opened the same day, with forty-two pupils and "seventy more spoken for."

ALSO IN 1888 Vancouver now has thirty-six miles of streets and twenty-four miles of wooden sidewalk.

ALSO IN 1888 White clamshells from a gigantic Indian "kitchen midden" in Stanley Park are used to pave the first roads in the park. The roads have been surveyed by Lauchlan Hamilton.

MARCH 26, 1889 A paid fire department is organized to replace the volunteers. John Howe Carlisle is appointed fire chief at seventy-five dollars a month. There are twenty-two others: two engineers, two stokers, two drivers, six permanent men, and ten call men.

Only three years before this photo was taken, this part of the city was still virgin forest with 100-foot-high trees. In this 1889 view from the first Hotel Vancouver there were still plenty of lots available in what was to become the very heart of downtown Vancouver. (VPL)

NOVEMBER 21, 1889 The first meeting is held of the Trades and Labor Council. The council has been formed after a resolution initiated by the Carpenters Union.

DECEMBER 1889 Benjamin Tingley Rogers, twenty-four, of New York, proposes a sugar refinery in Vancouver. He has experience in sugar refining, and his plans intrigue the CPR's William Van Horne and his associates. They subscribe more than $80,000 to the project. The Rogers Sugar Refinery has become a waterfront landmark.

DECEMBER 5, 1889 The first Shakespeare play is seen in Vancouver when *Richard III* is presented at the Imperial Opera House. (The building doubles as roller skating rink.) The Imperial Opera House opens this year, and is the second in the city.

ALSO IN 1889 Market Hall opens at the northeast corner of Main and Pender. The main floor is a public market for poultry and produce, the lane outside is for horses, cattle, and swine. The second floor is a theatre, used for concerts and political meetings.

ALSO IN 1889 A lot at the corner of Hastings and Cambie sells for $7,600.

ALSO IN 1889 The Marpole Midden is discovered by workmen extending Granville Street. Tools, weapons, and other artifacts are found in what later proves to be the largest village midden discovered in North America to that date. It extends over 4.5 acres. In 1898 the American Museum of Natural History carries out excavations. Vancouver anthropologist Charles Hill-Tout examines the midden and mistakenly identifies the midden people as Eskimoid. They are,

Hastings Sawmill employees in dark-face dressed up as the "Dark Town Fire Brigade" for the 1889 Dominion Day parade. Such displays were symptomatic of the racist attitudes that led to the formation of organizations like the Asiatic Exclusion League which later caused the 1907 riots in Chinatown. (VPL)

in fact, Salish. They abandoned the site as land built up by the river began to isolate it from the sea.

JANUARY 3 OR 4, 1890 Fraser River ice causes a partial collapse of the North Arm Bridge, completed a few weeks earlier by the San Francisco Bridge Company. It is repaired quickly.

JANUARY 13, 1890 Central School opens on Pender between Hamilton and Cambie. It has eight rooms, and is the city's first brick school. It will be demolished in the spring of 1948.

JUNE 26, 1890 The Vancouver Electric Railway and Lighting Company sends its first electric streetcar for a test run along Main, Cordova, Granville, and Pender. The car travels at six miles an hour, and a ride is five cents. Operations begin officially June 28.

OCTOBER 6-11, 1890 The Vancouver Art Association holds its First Annual Exhibition, in the Vancouver Philharmonic Society's rooms in the Lefevre Building. Three hundred and thirty-eight works of art are on display, eighty-three of which are by fifty-nine local artists. At the grand opening association president David Oppenheimer says the exhibition "paved the way for the creation of a permanent art gallery in Vancouver."

The Marpole midden was first discovered by a road-building crew in 1889 while in the process of extending Granville Street. This "kitchen" midden was made up primarily of discarded shells but also contained bone tools, stone weapons, and the human skeletal remains pictured here. The site was inhabited by the Coast Salish around the year 400 B.C. but is now occupied by the Fraser Arms Hotel. (VPL)

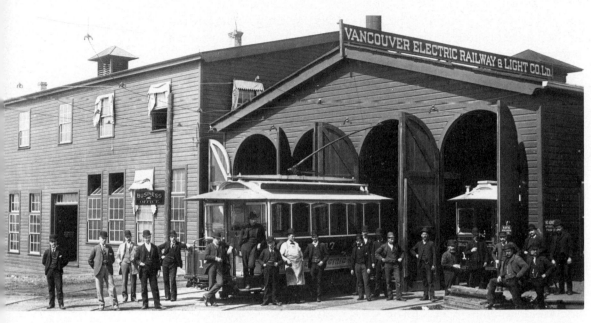

Vancouver's first streetcars began rolling in the year 1890. From its inception the system utilized what was then very high-tech electrical traction equipment rather than the conventional horse-drawn cars found in other cities. (VPL)

DECEMBER 22, 1890 H.O. Bell-Irving forms the Anglo-British Columbia Packing Company (ABC Packing). By April 1891 the company has purchased seven canneries on the Fraser River, and two on the Skeena. ABC Packing produces slightly more than one quarter of the province's total salmon pack for the year 1891. ABC goes on to become the largest sockeye-packing company in the world.

DECEMBER 27, 1890 The first vessel is registered in the port of Vancouver. The *Alpha* will be destroyed by fire September 24, 1891.

ALSO IN 1890 Vancouver's population is 12,500.

ALSO IN 1890 A telephone link is established between the Vancouver Waterworks and the Capilano Dam.

ALSO IN 1890 Philip Oben clears the western portions of the West End, rolling the logs into the water at the north foot of Denman Street.

ALSO IN 1890 Judge Gray names the Lions. The twin mountains, a Vancouver landmark, have been known as the Sisters, or more rudely, Sheba's Paps. The judge fancies a resemblance to sleeping lions and suggests the name. This leads to the entrance to the harbor becoming known as the Lion's Gate.

FEBRUARY 9, 1891 The Vancouver Opera House holds its grand opening. Built by the CPR at a cost of about $100,000, the 1,600-seat opera house is on Granville at the location presently occupied by Eaton's. The first production is Wagner's *Lohengrin,* with the Emma Juch Grand English Opera Company. A sign reads: "We do not require Ladies to remove their hats in the theatre, as is the custom in the United States. It is not necessary. Ladies in British Columbia know that Gentlemen cannot see through felt and feathers." No expense has been spared in the opera house's construction, and Miss Juch says, "I question if there is an opera house that can equal it."

APRIL 28, 1891 The *Empress of India* comes to Vancouver on her maiden voyage. She brings 131 first class and 355 Chinese steerage passengers. This is the first visit of the CPR's White Line *Empress* ships. The *Empress of India* brings the first Royal Mail to the city.

AUGUST 22, 1891 The district municipality of Coquitlam is incorporated.

SEPTEMBER 11, 1891 The interurban begins running to New Westminster. Its first stop is at Cedar Cottage (near today's John Hendry Park). Mayor Oppenheimer and other dignitaries are aboard, including William Van Horne and Lord Mount Stephen. The interurban will eventually offer hourly service, fifty cents one way, seventy-five cents return.

The Hastings Sawmill (originally known as Stamp's Mill) ran from 1865 to 1930, and is shown here circa 1890. Before the coming of the Canadian Pacific Railway (CPR) it was the major employer of the townsfolk of Granville. The Hastings Mill Store (on the left) was moved to Pioneer Park on Alma Street and today serves as a museum run by the Native Daughters of BC. (VPL)

SEPTEMBER 26, 1891 The provincial government grants the CPR 6,000 acres, including 160 acres on the Kitsilano waterfront occupied by squatter Sam Greer. He refuses to move, and Sheriff Tom Armstrong is sent to evict him. Sam shoots the sheriff, wounding him, and is convicted of assault and sent to jail. "Sam made one terrible mistake," a contemporary tells Major Matthews. "If he had not fired that gun at Tom Armstrong, he would have held his property. Public opinion was so strong that the CPR would have had to give in; the people would have torn up the rails."

ALSO IN 1891 Charles Hill-Tout arrives in Vancouver from Toronto. He becomes a leading Canadian anthropologist and ethnologist. The Devonshire-born Hill-Tout opens a boys' school, Buckland College, in Vancouver. Around 1905 he will suggest to the CPR that it name its newest subdivision Kitsilano, a modification of the name of the Squamish chiefs' hereditary name, Khahtsahlano.

SPRING 1892 Hastings Street is paved from Cambie to Granville, the first street in the city to advance beyond wooden planks.

APRIL 13, 1892 The municipality of South Vancouver is incorporated. Comprising 14.5 square miles, it contains all the area west of Boundary Road, including the Point Grey peninsula, and south of 16th Avenue.

SEPTEMBER 8, 1892 Burnaby is incorporated. The population is 200.

The Kitsilano Indian Reserve was known to the Native people as Snauq. It is now the location of Vanier Park. This photo was taken August 15, 1891, behind the house of Jericho Charlie. Left to right, standing, are Jericho Charlie Chinnalset, William Green, Peelass George of the Chilcotin, and Jimmy-Jimmy. Seated are Mary Yam-Schloot and paddle maker Jack Towhuquamkee. Courtesy, City of Vancouver Archives

OCTOBER 10, 1892 The Women's Christian Temperance Union opens a Children's Home at Dunsmuir at Howe. The WCTU is responsible for the creation of the Children's Aid Society in Vancouver.

NOVEMBER 16, 1892 The first Vancouver assizes, with Judge McCreight presiding, are held in the old courthouse (on today's Victory Square). There are no cases to be heard.

JUNE 9, 1893 The Canadian-Australian Line, with its motto "Hands Across the Sea," begins to call in at Vancouver. The first vessel to visit is the *Miowera*. The line is intended as an "all-red" (all British) service for passengers travelling between the U.K. and its South Pacific possessions via Canada.

OCTOBER 26, 1893 The first meeting of the Vancouver Pioneer Society is held for citizens who have been here since before the Great Fire. There are seventy names on the list of charter members, including Malcolm MacLean as president and David Oppenheimer as a member of the executive board.

JANUARY 16 OR 17, 1894 An oath of loyalty is administered to Number Five Company, B.C. Brigade Garrison Artillery. The BCBGA, with 100 men, is the first Vancouver-based military unit. At their first public parade, on May 10, the men are displeased when two civilians, intoxicated, attempt to take command.

APRIL 14, 1894 At a special meeting of the school board it is

By the 1890s steam power had replaced ox power in the forests. Except for Stanley Park the woods on the downtown Vancouver peninsula were cleared by 1890 and logging operations moved eastward to camps like this at Royal City Mills or south to the tallest timber on Point Grey. (VPL)

resolved to suspend the principal of West End School for thirty days for being drunk on a city street.

APRIL 17, 1894 At a meeting in O'Brien Hall called by Captain and Mrs. Mellon, it is agreed to form the Art, Historical and Scientific Association. The AHSA has partially evolved from the Vancouver Art Association, founded in 1889.

MAY 1894 Serious flooding in the Fraser Valley causes the bloated bodies of horses, cows, pigs, and sheep to come floating down the river. They back up into False Creek.

NOVEMBER 10, 1894 A local Council of Women is formed, founded by Lady Aberdeen, who has aided in its inauguration. The council holds its first annual meeting November 5, 1895, and describes itself as "a federation of associations that band themselves together to further the application of the Golden Rule to society, custom and law."

NOVEMBER 22, 1894 St. Paul's Hospital opens, founded by the Catholic Sisters of Charity of Providence. It is a wooden structure with twenty beds.

ALSO IN 1894 The Nine O'Clock Gun is installed at Stanley Park. Richard Steele's book, *The Stanley Park Explorer,* gives what seems to be the most accurate account of the gun's original purpose: to provide a signal to sailing vessels in need of accurate time readings to utilize the tides effectively. The lighthouse keeper at Brockton Point, William D. Jones, complained that the traditional method—blowing up a stick of dynamite—was dangerous. The Nine O'Clock

Three bachelors share the same bed (and bottle) in a typical early Vancouver workingman's abode of the 1890s. (VPL)

43

St. Paul's Hospital was founded in 1894 by the Sisters of Charity of Providence and stood on the same site as the present-day facility at 1081 Burrard Street. (VPL)

Gun, cast in England in 1816, was installed at Brockton Point, not far from its present location, in 1894, and Jones wrote, "The report is not the important thing. It is the flash that counts. A ship's captain never waits for the sound to reach him. He goes by the flash."

FEBRUARY 1, 1895 After a petition asking for daily mail service is sent to Ottawa (310 names are obtained in one day), daily home delivery begins north of False Creek between Campbell Avenue and Nicola Street. Jonathan Miller is the postmaster. About a dozen men will be hired to deliver the mail.

AUGUST 15, 1895 Mark Twain lectures at the Vancouver Opera House, and, despite a bad cold, is a smash. The audience laughs so loudly that portions of his talk cannot be heard.

ALSO IN 1895 The first book of poems by Pauline Johnson appears.

ALSO IN 1895 The first letterboxes are installed on city streets.

JULY 13, 1896 A by-law is passed to regulate the speed of bicycles. Henceforth they must not exceed eight miles per hour.

AUGUST 16, 1896 Gold is discovered in the Klondike. Vancouver will become a way-station for gold-seekers needing supplies.

SEPTEMBER 13, 1896 Chinese ambassador to Canada Li Hung Chang visits Vancouver, and Chinatown builds an elaborate arch in celebration. Li arrives by special CPR train and is met by a guard of honor from HMS *Comus* and Chinese musicians and merchants.

SEPTEMBER 17, 1896 Louis Denison Taylor, born in Ann Arbor, Michigan, comes to Vancouver as circulation manager for the *Province.* "L.D." will become a power in the city, as publisher of the *World* and as—five times—mayor. His famous trademarks are a red tie and a cigar.

OCTOBER 26, 1896 City council limits to two the number of cows permitted each family.

ALSO IN 1896 CPR lots that sold for $1,200 in 1886 are now as high as $20,000.

APRIL 3, 1897 The B.C. Electric Railway is incorporated, with Frank Barnard as first general manager. The BCER takes over the property of the Consolidated Railways and Light Company.

AUGUST 2, 1897 A Kinetoscope exhibition at Market Hall shows motion pictures, together with Edison's "wonder speaking phonograph."

In 1892 the Philp Brothers' fruit and game store on Cordova Street offered a broad selection of local game: ducks, geese, grouse, pheasant, deer, fish, and shellfish. Fruits and vegetables were imported from around the world, though some locally grown produce was available. (VPL)

OCTOBER 2, 1897 News reaches Vancouver of the death in the Yukon of former mayor Fred Cope. On the boat bringing Cope's body home, his coffin is inadvertently switched with one containing the body of a notorious outlaw, Soapy Smith, slain in a gunfight in the Yukon. Vancouver gives Soapy a grand civic funeral. The mistake is only discovered when they open the other coffin in Seattle.

OCTOBER 21, 1897 Pauline Johnson reads her poetry at the Homer Street Methodist Church to an audience including Sir Charles Tupper.

DECEMBER 31, 1897 The city's chain gang goes on strike, protesting their forced labor clearing lanes. They are taken back to the city jail and put on a diet of bread and water until they change their minds. After three days of this they go back to work. The chain gangs will last from about 1889 to 1910.

MARCH 1, 1898 Crofton House School is established by Jessie and Mary Gordon at the corner of Nelson and Jervis streets, the "highest and healthiest portion of the West End."

MARCH 26, 1898 The *Vancouver Daily Province* begins in the B.C. Lithograph building on Hastings Street. The staff numbers seventeen, five of them in editorial. The owner is Hewitt Bostock, who hires Walter Nichol as publisher.

MARCH 28, 1898 The first long-distance telephone in Vancouver goes into operation at the *Province.*

JUNE 24, 1898 Bloomer-wearing ladies are censured in Vancouver. Lady cyclists wearing bloomers find it difficult to gain admission to respectable places.

AUGUST 6, 1898 The first pay phones in the city begin operation at English Bay. They cost five cents.

SEPTEMBER 10, 1898 New Westminster suffers a bad fire. Two hose reels and a crew under Chief Carlisle arrive from Vancouver in seventy-five minutes. The entire business district is destroyed, and hundreds are left homeless.

NOVEMBER 3, 1898 James Skitt Matthews, twenty, comes to Vancouver. He will begin an unofficial archives in 1929, see it become official, and run it for more than thirty years.

ALSO IN 1898 The second CPR station is built in "railway baronial" style at the foot of Granville Street. It will exist until 1914.

ALSO IN 1898 The Socialist Labor Party is organized by a railway worker influenced by Eugene Debs and the American Railway Union.

FEBRUARY 14, 1899 Theodore Ludgate is granted a twenty-five-year lease on Deadman's Island for the purpose of logging. There are protests, and the board of trade comes out against the lease. In 1906 the lease is overturned. In 1909 Ludgate and a group of men return to the island and, in an act of vandalism, destroy trees. They are arrested and fined. In 1912 Ludgate is a member of a group that burns squatters' shacks on the island.

AUGUST 25, 1899 Work on the Davie Street tramline begins. By 1900 rails will run on Davie from Granville to Denman, and along Denman from Davie to Robson. Cars can now run all the way from Main and 16th to the West End.

OCTOBER 24, 1899 Seventeen volunteers leave Vancouver to fight in the Boer War, the first Vancouverites ever to go to war. Among them are Victor Spencer, Jack Leckie, and H.S. Tobin. Upon their departure they are presented with twenty-five dollars each on behalf of the citizens.

As Vancouver became more established, sturdy brick and stone buildings began to replace wooden structures in the downtown area. This flatiron building, erected in 1895 at the intersection of Water and Cordova streets, stands today as a testimony to its solid construction. (VPL)

ALSO IN 1899 Vancouver High School, at Dunsmuir and Cambie streets, affiliates with Montreal's McGill University and becomes Vancouver College of McGill University. It offers one year of arts and science, graduates of which will then be eligible for admission to McGill. Mrs. Duncan Reid has led the negotiations with McGill.

FEBRUARY 27, 1900 The first Vancouver soldiers to be killed in the Boer War die at the Battle of Paardeberg.

AUGUST 13, 1900 Vancouver College's academic year begins. The school will offer commercial training, teacher's certificates, matriculation certificates, and the first year of arts.

OCTOBER 19, 1900 Thomas Cunningham, collector of votes in Vancouver, refuses to put Tomey Hamma's name on the voting list. Hamma is Japanese. In November the B.C. Supreme Court rules the 1895 legislation disenfranchising Chinese, Japanese, and native Indians is ultra vires, and orders Hamma's name be added. But on December 17, 1902, the Privy Council reverses the decision. The *Victoria Colonist* rejoices: "We are relieved from the possibility of having polling booths swamped by a horde of Orientals who are totally unfitted either by custom or education to exercise the ballot. . . ."

NOVEMBER 12, 1900 The first civic building by-law is passed by Vancouver council. It defines fire limits, regulates erection of buildings, and provides for the appointment of a building inspector.

DECEMBER 31, 1900 The Royal Canadian Regiment returns from South Africa, with at least one killed and one wounded. There is a

When the Klondike gold rush hit in 1898, Vancouver became one of the main sources of supply for sourdoughs on their way to that frozen Yukon pay dirt. Prospectors were expected to carry all their own supplies to the goldfields and it's doubtful if anyone but a greenhorn would have bought this rig with its Sunday School sled powered by four tortured looking strays. (VPL)

Grand Illumination of city streets, and schoolchildren sing songs of welcome.

ALSO IN 1900 Less militant members of the Labor Socialist Party split away and form the United Socialist Labor Party.

MARCH 8, 1901 The Carnegie Foundation offers $50,000 to Vancouver for a library if Vancouver will provide a site and $5,000 a year for maintenance. Building begins in November 1901, and the library will open to the public in November 1903.

SEPTEMBER 19, 1901 Normal School opens a week later than scheduled because of extreme summer heat. There are thirty-four students, including thirty girls. William Burns will be principal to September 1920.

ALSO IN 1901 Upon the death of her husband, J.C. McLagan, Sara Ann McLagan becomes the first female editor/publisher of a newspaper in Canada, the *World*. Mrs. McLagan was also the first woman telegraphist in British Columbia.

ALSO IN 1901 W.H. Malkin marries Marion Dougall of Windsor, Ontario. They make their home at Southlands, a large and handsome mansion at Blenheim and Marine Drive. When she dies in 1934 he will donate the money to build Malkin Bowl in Stanley Park in her

Stevedores unload bales of hemp from a ship on Vancouver's waterfront around 1901. This was before the days of bulk carriers and, depending on the cargo, it often took a week or more to pack a ship's hold. (VPL)

The composing room of the *News-Advertiser* in 1895 boasted the first linotype machines in British Columbia. The *Advertiser,* which became the *News-Advertiser* in 1887, was Vancouver's earliest newspaper and was known for its modern practices, including classified ads and the first electric-powered presses in North America. (VPL)

name. W.H. Malkin, with his two brothers, creates W.H. Malkin & Company.

ALSO IN 1901 The Vancouver chapter of the Red Cross is formed.

ALSO IN 1901 Men still form nearly 60 percent of Vancouver's population.

JANUARY 20, 1902 The Royal Brewing Company begins brewing at Cedar Cottage, at the corner of Kingsway and Dumfries. Their specialty is a heavy English ale.

JUNE 1902 Vancouver General Hospital is incorporated as a private, non-profit medical institution. There is accommodation for fifty patients in what has been the old city hospital building. In 1905 the hospital will relocate in Fairview.

AUGUST 9, 1902 The International Order of Daughters of the Empire (IODE) is formed in Vancouver on Edward VII's coronation day. The city's chapter is organized by Mrs. J.M. Lefeure.

OCTOBER 31, 1902 The Pacific Cable opens. Mayor T.F.

Neelands sends a message via the cable to newly crowned King Edward VII: "Your loyal subjects in the city of Vancouver, British Columbia, send greetings via Australia, and pray that the electric bond this day completed may more firmly assure the blessings of peace and prosperity throughout Your Majesty's empire."

ALSO IN 1902 Vancouver's population is 30,000.

ALSO IN 1902 Dr. Glen Campbell begins eye tests for Vancouver children. He is Vancouver's first eye, ear, nose, and throat specialist. In 1932 he will establish "sight saving" classes in Vancouver schools.

ALSO IN 1902 Charles Woodward opens a department store at Hastings and Abbott streets after his dry goods store on Main Street is a success.

JANUARY 6, 1903 Vancouver Business College opens with four students. In one year there are sixty-five. The college guarantees that a student will gain employment after graduation at a salary of not less than thirty dollars a month.

FEBRUARY 2, 1903 The city crest is redesigned, retaining the motto "By Sea and Land We Prosper." The first city crest was designed by Lauchlan Hamilton about 1886. The new, simpler design is by James Bloomfield.

The Vancouver Cycling Club takes a breather for a photo in Stanley Park in 1900. (VPL)

AUGUST 26, 1903 The Art, Historical and Scientific Association becomes an official department of the city, and becomes known as the Vancouver Museum.

OCTOBER 1, 1903 The Vancouver Public Library moves into the Carnegie Building at Main and Hastings from the YMCA building at 169 West Hastings. It will open to the public in November, with Canon L.N. Tucker officiating, and will have 8,000 books on the shelves.

NOVEMBER 18, 1903 The first military cadet corps in the city, the Vancouver High School Cadet Corps, is gazetted to the militia as a unit.

ALSO IN 1903 The first taxi is driven in the city, by H. Hooper.

ALSO IN 1903 Construction starts on a tunnel to bring water to Vancouver Power Company. The two-and-a-quarter-mile-long tunnel, fourteen feet in diameter, is blasted through the mountains north of what is now Ioco to provide a continuous supply of water from Lake Coquitlam to Buntzen Lake. Then penstocks direct the water down the final 400 feet to the edge of Indian Arm. Two powerhouses will be built there. Water begins to flow in 1905.

JANUARY 1, 1904 Vancouver goes from five wards to six. Two "fit and proper" persons represent each ward.

Vancouver's first automobile, circa 1900, was nothing more than a converted wagon with a steering wheel and an engine. (VPL)

ALSO IN 1904 The Great Northern Railway reaches Vancouver. Now travellers can go to Seattle and other U.S. points by train.

JUNE 1, 1905 L.D. Taylor and a syndicate buy the *World* from Sara McLagan. The syndicate is a complicated financial affair, and includes Taylor, Mrs. A.H. Berry (daughter of Jonathan Miller), and Victor Odlum. Victor Odlum is treasurer of the *World,* and will go on to become editor-in-chief.

JULY 2, 1905 The parks board opens the English Bay Bathhouse, built for $6,000.

AUGUST OR SEPTEMBER 1905 Street lighting comes to North Vancouver, supplied by the Vancouver Power Company.

SEPTEMBER 1905 The first Auto Club race is held around Stanley Park. Eleven cars start, five finish. All who finish are driving Oldsmobiles. Among the racers are John Hendry, Harry Stevens, F.R. Stewart, and Harry Hooper.

ALSO IN 1905 Vancouver General Hospital moves to its present Fairview location.

The Hollow Tree is a famous Vancouver landmark. The tall woman on the right is the poet of Stanley Park, E. Pauline Johnson, whose book *Legends of Vancouver* romantically extolled the virtues of the city's favorite park. (VPL)

MARCH 11, 1906 The Children's Aid Home burns, and the children are moved to a vacant hospital at 1530 Cambie. In August 1907 they will move to a new home on Wall Street, in Hastings Townsite.

JULY 3, 1906 Chief Capilano goes to London to meet Edward VII and Queen Alexandra at Buckingham Palace. He goes with Chief Charlie Tsipeymult of Cowichan and Chief Bazel David from the Cariboo to discuss Indian problems. The chiefs wear native costume. The King says, "Welcome, my loyal chiefs. Rise, and let me shake your hands. You are in London, the capital of the British Empire. The city is yours." The visit lasts half an hour, and they are presented with the gold Queen Victoria medal in commemoration of their visit.

JULY 21, 1906 The tugboat *Chehalis,* belonging to the Union Steamship Company, is cut in half in a collision off Brockton Point and sinks in First Narrows. Nine lives are lost, and no bodies are ever recovered. The other ship, the *Princess Victoria,* is later determined to have been travelling too fast.

AUGUST 1906 David Spencer, who has bought a dry goods store on Hastings in the spring, changes its name to David Spencer, Ltd. Spencer's will become a famous city store.

SEPTEMBER 25, 1906 The Vancouver Canadian Club has its

In this 1908 view it is easy to see how the CPR dominated the Vancouver waterfront with its station (left) and extensive railyards and docks (right). The Hastings Sawmill and a couple of sailing ships can be seen just to the upper right of the station roof. (VPL)

inaugural luncheon, with Governor General Grey as the guest of honor. During his remarks the governor general says, "It requires no inspired prophet to foretell the greatness of Vancouver now. Vancouver is now the recognized gateway between the East and West."

ALSO IN 1906 Electric street lighting is installed on Granville Street, electric standard lights replacing the old arc lights. Granville is the first street in the city to be so lighted, and will have 118 of the cluster-type globe standards installed.

FEBRUARY 25, 1907 Talking "too eloquently" about the results of Chief Joe Capilano's visit to Edward VII, Chief Jospeh Bradley of the Tsimpseans is charged with sedition. In April Chief Capilano is threatened with a charge of "inciting the Indians to revolt" after he makes a report of statements alleged to have been made by the King.

APRIL 12, 1907 The Vancouver Stock Exchange is incorporated by a special act of the B.C. legislature. The VSE opens August 1 at 849 West Pender Street, with twelve charter members. Seats on the exchange sell for $125.

MAY 13, 1907 The city of North Vancouver is incorporated, having split away from the municipality of the same name.

SEPTEMBER 30, 1907 A number of street names are changed: Richards Street becomes Balaclava, Cornwall is changed to Blenheim, Boundary Street becomes Trafalgar. Dupont Street (location of a notorious red-light district) disappears, and becomes an extension of Pender. Landsdowne Street becomes Waterloo.

Above: This police constable patrols his beat along Granville Street in 1907. The police force, which at this time numbered fewer than fifty men, had to take care of a population of over 50,000 people. (VPL)

Above left: These storefronts on Carrall Street in Chinatown were boarded up after Vancouver's worst race riot, which occurred on the night of Saturday, September 7, 1907. A rally held by the Asiatic Exclusion League had incited a mob of 5,000 that poured into Chinatown after the meeting, breaking windows and attacking Chinese citizens. (VPL)

Left: Edith Jackson was one of several "first white babies" born in Vancouver. She was later disqualified when the real "first baby," Margaret McNeil, born April 29, 1886, was discovered living in the U.S. (VPL)

Below: When the City Market opened in 1908 it was the place to shop for not only fruits and vegetables but also horses, which were auctioned on the wharf behind the market. (VPL)

ALSO IN 1907 Vancouver's boundaries are extended west to Alma Street.

JANUARY 1, 1908 The municipality of Point Grey is formed out of the western portions of South Vancouver.

ALSO IN 1908 The University of British Columbia is founded.

JANUARY 7, 1909 The first shipment of grain is exported from Vancouver.

MARCH 15, 1909 The first freight via the Great Northern Railway arrives in Vancouver.

MARCH 29, 1909 Longshoremen strike for higher pay. They want thirty-five cents an hour for day work and forty cents an hour for night work.

SEPTEMBER 6, 1909 The first Granville Street Bridge opens. It is in pretty much the same alignment as the present bridge, although much shorter.

As soon as there were cars in Vancouver there were car rallies. The object of this 1909 rally was to drive out to Burnaby and then return to Vancouver in one piece. Here we see one of the more unfortunate drivers having to stoop to a horse-powered assist in the darkest depths of backwoods Burnaby. (VPL)

OCTOBER 6, 1909 Vancouver's first ambulance is taken out for a test drive, and runs over and kills an American tourist.

ALSO IN 1909 English Bay Pier is built.

ALSO IN 1909 The Chinese Benevolent Association is founded.

ALSO IN 1909 Vancouver gets its first skyscraper, with the construction of the Dominion Trust Building at Hastings and Cambie.

ALSO IN 1909 Ferry service begins to West Vancouver.

ALSO IN 1909 The Vancouver Athletics baseball club is formed by Bob Brown.

AUGUST 15, 1910 The first Exhibition opens. It runs six days at Exhibition Park and is a huge success. Prime Minister Wilfred Laurier officiates at the opening. A celebration is held marking the Golden Jubilee of the arrival of the first Oblate Missionaries.

DECEMBER 21, 1910 Hastings Townsite ratepayers vote to join Vancouver.

ALSO IN 1910 Women get the civic vote in Vancouver. Janet Kemp and a delegation of women's organizations have led the struggle, and argue eloquently before city council.

Above: The awesome size of the cedar trees that once grew in Vancouver is graphically illustrated by this stump house built by a pioneer named Berkman near present-day 27th Avenue and Prince Edward Street. The large stump at left served as the living room and the smaller stump on the right was used as the kitchen. Courtesy, City of Vancouver Archives

Above, left: Seraphim "Joe" Fortes stands in front of his English Bay cottage around 1910. Joe was born in Barbados and came to Vancouver in 1885. He survived the 1886 fire and went on to work as a bartender until the mid-1890s when he became the self-appointed guardian of the beach at English Bay. (VPL)

ALSO IN 1910 Construction begins on the Vancouver Block.

ALSO IN 1910 Construction begins on the courthouse, designed by Francis Mawson Rattenbury.

ALSO IN 1910 The BCER completes its line to Chilliwack.

ALSO IN 1910 Westminster Avenue becomes Main Street.

FEBRUARY 1911 George Cunningham opens his first drugstore, at Denman and Nelson.

ALSO IN 1911 The CPR builds piers A and B.

ALSO IN 1911 The first suffrage convention is held in Vancouver at O'Brien Hall. Mayor L.D. Taylor is chairman.

JANUARY 5, 1912 The first professional hockey game is played in Vancouver at the Denman Arena. The Vancouver Millionaires, in white and maroon sweaters, beat the New Westminster Royals eight to three.

Who said aerobics were new? This 1909 dance class is learning the latest. (VPL)

MARCH 30, 1912 The Vancouver local of the International Longshoremen's Association (ILA) is formed, with sixty charter members. Paddy Coyle buys the first membership book and button sold in Vancouver.

Left: A group of Vancouver's finest relax from the rigors of maintaining law and order in 1909. Although there are no smiles they are actually having a good time— one cracks an egg with a hammer and another cuts a roast with a saw. (VPL)

MAY 3, 1912 The Morning Sun is first published, by Jack P. McConnell and R.S. Ford (the latter is the publisher of the *Saturday Sunset*). *The Morning Sun* has a circulation of about 10,000.

SEPTEMBER 1912 Ten arches are erected along the route of a city tour to be taken by the Duke and Duchess of Connaught. One of the arches is later moved to Stanley Park where it becomes a famous landmark, Lumberman's Arch.

SEPTEMBER 18, 1912 The Duke and Duchess of Connaught visit. On September 19 they officially open the Connaught Bridge on a day declared a public holiday. Everyone calls it the Cambie Street Bridge, and it will be used until 1895, when it's torn down and replaced by the present bridge.

DECEMBER 20, 1912 The Rex Theatre opens on Hastings to show movies. Opened for business twenty minutes after the final nail is hammered in and the final curtain hung, the 999-seat Rex—all gold leaf and plush velvet—is called by the *Province* the "most modern movie house in the world."

ALSO IN 1912 Post Number Two, the first Vancouver post of the

English Bay beach was Vancouver's recreational playground in 1907, offering a pleasure pier, changing rooms along the beach, and a roller skating rink on Denman Street. (VPL)

Native Sons of B.C., is formed. Dr. F.J.N. Nicholson is the first chief factor. There are about 100 members. The interests of the group are history, citizenship, and the exclusion of Orientals.

ALSO IN 1912 China's Kuomintang (Nationalist Party) is founded and a Vancouver branch established.

ALSO IN 1912 The Sam Kee Building, at the southwest corner of Carrall and Pender, is erected by businessman Chang Toy. It occupies a space only six feet wide. Chang has put this curious building up on a narrow strip of land facing Pender Street, a strip left him by the city after they expropriated his land to widen the street. It is the narrowest commercial building in the world.

The Sam Kee Building—only four feet eleven inches deep and known as the narrowest building in the world—was built by Kee to spite the city which had expropriated his property to widen Pender Street, leaving him with only a sliver of land. (VPL)

ALSO IN 1912 Karno's Comedians, a music hall troupe from England, perform in Vancouver. Among the cast are Charlie Chaplin and Stan Laurel.

FEBRUARY 16, 1913 Dr. F.F. Wesbrook is named the first president of UBC. He has been dean of the medical college at the University of Minnesota.

MARCH 7, 1913 Poet Pauline Johnson dies in the Bute Street Hospital. On March 10 a Church of England memorial service is read to a packed Christ Church, while hundreds more gather outside. In a simple ceremony at Siwash Rock, with just her closest friends present, one of her poems is read and her ashes are buried at the rock.

The Japanese steamer *Komagata Maru* arrived in Vancouver May 23, 1914, with 376 East Indian men aboard seeking immigration to Canada. Racism prevented them from landing, and they were forced at gunpoint to return to India. Once back in India, a riot ensued in which 26 of these men were killed and 200 imprisoned. (VPL)

APRIL 18, 1913 Athletic Park is dedicated. The private park has been built by Bob Brown, who has leased the land from the CPR, and who will build a stadium, later named Capilano Stadium. Baseball is the game here.

OCTOBER 1, 1913 Kingsway is completed. "The new highway between Vancouver and New Westminster, passing through South Vancouver and Burnaby, is now complete.... It is a broad, magnificent road, and by none will it be more appreciated than by motorists, who, to the number of 600, made the trip between the two cities on the day the road was opened." Before becoming a highway, this route was known as Westminster Road, which in turn evolved from "the Black Trail," so named because of an early forest fire.

ALSO IN 1913 Lumberman's Arch is floated by barge down to Stanley Park and re-erected. Its official name will become Bowie Arch in 1915, after the death of George P. Bowie, who designed the arch.

ALSO IN 1913 Construction starts by the CPR on the second Hotel Vancouver. It will not open until 1916. This gorgeous building, designed by Francis Swales, features 500 rooms, and 456 have an exterior view. The Roof Garden restaurant, Oak Room, Peacock Gallery, and Spanish Grill will become favorite haunts, and everyone who is anyone stops at the Hotel Vancouver.

ALSO IN 1913 The World Building, tallest in the British Empire, is completed.

FEBRUARY 1914 Famed English music hall performer Marie Lloyd appears at the Orpheum. Mayor T.S. Baxter orders one of her songs,

A 1905 Sunday afternoon auto jaunt around Stanley Park stops to let the radiators cool at Prospect Point. In 1907, the first year cars were registered in the province, British Columbia had a grand total of 175 automobiles. (VPL)

"The Ankle Watch," cut from the show because during the song she lifts her dress slightly to reveal the watch. The mayor finally closes her show, and she gives a warmly received performance before the "smart set" at the Hotel Vancouver.

MAY 23, 1914 The *Komagata Maru* arrives in Vancouver carrying 376 East Indian passengers, who are refused entry on the grounds they have not come directly from India. The ship anchors near Coal Harbor and begins a long wait as negotiations drag on to permit the passengers entry. On July 17 they are ordered away, and the passengers take over the ship. Soldiers are ranged for duty on the pier, and the warship HMCS *Rainbow* enters the harbor. Finally, on July 23, the *Komagata Maru* departs. On its arrival back in India there is a riot, and many people die.

AUGUST 4, 1914 Britain declares war on Germany. Canada is automatically included. In the Orpheum Theatre, the manager interrupts the performance to announce that war has been declared.

The original Lumberman's Arch erected in Stanley Park was built to display the diverse variety of trees growing in B.C.'s forests. Each of the pillars of the arch was made from a different species of conifer: Douglas fir, spruce, red cedar, yellow cedar, hemlock, tamarack, etc. (VPL)

PART III

AUGUST 10, 1914 Dr. Leonard S. Klinck, dean of agriculture, is the first faculty member appointed by UBC. He and his wife spend their first summer in Vancouver living in a tent. His first lecture is held in an old horse barn.

AUGUST 18, 1914 Two 4.7-inch naval guns in Stanley Park, close to Siwash Rock, are test-fired. The Stanley Park battery will remain in place until armistice.

AUGUST 21, 1914 The first troop train leaves Vancouver, heading for training camps before the troops are sent overseas. Among the many local regiments on board are the Seventy-second Canadian Infantry Battalion Seaforth Highlanders.

AUGUST 24, 1914 King George High School opens at 1070 Burrard. Thomas Pattison is the first principal of the red brick schoolhouse, which boasts a staff of six and an enrolment of 196 pupils.

NOVEMBER 1, 1914 The Twenty-ninth Vancouver Battalion CEF, known as Tobin's Tigers, forms at Hastings Park, with 1,100 recruits. Colonel H.S. Tobin establishes a minimum height requirement of 5'10." Tobin's Tigers leave for active service on May 14, 1915. Six thousand men will eventually serve in the battalion, seeing action in virtually all the major battles of the war. The battalion will suffer 800 casualties.

Preceding pages: By the end of World War I the hospitals were overflowing with the maimed and mutilated young men who'd gone off to fight for the British Empire. Groups such as the Returned Soldiers Club raised money to aid the victims of modern chemical and mechanized warfare. (VPL)

Below: In late 1914 the 29th Overseas Battalion of the Canadian Expeditionary Forces used Hastings Park for practice drills and continued to do so throughout World War I. Because of this they soon became known as "the knights of the roller coaster"—one of the most feared fighting units in Canadian history. Courtesy, City of Vancouver Archives

ALSO IN 1914 The Marine Drive bridge over the North Shore's Capilano River is built.

ALSO IN 1914 Imperial Oil opens its IOCO refinery on Burrard Inlet.

FEBRUARY 14, 1915 The first trans-Canada telephone call, between Vancouver and Montreal, is placed.

FEBRUARY 15, 1915 The Imperial Theatre opens a brand-new musical comedy, *Fifty Years Forward.* Among the amusing predictions for 1965: a lady mayor in Vancouver.

MARCH 26, 1915 The Vancouver Millionaires win the Stanley Cup, the first Western Canadian team to do so. Each of the Millionaires receives a bonus of $300 for defeating the Ottawa Senators three games straight in a best-of-five series. Fred "Cyclone" Taylor is the star forward.

APRIL 29, 1915 Simultaneous fires break out on the Granville and Cambie Street bridges. Authorities suspect sabotage.

In 1916 Hastings Street was the main business and shopping district of the city. The drivers seem to be piloting their cars down the wrong side of the road but they're just obeying the English "left-hand rule" which was practiced in Vancouver up to the year 1922. (VPL)

MAY 4, 1915 Louis D. Taylor, prominent businessman and many-time mayor of Vancouver, sells the *World* newspaper to John Nelson.

JULY 1, 1915 The Georgia-Harris Street Viaduct opens to traffic.

AUGUST 28, 1915 The first Canadian Northern Pacific Railway train (later to become the CNR) arrives in Vancouver.

SEPTEMBER 30, 1915 The University of British Columbia opens for classes in a temporary structure at 10th and Laurel.

OCTOBER 11, 1915 CP's SS *Monteagle* burns in the harbor, with $100,000 damage.

OCTOBER 12, 1915 The UBC Alma Mater Society forms.

DECEMBER 15, 1915 William J. Bowser takes office as premier of British Columbia.

ALSO IN 1915 Granville Island opens for business after a federal government works project has False Creek drained at the eastern end.

In August 1916 the 242nd Foresters Battalion set up a make-shift recruiting office on Pender Street. Men from all walks of life and of all ages passed through the front door as civilians and, after signing up, left through the back door as completely uni-formed cannon fod-der bound for the trenches. (VPL)

ALSO IN 1915 The Chinese Canadian Club is founded by a group of young Chinese emigrants and students.

MARCH 8, 1916 Today is Sock Day in Vancouver. The IODE asks for socks for the soldiers fighting overseas.

MARCH 11, 1916 Several complaints are made of the reckless manner in which some jitney drivers crowd citizens who are about to board streetcars. It will be a year before B.C. Electric Railway asks Vancouver City Council to review the jitney problem. The ensuing Shortt Report recommends banning jitneys from Vancouver streets.

NOVEMBER 23, 1916 A provincial election is held, with a referendum on the enfranchisement of women. Women win the vote, and Liberals win the election.

DECEMBER 19, 1916 On the eve of Prohibition, the Strand Hotel sets an all-time record for bar receipts.

DECEMBER 23, 1916 The first annual children's Christmas tree party is held in the Beatty Street drill hall.

Harold Smith (left) was Vancouver's official regimental photographer during World War I. He and his employees made thousands of individual soldiers' portraits and also photographed huge groups of troops with a banquet camera (seen here behind the motorcycles). (VPL)

ALSO IN 1916 The second Hotel Vancouver opens at Granville and Georgia.

ALSO IN 1916 Holy Rosary Church is declared a cathedral.

ALSO IN 1916 Vancouver City Council votes to open civic offices to women.

ALSO IN 1916 Stephan Raymur uncovers a German spy ring in Vancouver, and arrests a German spy.

ALSO IN 1916 The first grain elevator is opened in Vancouver.

JANUARY 15, 1917 The Ballet Russe opens at the Opera House. The famed Russian troupe stars Nijinsky among the more than forty performers. The repertoire for the North American tour contains a dozen ballets. A full orchestra, conducted by Pierre Monteux, accompanies the troupe during its Vancouver appearance.

JANUARY 18, 1917 An income tax is introduced as a temporary war measure.

The men and women at Vancouver Iron and Engineering Works in 1917 were contributing to the war effort by manufacturing artillery shells to be used by troops on the western front, over 6,000 miles away. (VPL)

The second Vancouver Hotel was built between 1912 and 1914 on the site of the first Vancouver Hotel—the southwest corner of Georgia and Granville streets. It was the largest hotel in the city and in its later years served as a home for soldiers returning from World War II. It was demolished in January 1949. (VPL)

JANUARY 20, 1917 The *Mabel Brown,* first of a class of wooden coastal schooners built by the Wallace Shipyard for the Canada West Coast Navigation Company, is scheduled for launch. The *Mabel Brown* gets stuck in the ways on the first launch attempt. The second (and successful) launch date is February 2.

MARCH 20, 1917 Police Chief Malcolm MacLellan and nine-year-old George Robb are killed during a raid on an East Georgia Street house. Gunman and suspected cocaine dealer Bob Tait kills himself.

APRIL 5, 1917 Women are enfranchised in British Columbia.

MAY 3, 1917 The first annual patriotic parade is held. The parades continue until 1922.

JUNE 13, 1917 The first strike by BCER workers begins, lasting nine days.

JUNE 17, 1917 The Beacon Theatre opens on Hastings Street, and is proclaimed as one of the best vaudeville houses on the continent. Owner Alex Pantages appears on stage to dedicate his theatre. The first program features Mlle. Bianca, formerly of the New York Metropolitan Opera, and vaudevillian Will Morrissey.

JULY 19, 1917 Helen McGill becomes the first woman to be appointed judge of the juvenile court.

SEPTEMBER 1, 1917 Robert J. Cromie buys the *News Advertiser*, amalgamates it with the *Morning Sun,* and begins the *Sun,* a morning paper. With a circulation of 16,000 the newspaper is the largest daily west of Toronto.

SEPTEMBER 4, 1917 The Bridge Hotel is demolished. The last known building to predate the Great Fire, the Bridge served as a temporary morgue for the city during the conflagration of 1886. The Bridge's Main Street location once placed it in a very fashionable part of the city. Not the least of its charms, the hotel verandah provided a favorite fishing spot.

OCTOBER 1, 1917 Faced with Prohibition, the Twenty-ninth Regiment commemorates the occasion with a Burial of Bacchus, a mock funeral service for the now illegal hootch.

NOVEMBER 12, 1917 Local East Indians, claiming they are not citizens of Canada with full rights, seek exemption from compulsory military service.

ALSO IN 1917 Evelyn Farris becomes the first woman to sit on UBC's board of governors.

ALSO IN 1917 War Dog, the first steel steamer from Wallace Shipyards, and the first steel ocean-going vessel to be built on Burrard Inlet, is launched.

ALSO IN 1917 Just three decades after the Great Fire, Vancouver's fire department is the first in Canada to be fully motorized.

JANUARY 13, 1918 The Amputations Association forms, the first in Canada.

JANUARY 24, 1918 Mary Ellen Smith is elected first woman MLA in B.C., winning her riding in Vancouver Centre with 3,000 votes. Her deceased husband, Finance Minister Ralph Smith, held it before her. Described as "one of the most outstanding women of the Dominion," she is also the first woman to hold a cabinet position— Minister without Portfolio, though she resigns the cabinet within a year. As a representative to Britain, she's elected, and reelected with the largest majority ever held in Canadian politics. She's instrumental in passing legislation for minimum wages, mothers' pensions, equal guardianship, and other issues concerned with sexual equality.

FEBRUARY 25, 1918 The business tax is approved.

B.C. Electric operated this open-air sight-seeing observation streetcar from 1909 to 1950. The man standing on the left is Teddy Lyons, who became quite a Vancouver personality throughout his many years' service on the tour. (VPL)

MARCH 6, 1918 Premier John Oliver takes office.

APRIL 14, 1918 Daylight Saving Time is introduced to Vancouver by Major Hart-McHarg, who had seen it in action in England. For the sake of Fraser Valley farmers who objected to the disruption of their milking schedules, the new system is called "War Time."

MAY 18, 1918 The first grain shipment from Vancouver via the Panama Canal departs. Five ships, loading at Steven's Folly, a grain elevator which had lain idle during the war, carry 800,000 bushels of wheat to Europe. The ships each carry chemists who check the wheat daily for spoilage in the tropical heat. The opening of the Panama Canal combines nicely with Vancouver's fine natural harbor and the railway terminus to make the city a natural choice as a seaport.

JUNE 17, 1918 Sarah Bernhardt is in Vancouver, appearing at the Orpheum Theatre for a week. Matinee tickets to see her cost fifteen to fifty-five cents. Evening tickets are priced from fifteen to eighty cents.

This quarter-ton sturgeon was pulled out of the Fraser River in 1918. (VPL)

AUGUST 2, 1918 The Vancouver Trades and Labor Council conducts a twenty-four-hour general strike to commemorate the death of Albert Godwin, former president of the B.C. Federation. Godwin was hit and killed on Vancouver Island while being pursued for draft evasion. He had been exempted from the draft because he was tubercular, but had been reclassified as fit after leading a strike for an eight-hour day. The response to the call from the VTLC for a general strike (the first in Canadian history) is overwhelming. Virtually no union employees remain on the job.

OCTOBER 5, 1918 The first case of Spanish Influenza in Vancouver is reported. During the epidemic, city health officers order bans on church services, theatre openings, and late shopping. By October 14, 200 cases of flu are reported. By November 14 there are 3,972 cases and 426 deaths. New burial space becomes necessary. The Vancouver General Hospital adds a temporary annex, opening the Heather Pavilion.

Top: The Vancouver Exhibition was the forerunner of today's Pacific National Exhibition. This ornate structure was the first building erected for the Vancouver Exhibition, which opened in 1910. (VPL)

Above: On October 28, 1922, UBC students conducted "The Great Trek" from their "Fairview Shacks" out to the site of the University Endowment Lands, demanding the provincial government complete their campus. (VPL)

OCTOBER 24, 1918 The *Princess Sophia* grounds on Vanderbilt Reef in Lynn Canal. Before rescue workers can reach the passengers, days later, 343 people die as the ship sinks.

OCTOBER 31, 1918 Harry Gardiner, the "Human Fly," scales the World Building. "Up and up he went until, at a great height, he reached the buttress, supporting the overhanging roof, and swung himself over it. The host, watching far below, gasped."

NOVEMBER 11, 1918 Armistice Day. Citizens throng the streets, celebrating the victory, and the "Gallant Boys Who Made It Possible." The newspaper headlines say it best: "Downtown Streets Maelstrom of Laughing Jubilant Flag-bedecked Humanity" ... "Most Extraordinary Scenes in City's History."

NOVEMBER 15, 1918 The flu epidemic continues to rage; schools and other public buildings close.

NOVEMBER 17, 1918 Alleged German spy Richard Wilkins is arrested in Vancouver Harbor.

Homicide detectives received an unusual amount of public attention in 1924 due to the spectacular Janet Smith murder case. Here detectives display a small weapons cache discovered beneath a grain elevator on the waterfront. Courtesy, City of Vancouver Archives

Above: Fleeing from accusations of corruption, U.S. President Warren G. Harding spent two weeks in Alaska. He passed through Vancouver July 26, 1923, on his way back to the states. He became ill and died of apoplexy one week later in San Francisco. (VPL)

Left: The highlight of the 1924 billiard season occurred when touring world's champion Ralph Greenleaf popped into town and made the rounds of the local billiard parlors displaying his tremendous talent to his fans. Courtesy, City of Vancouver Archives

DECEMBER 7, 1918 An earthquake stops the clock atop the Vancouver Block.

DECEMBER 15, 1918 Vancouver establishes its first traffic department. Under Inspector George Hood, constables direct traffic at major intersections, wearing white gloves and wielding batons.

ALSO IN 1918 Harry Green organizes the first Vancouver Symphony Orchestra, which disbands in 1921.

JANUARY 25, 1919 The *Empress of Asia* brings home the first contingent of soldiers. The nearly 1,400 men, fresh from the battlefields of France, receive a tumultuous welcome.

JANUARY 30, 1919 The Native Daughters of B.C. form. Mrs. Paul Smith is the first chief factor. The group's objectives are to pay tribute to the pioneers and the history of B.C., and to engage in patriotic and charitable activities.

MARCH 3, 1919 The first commercial seaplane takes off from Vancouver, carrying airmail for Seattle.

NOVEMBER 1, 1919 The CNR station on Main Street opens. Mayor Gale conducts the ceremonies immediately following the arrival of the first transcontinental CNR train at 7:00 p.m.

ALSO IN 1919 Dr. George H. Worthington, a city alderman, forms the Vancouver Drug Company, which later becomes Cunningham's Drugs.

FEBRUARY 3, 1920 The harbor police are formed.

Mayor L.D. Taylor sits behind his desk at city hall on May 19, 1925. Taylor was Vancouver's most popular mayor and held the office off and on for a total of eleven years between 1910 and 1934. Taylor's trademarks were his red neckties and his constant cigars. (VPL)

This 1925 cartoon by Fitzmaurice pointed out the voting public's boosterism and political generalities which Mayor L.D. Taylor was fond of dishing out. (VPL)

FEBRUARY 15, 1920 The first direct shipment of lumber to Cuba is sent.

MARCH 14, 1920 Gasoline prices are advanced two cents per gallon in the city. The new rate is thirty cents per gallon, of which three cents is for tax.

OCTOBER 17, 1920 A trans-Canada flight, piloted by two RCAF pilots, ends in Vancouver. The feat demonstrates that regular transcontinental service is a practical possibility.

ALSO IN 1920 CKMO radio, later to become CJOR, goes on the air.

ALSO IN 1920 Vancouver fire department equipment, originally white, is painted red.

JANUARY 1, 1921 Alex Pantages founds the Polar Bear Club.

MARCH 25, 1921 The Capitol Theatre opens on Granville. The program includes a main feature, continuous from noon until *Midnight Madness*, accompanied by newsreels, an operatic selection, a comedy routine, and an "idyllic prelude" entitled *Woman's Four Ages of Romance. Brewster's Millions,* starring Fatty Arbuckle, is the coming attraction.

MAY 1, 1921 Prohibition ends in Canada.

AUGUST 29, 1921 CPR's *Princess Louise,* the largest passenger ship built in B.C., is launched.

JANUARY 1, 1922 As of 6:00 a.m. Vancouver drivers move over to the right side of the road.

FEBRUARY 17, 1922 CPR's Pier H collapses, hurtling 385 tons of copper bars into Burrard Inlet. The pier was one of the oldest owned by CPR. It is believed that the underpinnings gave way under the heavy load.

FEBRUARY 18, 1922 Brothers M.J. Lannon and P.J. Ryan found Vancouver College.

MARCH 1, 1922 The first radio broadcast in Vancouver is a program of news and music from Province Radiophone.

OCTOBER 28, 1922 The UBC Great Trek (also known as the Pilgrimage) draws attention to the crowded facilities in Fairview. Students march en masse to the Point Grey site long promised as a permanent home for the university. The trek is the final stage in a Varsity Week campaign that convinces legislators to loosen purse strings and complete the new buildings within two years.

NOVEMBER 9, 1922 UBC gets a grant to continue construction on the new facilities.

ALSO IN 1922 Judge Emily Gowan (Ferguson) Murphy writes *The Black Candle,* a sensational expose of the drug trade in Vancouver. Mrs. Murphy, who more often wrote under the pen name "Janey Canuck," takes a harsh stand against drug dealers: "All honest men and orderly persons should rightly know that there are men and women who batten and fatten on the agony of the unfortunate drug-addict—palmerworms and human caterpillars who should be trodden underfoot like the despicable grubs that they are."

FEBRUARY 19, 1923 Bandits gag and bind the employees of the Capitol Theatre on Granville, and escape with $2,500 from the theatre's safe.

MARCH 19, 1923 BCER inaugurates the first bus line on Grandview Highway. Mayor MacLean and members of council, along with BCER officials, go along for the ride. Service extends from Commercial and Broadway via Grandview Highway, Renfrew, and Rupert to 22nd and Rupert.

JULY 1, 1923 Ottawa passes the Oriental Exclusion Act, otherwise known as the Chinese Immigration Act. The thousands of Chinese laborers who entered Canada during the late nineteenth century were subject to a head tax, imposed because Canadian workers worried about being displaced by Orientals who were willing to work for less

Facing page: This B.C. Telephone Company crew loads the hold of an old ship with thousands of feet of undersea telephone cable on January 29, 1927. Courtesy, City of Vancouver Archives

During the off-season, American baseball slugger Babe Ruth toured the Pantages Theatre circuit, making public appearances and drawing huge crowds. Wherever there's a crowd you'll find a politician—in this case Vancouver's mayor L.D. Taylor, faking it as the catcher while Police Chief Long looks on as umpire at the Pantages Theatre, November 29, 1926. (VPL)

pay. In 1901 this head tax rose from $50 to $100, then to $500 in 1904. The Exclusion Act further discouraged immigration—in fact limiting it to a trickle of fifteen immigrants allowed entry into Canada over eighteen years. From a population of 44,000 in 1923, the Chinese community in Canada dwindled to 34,627 by 1941. Canadian Chinese refer to this day as Humiliation Day. The discriminatory legislation is not repealed until 1947.

JULY 26, 1923 President Warren G. Harding becomes the first U.S. President to visit Canada. Just a month after his trip to Vancouver, Harding dies suddenly, while on a goodwill tour.

AUGUST 4, 1923 Southam interests assume control of the *Vancouver Daily Province,* a newspaper which had become one of the most prosperous dailies west of Winnipeg.

OCTOBER 1, 1923 The first Canadian government Merchant Marine ship departs with grain for Britain.

DECEMBER 13, 1923 Alderman W.R. Owens wins the mayoralty from Louis D. Taylor by a margin of fifty-three seats.

ALSO IN 1923 James Butterfield begins writing a column in the *Province.*

ALSO IN 1923 Harry Houdini escapes from a straitjacket while hanging by his heels from the Sun Tower.

ALSO IN 1923 Children's Hospital is created when members of the Women's Institute become concerned that there is no organized centre to which they can apply for assistance for a young girl who needs a leg brace which her parents cannot afford. The group, in cooperation with other Women's Institutes, starts the Children's Hospital Fund to provide assistance to children hospitalized in wards for adult patients. Starting with a one-room clinic, the group moved into the John McCallan house on Hudson Street in 1927. Thirty-five patients were admitted the first year.

MARCH 11-12, 1924 The *Vancouver Sun* buys the *Vancouver World,* and moves into both the morning and evening markets.

JULY 26, 1924 Janet Smith, a Scottish nanny, is found murdered in the Shaughnessy home of her employers. The Chinese house boy is kidnapped and later accused of murder. He is acquitted, and the murder remains a mystery.

ALSO IN 1924 Victor Odlum buys the *Vancouver Star.*

FEBRUARY 7, 1925 Eleven crew members from a Japanese ship drown in Vancouver's harbor.

An estimated 25,000 people crowded Vancouver's streets on September 14, 1928, to welcome home Percy Williams, the city's first Olympic gold medal winner. At the Brockton Oval he was awarded this snappy new roadster by an appreciative city council and Mayor L.D. Taylor. Courtesy, City of Vancouver Archives

FEBRUARY 11, 1925 Memorial services are held for the drowned Japanese sailors.

JUNE 10, 1925 Inaugural services at St. Andrew's Presbyterian Church mark the formation of the United Church.

JULY 16, 1925 Six new two-car multiple-unit streetcars go into service with B.C. Electric's fleet. Four of the new units take on the Fraser-Kerrisdale route, and two are put on the Grandview-Fourth Avenue route.

AUGUST 11, 1925 The Japanese ship *Kaikyu Maru* rams and sinks the tug SS *Hustler*. Three water mains under the Second Narrows Bridge are broken, and Vancouver's water supply is endangered.

AUGUST 11, 1925 Radio station CNRV begins broadcasting from a studio in the CNR depot. Sir Henry Thornton, president of the CNR, officially opens the facility, which is the first radio station to meet the requirements of the new radio law. The station broadcasts on Tuesday and Friday evenings only.

OCTOBER 30, 1925 The Invisible Empire of the Kanadian Knights of the Ku Klux Klan holds an informal reception at its Imperial Palace, 1690 Matthews Street. The Klan's residence is the former Glen Brae House, the first house in the city to have an elevator.

NOVEMBER 7, 1925 The Second Narrows Bridge opens.

ALSO IN 1925 Walter F. Evans, impressario and musician, builds the Devonshire Hotel.

ALSO IN 1925 The first neon sign is erected in Vancouver.

ALSO IN 1925 The UBC campus opens in Point Grey.

APRIL 24, 1926 Famed tenor John McCormack performs in Vancouver.

JUNE 29, 1926 Prime Minister Arthur Meighen takes office.

ALSO IN 1926 W.C. Shelley puts a road up Grouse Mountain, and construction starts on Grouse Mountain Chalet, which opens in September.

MAY 3-7, 1927 Noel Coward's *Hay Fever* is performed in Vancouver for the first time.

MAY 9, 1927 The Hotel Georgia opens.

JUNE 25, 1927 South Vancouver and Vancouver approve amalgamation.

JULY 1, 1927 Vancouver celebrates the Diamond Jubilee of Confederation.

JULY 4, 1927 CPR piers B and C open as part of the Jubilee celebration.

SEPTEMBER 2, 1927 The sale of the Rogers Building to General "One Arm" Sutton for one million dollars is reputed to be the city's largest real estate transaction.

A telephone company lineman stands on the running board of his solid-rubber-tired truck in 1928. Courtesy, City of Vancouver Archives

Far left: The daring British aviator, the Honourable Mrs. Victor Bruce, arrived in Vancouver in mid-December 1930, aboard the CPR steamer *Empress of Japan.* Because of the short flying range of her biplane (1,000 km) it couldn't make it across the Pacific Ocean so it had to be sent by ship from Japan and reassembled in Vancouver for resumption of her global solo flight. (VPL)

Left: Billy Townsend weighs in on December 13, 1929, for his big fight against Al Foreman. Three thousand people paid ten cents a head to see Townsend mash Foreman in a full twelve rounds to become the new Canadian lightweight champion. Courtesy, City of Vancouver Archives

SEPTEMBER 4-5, 1927 The World Sculling Championships are held in Burrard Inlet.

OCTOBER 2, 1927 Grace Hospital opens.

NOVEMBER 2, 1927 Port exports reach a record seventy-five million bushels of grain.

NOVEMBER 9, 1927 The new Anglican Church College building at UBC is opened.

ALSO IN 1927 Spencer's Store opens at Hastings and Richards.

ALSO IN 1927 Vancouver Iron and Engineering Works is founded.

ALSO IN 1927 Mrs. Norman Porter organizes the "Miles of Dimes" campaign to support the Vancouver Children's Hospital.

ALSO IN 1927 The Hudson's Bay Company gets the city's first postage meter.

ALSO IN 1927 The Kitsilano Branch Library, the first in B.C., opens.

ALSO IN 1927 The *Province* newspaper establishes the *Empress of Japan* figurehead in Stanley Park.

JANUARY 28, 1928 Point Grey and Vancouver approve amalgamation.

FEBRUARY 5, 1928 Francis Bursill, who wrote under the pen name "Felixe Penne," dies. Bursill founded the Collingwood Free Library, the Dickens Fellowship, and the Vancouver Shakespearean Society.

APRIL 24, 1928 The Second Narrows Bridge is damaged when the freighter *Norwich City* collides with it. This is the eighteenth major bridge mishap in three years.

JULY 18, 1928 A Conservative vote sweeps B.C., as the MacLean government loses the election, and Simon Tolmie takes over as premier.

AUGUST 1, 1928 Percy Williams wins the second gold medal at the Olympic Games in Amsterdam. A civic parade will be held later.

OCTOBER 17, 1928 W.H. Malkin defeats Taylor to become mayor of Vancouver.

OCTOBER 18, 1928 The city gets its first traffic light, at Hastings and Main.

OCTOBER 20, 1928 The Capitol Theatre brings Vancouver its first "talkie," *Mother Knows Best.*

During the Depression men rode the freight trains west, looking for work. When no jobs were found, most just hung out on the coast. It was better to starve to death at forty degrees above zero than at forty degrees below. (VPL)

The *Province* newspaper's radio station CKCD erected this giant radio in Victory Square, across from its offices on Cambie Street. Throughout the month of December 1931 the *Province* relentlessly pumped Christmas music through the radio as a promotion for the newspaper's Santa Claus Fund. Courtesy, City of Vancouver Archives

DECEMBER 4, 1928 Construction begins on the Hotel Vancouver at its present Georgia and Burrard location.

ALSO IN 1928 The Alma Academy opens at Alma and Broadway as a dance spot.

ALSO IN 1928 St. Joseph's Oriental Hospital opens.

JANUARY 1, 1929 South Vancouver and Point Grey amalgamate with Vancouver. With amalgamation, Vancouver's population climbs to 240,000.

JANUARY 2, 1929 Mayor W.H. Malkin presides over the first council of a bigger Vancouver.

JANUARY 2, 1929 Vancouver's police force management is shaken up by "striking" reorganization. Problems had been building since 1928, with corruption rampant among the senior officers. As many as twelve senior officers are either demoted or dismissed, with three taking early retirement. It will take until the mid-1930s to restore stability to the VPD leadership.

JANUARY 23, 1929 Two seats on the Vancouver Stock Exchange sell for a record $25,000 each.

FEBRUARY 1, 1929 Famed evangelist Aimee Semple McPherson is en route to Vancouver to speak to a women's group.

FEBRUARY 7, 1929 Movies shot in living color (not tinted) come to Vancouver.

MARCH 9, 1929 The VSE has a record trading day, with shares reaching nearly $1.5 million.

APRIL 6, 1929 The northwest corner of Pender and Hornby sells for $140,000.

JULY 27, 1929 The Union Steamship Wharf burns.

JULY 27, 1929 Charles Lindbergh refuses an invitation to fly into Vancouver because Vancouver lacks an adequate airport.

AUGUST 7, 1929 Hastings Park is the site of the first annual B.C. High Schools Olympics.

AUGUST 24, 1929 Boeing of Canada opens a plant in Vancouver at Coal Harbor.

AUGUST 27, 1929 The Graf Zeppelin visits Coal Harbor.

SEPTEMBER 19, 1929 A log-carrying freighter, the *Pacific Gather-*

Henry Lund and Iris Palethorpe were chosen as the Suntan King and Queen of the 1932 Vancouver Exhibition. They are here surrounded by the members of the Home Gas Orchestra. In a city that receives fewer than 2,000 hours of bright sunshine annually, cultivating a suntan requires total commitment. Courtesy, City of Vancouver Archives

er, knocks out a span on the Second Narrows Bridge, closing the bridge for three and a half years.

OCTOBER 2, 1929 Lauchlan Hamilton, former CPR surveyor and commissioner, and the man who designed Vancouver's street system, visits the city. Hamilton answers critics of Vancouver's plan by pointing out that the plan had to conform to portions of Granville Townsite and Lot 185—the West End—which had already been laid out.

OCTOBER 18, 1929 The Privy Council of Canada rules that women are "persons," and are thus entitled to sit in the Senate.

OCTOBER 29, 1929 Wall Street crashes.

DECEMBER 17, 1929 The unemployed raid the city relief office.

DECEMBER 18, 1929 Several hundred unemployed march in protest.

JANUARY 1, 1930 An order-in-council approves a ninety-nine-year lease on Deadman's Island, and stipulates that the name be changed.

FEBRUARY 14, 1930 A *Sun* contest results in the suggestion that Deadman's Island be renamed Park Island, but the parks board announces that the name Deadman's Island will continue in use for the time being.

FEBRUARY 22, 1930 A 25-by-120-foot lot on the 600 block of Granville sells for $210,000.

APRIL 24, 1930 The freighter *Losmar* tears off the south span of the Second Narrows Bridge, causing $100,000 damage.

JULY 12, 1930 The city market opens at Main and Pender, near the old city hall.

JULY 28, 1930 The Hastings Mill Store is towed by barge to Alma Park as a museum.

AUGUST 6, 1930 Percy Williams wins the 100-yard dash in the Dominion Police Games in Toronto.

AUGUST 7, 1930 Premier Richard B. Bennett, elected July 29, takes office.

AUGUST 21, 1930 With a per capita income of $4,339, B.C. is the wealthiest province in the country.

Above: This rocket won the first prize as a parade float in the 1936 Vancouver Jubilee Parade and was so popular that it was installed at the Vancouver Airport. In recent years it completely rotted and was removed. A group of Vancouverites is now in the process of rebuilding it for Expo 86. (VPL)

Far left: Huge advances in car tuning occurred in the 1930s. Gizmo fetishists paid $2.50 to have their motors read on one of these meter machines—the equivalent of thirteen days' relief camp wages. Courtesy, City of Vancouver Archives

Left: This unbelievable bamboo arch tower was constructed to commemorate Vancouver's fiftieth year and was part of a Chinese village display located between Chinatown and the Georgia Street viaduct right off Carrall Street. (VPL)

AUGUST 23, 1930 Stan Leonard wins the Caddy's Golf Championship.

OCTOBER 5, 1930 The Vancouver Symphony Orchestra holds its first concert at the Orpheum.

OCTOBER 21, 1930 Vancouver's first relief gang works on clearing in Point Grey.

NOVEMBER 21, 1930 The first Lillibet dolls, modelled after Princess Elizabeth, become available in Vancouver.

NOVEMBER 30, 1930 The jobless are pouring into Vancouver at a rate of forty to fifty per day.

DECEMBER 6, 1930 Air mail is shipped to the Orient via Vancouver.

DECEMBER 8, 1930 Work begins on Burrard Bridge.

ALSO IN 1930 Two hundred skeletons are discovered in a Marpole midden.

ALSO IN 1930 Vancouver lists 7,000 unemployed. Federal and provincial governments agree to provide relief.

JUNE 1, 1931 The new CPR pier is built.

JUNE 15, 1931 The government takes over the sale of liquor.

JULY 2-3, 1931 In a two-day debate, Vancouver council bans walkathons and similar contests of endurance forever. Concerns over the potential injuries participants face, as well as charges of offending public decency and violating the Lord's Day Act and factory laws are all part of the "walkies" controversy.

JULY 3, 1931 Canada's first baseball game to be played under the lights is held at Athletic Park (later to be called Capilano Stadium).

JULY 22, 1931 Vancouver Airport and Seaplane Harbor officially opens.

False Creek in 1936 was a place of sawmills, sawdust burners, industrial waste, and pollution, an unhealthy place to be. For most people though, the smell of smoke from the mills was the smell of money and during the Depression many were willing to put their health at risk to have a job. Courtesy, City of Vancouver Archives

AUGUST 15, 1931 Kitsilano Swimming Pool opens officially.

OCTOBER 5, 1931 Lieutenant-Governor Fordham Johnson officiates at the opening of the Vancouver Art Gallery.

NOVEMBER 3, 1931 South Vancouver opens a new municipal hall on Fraser Street.

ALSO IN 1931 Sculptor Charles Marega is commissioned by the Vancouver Art Gallery to sculpt the frieze for the gallery facade.

ALSO IN 1931 Fisherman's Wharf is completed.

FEBRUARY 22, 1932 Six thousand unemployed march from Powell Street grounds to Cambie Street grounds.

MARCH 31, 1932 Vancouver is named Canada's leading port.

APRIL 13, 1932 Paderewski performs in recital at the Vancouver Arena.

MAY 4, 1932 The unemployed demonstrate at city hall.

AUGUST 1, 1932 Duncan McNaughton wins the high jump at the Los Angeles Olympics.

AUGUST 20, 1932 Vancouver beer parlors are now open from 9:30 a.m. to 11:30 p.m.

In 1936, three years before the opening of the Lions Gate Bridge, the North Vancouver Ferry, which left from the foot of Main Street, was the fastest way to get to the North Shore. The only surface connector to the northside of Burrard Inlet at that time was the Second Narrows Bridge. (VPL)

AUGUST 29, 1932 Governor General Bessborough opens the Canadian Pacific Exhibition.

ALSO IN 1932 Thirty-four thousand people in Vancouver are on relief. Provincial government lowers the relief rate to $12.50.

JANUARY 13, 1933 Two bank clerks are shot during a hold-up in Kitsilano, as bandits take off with $3,500.

JANUARY 25, 1933 Mayor Telford suspends Police Chief C.E. Edgett, accusing him of involvement with pimps and gamblers.

JANUARY 27, 1933 Blackburns Farmers' Market opens at Seymour and Robson.

FEBRUARY 7, 1933 Police Chief Edgett is dismissed.

FEBRUARY 11, 1933 Edgett sues the Police Commission.

MARCH 20, 1933 A bomb destroys the lobby of the Royal Theatre, hurling the manager and his wife from their bed as they sleep in their suite above the theatre.

APRIL 11, 1933 Vancouver council votes to ban slot machines.

APRIL 24, 1933 The *Vancouver News Herald* publishes its first edition.

The waiting room of the tram station at Hastings and Carrall was a familiar place for commuters who caught the trains to locations in Richmond and the Fraser Valley. Courtesy, City of Vancouver Archives

JUNE 9, 1933 A city by-law amendment allows men to wear bathing trunks on city beaches and to dispense with tops.

JULY 3, 1933 Unemployed and police fight over evictions.

JULY 10-15, 1933 Shaughnessy Golf Club hosts the first Canadian Amateur Golf Championships to be played in B.C.

NOVEMBER 2, 1933 The CCF forms the official opposition as thirty Liberals are elected and the Tolmie group is crushed.

NOVEMBER 15, 1933 Premier Thomas Duff Pattullo takes office.

JANUARY 5, 1934 The reading room in the public library, closed in 1933 for a lack of funds, re-opens.

MARCH 2, 1934 The government approves a rise in food relief rates to thirty dollars a month for a family of five.

MARCH 5, 1934 Council approves a rise of 10 percent per month for residents receiving food relief.

JULY 8, 1934 The Vancouver Symphony Orchestra performs at the opening of the Malkin Bowl.

A lighter moment in the relief camps: a group of musicians get together to play a few Woody Guthrie songs and labor tunes by Joe Hill. (VPL)

DECEMBER 8, 1934 Tokyo and Vancouver are linked by radio and telephone.

DECEMBER 13, 1934 G.G. McGeer is elected mayor with the largest lead in Vancouver history. McGeer sweeps into office with 25,000 votes out of the 44,000 ballots cast. Another old favorite, L.D. Taylor, is eliminated in the landslide.

DECEMBER 22, 1934 The Bank of Vancouver is liquidated.

ALSO IN 1934 The Bank of Canada is established.

JANUARY 6, 1935 Mayor McGeer orders a day of prayer for forgiveness of city sins.

JANUARY 21, 1935 The roof on the Hastings Park Forum collapses under a heavy snowfall.

APRIL 19, 1935 Strikers rally at the Cambie Street grounds and march to Stanley Park.

APRIL 23, 1935 Relief camp men demonstrate with a parade through the Hudson's Bay Company, causing thousands of dollars in damage. Mayor McGeer reads the Riot Act in Victory Square.

The Guinness Company was eager to develop the slopes above West Vancouver and after ten years of negotiations received that right. The deal included the construction of a $6-million toll bridge across the First Narrows (paid for by Guinness) which opened in late 1938 and is to this day known as the Lions Gate Bridge. (VPL)

APRIL 28, 1935 The CCF holds the largest political relief rally in Vancouver in the Arena.

MAY 1, 1935 B.C.'s relief bill hits $8,020,000.

MAY 6, 1935 King George's Jubilee is celebrated at the Brockton Oval.

MAY 18, 1935 Relief strikers occupy Carnegie Library.

JUNE 3, 1935 The first unemployed Ottawa trekkers leave for Ottawa by train.

JUNE 11, 1935 The first baby bonds worth $1.5 million for the city of Vancouver are issued.

JUNE 15, 1935 General strikers call on the longshoremen for support.

JUNE 15, 1935 Tear gas bombs are used to quell rioters at the Ballantyne Pier. The leader of the longshoremen is jailed.

OCTOBER 23, 1935 Prime Minister William Lyon Mackenzie King takes office.

JANUARY 24, 1936 The parks board recommends that the Stanley Park hollow tree be destroyed.

JANUARY 28, 1936 A civic memorial service for King George V is held at Malkin Bowl.

FEBRUARY 1, 1936 Two thousand women sign a petition for free government-run birth-control clinics.

FEBRUARY 22, 1936 The Seaforth Highlanders Regimental Band is formed.

MAY 1, 1936 Sales tax is set at 8 percent.

MAY 6, 1936 Poet Dorothy Livesay moves to Vancouver.

MAY 24, 1936 Civic Golden Jubilee celebrations start. Newspapers publish Jubilee souvenir editions.

JUNE 28, 1936 Eight thousand attend dedication services for the Jubilee at the Exhibition Forum.

JULY 4, 1936 Brighton Pool is opened.

Left: Men from the relief camps stopped receiving their twenty cents a day in early 1938 and as a protest occupied the Vancouver Art Gallery and post office. The men in the VAG were persuaded to leave peacefully but those in the post office were forced to run through a police gauntlet of swinging clubs. (VPL)

Lower left: Steve Brodie, "Champion of Labor" and leader of the unemployed workers' occupation of the Vancouver Post Office, was singled out for "special questioning" by police officials. (VPL)

JULY 6, 1936 Telegraph wires link Vancouver to London, England.

JULY 15, 1936 W.L. "Biff" McTavish becomes editor of the *Daily Province.*

JULY 18, 1936 Chinese Carnival Village opens.

AUGUST 5, 1936 Mayor McGeer is made honorary chief of the Squamish Indian Band.

AUGUST 10, 1936 Mayor McGeer wears the Chain of Office for the first time in public service since 1912, to greet the Lord Mayor of London.

AUGUST 20, 1936 Fire destroys the Auditorium and Denman Arena.

AUGUST 29, 1936 Governor General Tweedsmuir officiates at the opening of the Seaforth Armories.

AUGUST 29, 1936 Gasoline sells for twenty-five cents a gallon.

DECEMBER 4, 1936 Vancouver's new city hall at 12th and Cambie is officially opened.

ALSO IN 1936 S. Ichie Hayakawa leads a delegation of Japanese-Canadian citizens to Ottawa in an unsuccessful appeal for enfranchisement.

FEBRUARY 16, 1937 The CBC begins broadcasting over radio station CRVC.

After being evicted from the post office the unemployed took to the streets and out of sheer frustration began breaking windows like this one at David Spencer's Department Store. A little more than a year later these same men would be lining up to defend their country. (VPL)

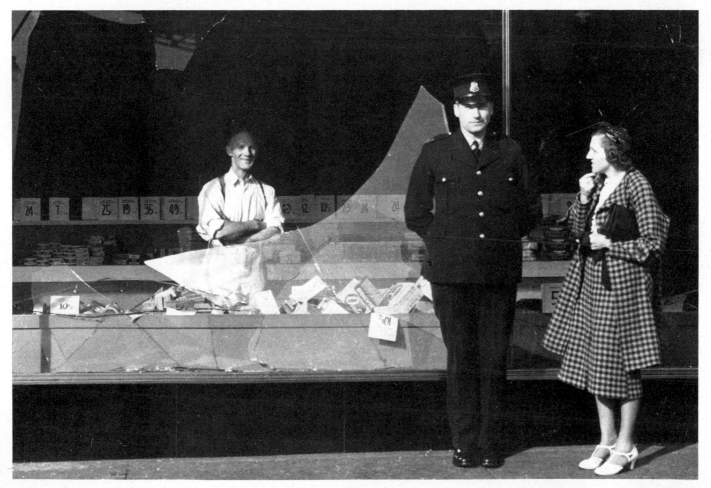

FEBRUARY 20, 1937 A snowslide on Grouse Mountain covers the chalet and many cabins.

MARCH 5, 1937 The first reference to marijuana in a Vancouver newspaper is made.

MARCH 22, 1937 *Vancouver Sun* offices are destroyed by fire.

MARCH 23, 1937 Helen Gutteridge becomes the first woman

elected to city council in the city's fifty-one-year history. Gutteridge is sponsored by the CCF, and her victory gives the party a three-seat block.

MAY 18, 1937 The *Vancouver Sun* purchases Bekins Tower, which becomes the Sun Tower and a heritage building.

JUNE 1, 1937 Pattullo's government is returned, but Paterson's revitalized Conservatives gain eight seats.

The view north from the top of the recently completed Hotel Vancouver number three shows that most of northwest downtown was still residential in July 1939. (VPL)

JUNE 16, 1937 The federal government contracts with Boeing for eleven warplanes.

JULY 19, 1937 Sliced bread comes to Vancouver.

OCTOBER 2, 1936 UBC Stadium opens.

NOVEMBER 15, 1936 Pattullo Bridge is officially opened.

ALSO IN 1937 The first *Sun* Salmon Derby is held.

MARCH 1, 1938 The B.C. Loggers' Association adopts an eight-hour day for their workers.

MARCH 25, 1938 Vancouver police crack down on Chinese gambling houses in the city, with late night and early morning raids on the dens to ensure that order was being rigidly obeyed.

JULY 27, 1938 Pier D burns.

JULY 29, 1938 Ann Mindigel is the first swimmer to swim from Vancouver to Bowen Island.

OCTOBER 14, 1938 A council suggestion for uniform spellings of surnames starting with Mc and Mac causes an uproar.

OCTOBER 18, 1938 Council rescinds the clause that would deny trading permits to Asians.

NOVEMBER 11, 1938 Lions Gate Bridge is opened by Mayor G. Miller. Mary Sutton is the first pedestrian, while Douglas Craig is the first driver.

ALSO IN 1938 Helen McGill is the first woman to receive an honorary degree from UBC.

ALSO IN 1938 The English Bay Pier is demolished.

ALSO IN 1938 Unemployed workers occupy the Vancouver Art Gallery, the post office, and the Hotel Georgia for a month. The forceable ejection of squatters results in a riot in which thirty-eight are injured and twenty-three jailed.

ALSO IN 1938 Angus Drive acquires a reputation as a "lover's lane."

JANUARY 23, 1939 Sculptor Charles Marega's lions are placed at the Lions Gate Bridge.

MAY 16, 1939 BCER extends the first bus line into the downtown city, mixing city buses with streetcars.

MAY 24, 1939 The CPR presents a musical farewell to the old Hotel Vancouver.

MAY 25, 1939 The new Hotel Vancouver opens on its present site.

MAY 29, 1939 King George VI and Queen Elizabeth visit Vancouver. The Associated Press releases the first wirephotos from Vancouver of the royal visit.

JUNE 19, 1939 St. Vincent's Hospital opens.

AUGUST 3, 1939 Radio telephones are installed in police cars.

AUGUST 26, 1939 Local militia man the guns at First Narrows in North Vancouver.

SEPTEMBER 3, 1939 Britain and France declare war on Germany.

SEPTEMBER 10, 1939 Canada enters World War II.

ALSO IN 1939 W.H. Malkin donates six acres of land to Vancouver for parks.

ALSO IN 1939 The Women's Auxiliary to the B.C. Regiment is formed.

The sideshow at the Vancouver Exhibition in August 1938 featured "boxers" and "wrestlers" a contestant could try to defeat for a big prize. Courtesy, City of Vancouver Archives

PART IV

WORLD WAR II AND THE FORTIES

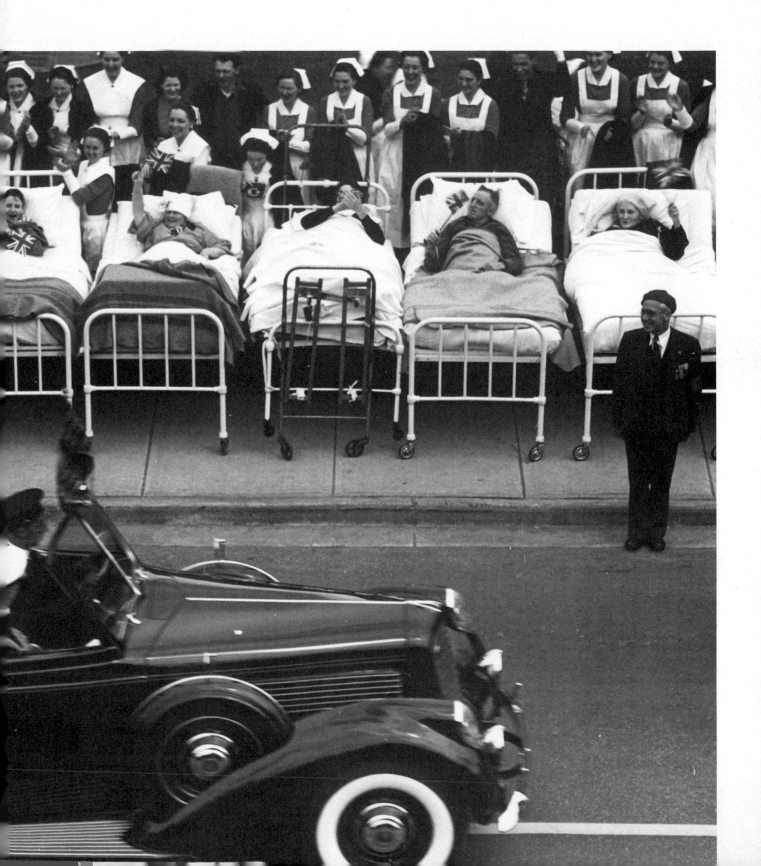

SEPTEMBER 1, 1939 The outbreak of World War II finds Vancouver citizens responding on all fronts. Hundreds join up and hundreds more become involved in volunteer organizations and fund-raising events.

OCTOBER 11, 1939 University president Dr. Leonard Klinck officially opens the first public aquarium, at the old English Bay Bathhouse. The star attraction is Oscar the Octopus.

NOVEMBER 5, 1939 Vancouver gets its first dial telephones. The switchover of about 3,300 telephones in the Marine exchange is accomplished in four minutes.

DECEMBER 14, 1939 Vancouver's "first lady," Ruth Morton, widow of John Morton, one of the Three Greenhorns, dies in Vancouver General Hospital at age ninety-one.

DECEMBER 18, 1939 Winston Churchill, First Lord of the Admiralty, announces that the first Canadian troops have landed on British soil.

Preceding pages: In late May 1939 Queen Elizabeth and King George VI made a royal visit to Vancouver. They opened the Hotel Vancouver number three and the Lions Gate Bridge. Patients from Vancouver General Hospital seem to enjoy the royal couple's curbside manner. (VPL)

Below: A common sight at English Bay in 1940 was this holy scripture cart, owned and operated by a religious eccentric who, among other things, devised a method for color-coding spirituality. (VPL)

FEBRUARY 22, 1940 Edward T. Rogers, a black shoemaker, wins the right in British Columbia Supreme Court to be served in city beer parlors. The Clarence Hotel is assessed damages of twenty-five dollars.

FEBRUARY 29, 1940 The *Vancouver Daily Sun* merges its pioneer radio station with CKWX. The station's power is increased to reach nearly all parts of British Columbia.

MARCH 2, 1940 A week-long gasoline war, which closed service stations and left automobiles abandoned all over the city, ends when prices are set at twenty-five cents per gallon.

MAY 11, 1940 Vancouver's airport is reported the busiest in Canada, with a take-off or landing every eighty-one minutes during daylight hours.

MAY 23, 1940 Masses of veterans converge on the Federal Building to enlist in the Veteran's Home Guard.

JULY 9, 1940 The first of thousands of children evacuated from Britain for the duration of the war arrive in Vancouver.

JULY 16, 1940 The Lord's Day Act is waived to allow theatres to stage a "Win the War" evening of free movies on Sunday. The sale of War Savings Stamps realizes $30,000.

AUGUST 6, 1940 Theatre Under the Stars (TUTS) gives its first performance at Malkin Bowl. Reserved seats cost fifty cents.

AUGUST 31, 1940 UBC librarian John Ridington retires. Students fondly called him "King John" and the library "King John's Palace."

SEPTEMBER 28, 1940 Fifteen-hundred male students register at UBC to begin compulsory military training.

OCTOBER 5, 1940 The Air Raid Patrol begins a house-to-house search in Vancouver looking for unregistered firearms.

DECEMBER 15, 1940 Indian princess Mary Capilano dies at age 105. She was the first Indian princess to welcome the Oblate missionaries ninety years before.

ALSO IN 1940 In the first two days following the draft of unmarried men, at least 434 marriage licences are issued in Vancouver.

JANUARY 2, 1941 Jonathan W. Cornett is sworn in as mayor.

One of the most dreadful appliances invented and used during the 1940s was the sawdust burning stove. They generated a lot of smoke and needed a dump truck load of sawdust for a single month's operation. (VPL)

APRIL 28, 1941 Ottar Novik and twenty-three relatives arrive from Norway. The family made its escape from war by crossing the Atlantic in a fishing vessel.

MAY 22, 1941 The city's first trial blackout is held between 10:00 and 10:15 p.m. Violators are subject to a $500 fine and a year in jail.

JUNE 2, 1941 A Victory Loan torch is lit at the head of the Stanley Park Causeway and is to burn until Vancouver meets its Loan quota.

JULY 8, 1941 The Victory Loan torch is taken to Britain and presented to Winston Churchill.

AUGUST 5, 1941 Vancouverite Isabel Guernsey is held as a prisoner of war in Germany after the ship *Zamzam* is torpedoed. She is released from an internment camp near Stuttgart on September 16.

SEPTEMBER 17, 1941 Women recruits enlist in the Canadian

Women's Army Corps (CWACS) at the Vancouver barracks.

NOVEMBER 6, 1941 Air raid sirens are tested throughout the city.

NOVEMBER 25, 1941 Local labor leaders call for equal pay for equal work for women who are replacing servicemen on assembly lines.

DECEMBER 7, 1941 U.S. naval base Pearl Harbor is attacked and Canada declares war on Japan. The RCMP immediately begin to tie up the Japanese fishing boats. Japanese schools are closed and newspapers are no longer allowed to publish in Japanese.

DECEMBER 9, 1941 Vancouver experiences its first total blackout. Stores are swamped with customers buying blackout covers.

DECEMBER 9, 1941 Mr. P.A. Woodward launches the "Canadian Aid to Russia" fund in the city. During the war years Canadians were to raise nearly ten million dollars for Russian aid.

The B.C. Electric Railway introduced a new line of streetcars that held nearly double the capacity of previous versions. Here they're being spruced up for their maiden voyage on Vancouver's streets in early January 1941. (VPL)

DECEMBER 10, 1941 Iwatichi Sugiyama, a naturalized British subject, is the only person of Japanese descent who dares to vote in the civic election.

DECEMBER 14, 1941 Gas masks go on sale to the general public.

DECEMBER 21, 1941 Butter becomes the first product to be rationed in Canada.

ALSO IN 1941 The closing of several mills results in a serious fuel shortage in the city. Potatoes are also in short supply due to a pricing dispute.

ALSO IN 1941 New regulations limit the purchase of liquor and curtail the hours of pubs and beer parlors. All beer parlors close for one hour over the supper hour, in an ill-considered attempt to get Dad home to the dinner table.

JANUARY 2, 1942 Vancouver's first anti-aircraft guns are installed. Locations of the installations are not made public.

JANUARY 7, 1942 City council refuses to debate a motion by Alderman Halford Wilson calling for all coastal Japanese to be moved. Council indicates it will wait for instructions from the federal government.

Civil defence drills became a normal part of the school day during World War II. Once these young women got home from school they would practice blackouts at home. (VPL)

JANUARY 14, 1942 Ottawa announces that all Japanese aliens are to be removed from defence areas of coastal British Columbia.

JANUARY 15, 1942 The population of Greater Vancouver is 337,000.

FEBRUARY 24, 1942 It is disclosed in Washington, D.C., that maps seized from the Japanese detail elaborate plans for an invasion of the west coast of North America.

FEBRUARY 28, 1942 All Japanese in Vancouver are forbidden to appear on public streets between dusk and dawn. Three days later a dozen are arrested for violation of the curfew.

MARCH 9, 1942 Police seize all radios from Japanese citizens to prevent them from hearing propaganda broadcasts from Tokyo.

MARCH 10, 1942 Restrictions are placed on men's clothing, banning fancy styles, cuffs, and pants pleats in an effort to save textiles.

MARCH 25, 1942 The Forum and Exhibition Park are closed to public events as Hastings Park is taken over for Japanese encampment.

APRIL 1, 1942 Gasoline rationing is in effect.

MAY 26, 1942 Tea, coffee, and sugar are added to the list of rationed goods.

ALSO IN 1942 Amateur gardeners are urged to use backyards and vacant lots to start "Victory Gardens" to provide food to war-torn Britain.

JUNE 3, 1942 All defence forces are on the alert after the Japanese bomb naval stations in Alaska.

AUGUST 31, 1942 The largest salmon run in thirty years is underway. The entire catch is canned for Britain and cannot be sold locally.

SEPTEMBER 19, 1942 Compulsory registration for the draft ends for single women between ages of twenty to twenty-four.

OCTOBER 2, 1942 Colonel Cecil C. Merritt, a hero of the Dieppe Raid, becomes the first Canadian in World War II to win the Victoria Cross.

OCTOBER 8, 1942 The last group of Japanese leaves Hastings Park for new homes in the interior.

NOVEMBER 3, 1942 Two bombs placed behind the haunches of one of the lions at the courthouse partially destroy it and shatter windows of nearby hotels. The responsible person is not found.

JANUARY 21, 1943 The army is called to cut wood as the city experiences a serious fuel shortage. Schools and laundries are closed.

FEBRUARY 8, 1943 Alderman Charles Jones is named head of a committee to dispose of Japanese properties on the Lower Mainland.

FEBRUARY 13, 1943 Liquor is rationed to one forty-ounce bottle per week per customer. By March 1 rations are changed to one bottle per month, and liquor stores open only one hour a day. Reports of line-ups, hijackings, and bootlegging follow.

FEBRUARY 16, 1943 A ban is placed on all new construction due to the serious lumber shortage.

World War II brought with it the threat of attack from the air and Vancouver's defences were tailored accordingly. In 1941 anti-aircraft guns and searchlights were stationed at secret (everything was secret) locations around the city. (VPL)

APRIL 6, 1943 Recruitment for a Land Army of agricultural workers begins. The first appeal is for women with experience in dairy farming. The school board approves a four-month summer vacation for pupils with a good academic standing to join the Land Army.

APRIL 28, 1943 A strike at Boeing, over the issue of rest periods, closes all four plants in the city until May 4.

MAY 4, 1943 Meatless Tuesdays go into effect in all restaurants and boarding houses.

MAY 5, 1943 Wednesday closing of retail stores goes into effect.

MAY 15, 1943 The ban on home construction is lifted and 1,500 permits are issued per month.

JULY 19, 1943 Men are asked to volunteer several hours a week of their leisure time to help alleviate a serious manpower shortage in essential industries.

JULY 22, 1943 Ration coupons representing the equivalent of 349,000 gallons of gasoline are stolen from the Union Oil station on Venables. This is one episode in a growing local black market for rationed goods.

A group of B.C. Telephone executives perform an ARP drill in October 1942. The Air Raid Protection organization was a volunteer group of about 10,000 citizens who regularly practiced civil defence skills throughout World War II. (VPL)

AUGUST 14, 1943 Married men ages twenty-seven to thirty are drafted.

OCTOBER 6, 1943 Under federal government instructions, the water supply is chlorinated. A front page of a local newspaper features a black-bordered box reading "In Memoriam, H2O." In subsequent weeks chlorine is blamed for everything from the death of fish fingerlings to canaries that no longer sing.

OCTOBER 7, 1943 The federal department returns Exhibition Park and the first nine holes of the Hastings Park Golf Course to city control.

NOVEMBER 20, 1943 Council enforces a 1923 by-law imposing a curfew on all children under sixteen.

DECEMBER 2, 1943 The first Canadians to be repatriated from Japanese prison camps reach Canada. Among them are forty-five Vancouverites.

DECEMBER 6, 1943 The city announces it will illuminate some evergreens for Christmas for the first time since the bombing of Pearl Harbor.

JANUARY 1, 1944 Approximately two dozen join Peter Pantages in the twenty-second annual Polar Bear Swim at English Bay.

After the bombing of Pearl Harbor in December 1941, Japanese Canadians were rounded up and sent off to camps in eastern British Columbia. Out of a population of about 10,000 before the war, fewer than 1,000 returned to Vancouver in 1949. (VPL)

JANUARY 13, 1944 The police commission orders a probe into prostitution and gambling problems in Vancouver.

FEBRUARY 25, 1944 Pre-fabricated housing comes to Vancouver. Homes sell for $3,600 each.

MARCH 3, 1944 Meat rationing, which since the previous May had been two pounds per person per week, is suspended indefinitely.

MAY 31, 1944 Vancouver faces a serious shortage of children's shoes.

AUGUST 3, 1944 Six thousand eight hundred jobs go unfilled in the city as a serious manpower shortage persists.

AUGUST 14, 1944 Odessa, USSR, is adopted as Vancouver's sister city. To mark the occasion the Vancouver Symphony Orchestra gives a concert of Russian music.

SEPTEMBER 16, 1944 Cecil C. Merritt, still a prisoner of war in Germany, is nominated by acclamation to run for the federal

In 1942 Japanese Canadians were first imprisoned at Hastings Park before being shipped out to camps in the Kootenays. Women and children were segregated from their men and all the work of cooking and cleaning was done on an unpaid basis by the prisoners themselves. (VPL)

117

Progressive-Conservatives in Burrard.

SEPTEMBER 18, 1944 Tea and coffee rationing ends.

OCTOBER 9, 1944 The *St. Roch* arrives in Vancouver having completed her historic two-way trip through the Northwest Passage from Vancouver to Halifax and back.

OCTOBER 11, 1944 The first day-care center for children of servicemen is opened in Vancouver to allow mothers one afternoon "off" a week.

OCTOBER 21, 1944 HMCS Discovery is offically opened on Deadman's Island and two ships are launched in Vancouver to mark the opening of the seventh Victory Loan campaign.

FEBRUARY 28, 1945 Fire destroys Capilano Stadium.

APRIL 20, 1945 Word is received in Vancouver of the release of Cecil C. Merritt from a German prison camp. He reaches Vancouver on May 22.

With the serious labor shortage during World War II many women found themselves working in traditionally male jobs. Here women are working in the Jones Tent and Awning Company making Venetian blinds. (VPL)

MAY 7, 1945 Air raid sirens ring at 7:04 a.m. to mark V-E day. The city erupts in a spontaneous celebration.

MAY 8, 1945 Vancouver declares a civic holiday to celebrate peace in Europe.

MAY 25, 1945 Gasoline rationing is eased, with one coupon buying four, rather than three, gallons of gas.

JUNE 20, 1945 The first special troop train bringing servicemen home arrives at the CPR depot. Throngs of citizens are on hand to greet the returning men.

AUGUST 4, 1945 The froth on beer glasses is limited by law to half an inch.

AUGUST 12, 1945 Vancouver celebrates V-J day prematurely when a recorded victory speech by Prime Minister Mackenzie King is accidently released. Vancouver newspapers bring out extras announcing the false peace.

Thousands of Vancouverites worked at the Boeing plant on Sea Island during World War II manufacturing military seaplanes. Boeing also had plants on False Creek and Coal Harbor where they made boats. Later the company moved to the U.S. (VPL)

AUGUST 14, 1945 Celebration of V-J Day results in some seventy-five minor injuries. Chinatown lights up with a display of fireworks which residents have hoarded since the outbreak of war.

AUGUST 16, 1945 Shipbuilding orders totalling twenty-two million dollars are cancelled, resulting in 2,500 layoffs in B.C.'s shipyards.

SEPTEMBER 10, 1945 A proposal is made at a Pacific Northwest Trade Association meeting that the new atomic bomb could be used to blow up submerged Ripple Rock, a hazard to navigation. Fortunately, cooler heads prevail.

OCTOBER 1, 1945 One hundred and forty Canadian war brides sail from Vancouver to join their husbands in Australia.

OCTOBER 3, 1945 Coal is rationed to one ton per household.

OCTOBER 7, 1945 The first battalion of the Seaforth Highlanders is welcomed home in what newspapers call "Vancouver's greatest celebration."

OCTOBER 18, 1945 Premier Hart announces that all B.C. Electric customers will receive one month's free electricity.

NOVEMBER 3, 1945 Vancouver is the first city in Canada to go over the top in the ninth and final Victory Loan Drive.

August 14, 1945, the day peace was declared at the end of World War II, was a great day in Vancouver. Things got so wild that police arrested dozens of people. These newsboys sold out in no time. Courtesy, City of Vancouver Archives

NOVEMBER 6, 1945 City council withdraws the order which set separate swimming days at Crystal Pool for "colored" and Orientals.

NOVEMBER 14, 1945 The wartime ban on operating ham radios is lifted.

FEBRUARY 19, 1946 Thousands are lined up before 6:00 a.m. to purchase nylon hose when Vancouver's first postwar shipment arrives.

MARCH 5, 1946 One of the largest funerals the city has seen is held for Sing K. Yip, believed to be the first Chinese immigrant to come to British Columbia.

MARCH 8, 1946 The operation of the Vancouver airport is returned to the city.

JUNE 6, 1946 A printers' strike begins against the *Vancouver Daily Province.*

JULY 1, 1946 Two weeks of festivities begin, celebrating the city's Diamond Jubilee. At Stanley Park members of the Kwakiutl Indian Band perform their secret Red River Bank Dance for the first time in public.

A B.C. Telephone employee displays her matchbook collection on May 30, 1944. For the duration of the war, with the boys overseas and rationing of everything from sugar to gasoline, young women took up hobbies like matchbook collecting to add a little excitement to their lives. (VPL)

JULY 16, 1946 Jack Scott writes his first column for the *Vancouver Sun*. He will become the best-loved of Vancouver columnists.

JULY 23, 1946 Violence erupts when the strike-bound *Vancouver Daily Province* attempts to publish.

AUGUST 15, 1946 National registration officially ends. It is announced in Ottawa that Canadian deserters and draft dodgers will not be prosecuted.

NOVEMBER 1, 1946 A simple ceremony marks the placing in the Canadian Memorial Church of a replica of Canada's Book of Remembrance. The book lists the 60,000 Canadians killed in the First World War.

NOVEMBER 15, 1946 Wartime restrictions are lifted from women's clothing. The "new look" featuring long skirts is slow to catch on in Vancouver.

DECEMBER 11, 1946 Senator Gerry McGeer, who is recuperating from surgery, is elected mayor of Vancouver. There are protests over his holding the two offices at once.

Soldiers and civilians alike whooped it up on V-J Day. The sounds and noises of that day were as memorable as the sights: air raid sirens screamed nonstop, car horns and ship whistles bleated incessantly, and people yelled and hollered themselves hoarse. Courtesy, City of Vancouver Archives

JANUARY 6, 1947 Mayor McGeer receives the first Certificate of Canadian Citizenship under the new Citizenship Act which came into force on January 1. Prior to the act's passing, the terms "Canadian national" and "British subject" were used to describe Canada's non-alien population.

JANUARY 11, 1947 Price controls on many goods and services are lifted but remain on rent, fuel, and food. Men's haircuts immediately rise to sixty-five cents.

JANUARY 25, 1947 An investigation of the police department is ordered by council and Walter Mulligan is named acting police chief.

JANUARY 27, 1947 The last troop train of World War II arrives at the CPR depot nearly two years after the war's end. Thousands are on hand to welcome the veterans.

FEBRUARY 2, 1947 At a sod-turning ceremony for a new synagogue at 19th and Oak, the ground is dedicated by Rabbi C.B. Ginsberg to Jewish veterans of World War II.

FEBRUARY 3, 1947 Beer rationing ends and beer parlors remain open until 11:30 p.m. for the first time in five years.

MARCH 27, 1947 Meat rationing ends.

APRIL 2, 1947 Liquor rationing ends.

MAY 7, 1947 A police raid at the Western Sports Club on East Hastings results in 142 arrests on gambling charges.

MAY 10, 1947 Vancouver schoolchildren circulate a petition calling on Ottawa to end the wartime excise taxes placed on candy.

JULY 1, 1947 Housing shortages persist but fifty veterans and their families find accommodation in converted huts at Seaforth Armories.

JULY 5, 1947 Candy bar prices are lowered to seven cents from eight cents.

JULY 23, 1947 With polio cases mounting in the worst outbreak in twenty years, paddling pools are closed and it is announced that school opening will be delayed two weeks.

AUGUST 1, 1947 Mayor McGeer opens a new bus terminal at Larwill Park and calls it a temporary structure which will be removed in ten years to make way for a civic centre. It is still there in 1986.

AUGUST 11, 1947 Residents are shocked to learn that Mayor Gerry McGeer, the man who "always fought for Vancouver," has died in his sleep. Over 20,000 turn out for his funeral on August 15.

SEPTEMBER 21, 1947 Mon Keong School, a high school to teach Chinese language, literature, and music, opens in Chinatown and is believed unique in Canada.

NOVEMBER 3, 1947 Sugar, the last rationed food in Canada, is removed from the restricted list. Prices immediately rise 10 percent.

NOVEMBER 10, 1947 Vancouver sets a goal of $20,000 to purchase fresh and tinned fruit for Britons, as the city's wedding gift to Princess Elizabeth and Prince Philip.

DECEMBER 4, 1947 The original Lumberman's Arch is demolished after a top joist crumbles with dry rot, making it a public menace.

Two women study the Emily Carr painting *Kitseukla* at the Vancouver Art Gallery in 1946. Carr, who was British Columbia's most famous painter, passed away March 2, 1945, and bequeathed her remaining work to the Vancouver Art Gallery. (VPL)

DECEMBER 10, 1947 Acting mayor Charles Jones defeats Effie Jones and Peter McAllister in the civic election's mayoralty race.

FEBRUARY 18, 1948 The twenty-month strike at the *Vancouver Daily Province* is found illegal by the British Columbia Supreme Court and $10,000 damages are awarded to Southam Company, owner of the *Province.*

APRIL 12, 1948 Chinese Canadians are registering for the first time to vote in a federal by-election. Over 60 percent of the eligible voters register.

MAY 27, 1948 The first refugees from the Fraser Valley floods reach Vancouver aboard a special rescue train run by the CPR. Damages run into millions of dollars as much of the valley's rich agricultural land is flooded. Thousands volunteer to build and maintain dikes.

Margaret McNeil, Vancouver's first white baby, was brought up from her home in Portland, Oregon, to cut the official cake commemorating the city's sixtieth birthday on April 6, 1946. The cake was topped with a light-bulb-illuminated replica of city hall. (VPL)

JUNE 6, 1948 Film and stage shows are allowed on Sunday to raise relief funds for Fraser Valley flood victims.

JULY 1, 1948 British Columbia imposes its first sales tax of 3 percent.

JULY 2, 1948 Rising meat prices evoke a consumers' protest. Only two pounds of sausage, a three-and-a-half pound rump roast, one pound of stewing meat, one pound of liver, and one and a half pounds of hamburger can be purchased for five dollars.

JULY 21, 1948 The first 107 veterans and their families vacate the old Hotel Vancouver and move to the Renfrew housing project.

SEPTEMBER 1, 1948 Vancouver loses a second mayor in a year when Mayor Charles Jones dies in Vancouver General Hospital.

SEPTEMBER 3, 1948 Alderman George C. Miller is named acting mayor of Vancouver.

SEPTEMBER 3, 1948 Council indicates it will allow Chinese Canadians to vote in the civic election if the Union of B.C. Municipalities passes a motion to that effect at its convention.

The prefabricated home was one solution to the postwar housing shortage. It could be slapped together in record time. This home at 2256 Kingsway, for example, was begun May 10 and completely finished down to the furniture and landscaping by June 25, 1948. (VPL)

OCTOBER 3, 1948 Hallelujah Point in Stanley Park is officially named to commemorate the work of the Salvation Army, who had often held services there.

NOVEMBER 25, 1948 Television is first seen in Vancouver, broadcast by KRSC-TV in Seattle.

DECEMBER 23, 1948 H.R. MacMillan presents the Vancouver City Archives with a letter written by Gassy Jack Deighton to his brother Tom on June 28, 1870. Gassy Jack advises Tom that you can "make an easy living with little work in the new world."

JANUARY 4, 1949 Police Chief Walter Mulligan warns that the police will raid nightclubs to stamp out the "under the table" liquor trade.

JANUARY 5, 1949 Demolition crews begin work at the old Hotel Vancouver. Bathtubs have proven the most popular items at the auction of furnishings.

Rabbi C.B. Ginsberg of the Schara Tzedeck congregation presided over the ground-breaking ceremony for a new temple at Oak and 19th on February 2, 1947. Mayor Gerry McGeer (seated centre) was among the dignitaries attending. The temple would be the largest and most modern west of Montreal. (VPL)

MARCH 24, 1949 Henry Blair, the last surviving "father of incorporation," dies.

MARCH 25, 1949 The Vancouver Board of Trade condones the return of Japanese Canadians to coastal regions.

MAY 11, 1949 Violence erupts at Lapointe Pier resulting in the arrest of twenty-nine members of the striking Canadian Seamen's Union.

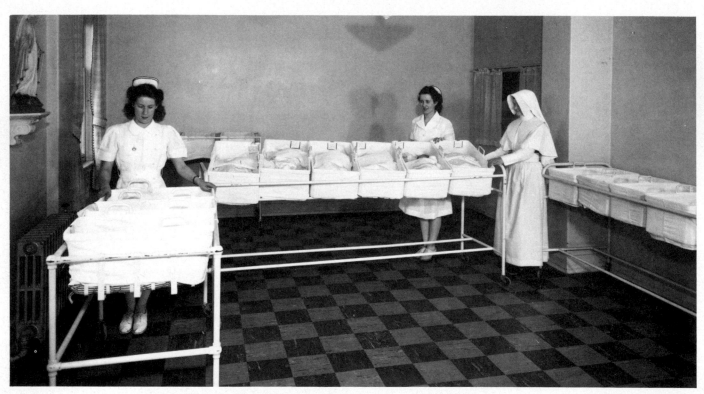

JUNE 15, 1949 A million-dollar four-alarm fire wipes out all industry on the False Creek waterfront bounded by 1st Avenue between Ontario and Main streets.

JUNE 27, 1949 The federal vote is given to persons of Japanese, Chinese, or East Indian descent, provided they are Canadian citizens or British subjects.

AUGUST 15, 1949 Kingsway becomes a six-lane highway between Vancouver and New Westminster.

SEPTEMBER 10, 1949 Registering in pre-medicine at UBC is Gloria Cranmer, the first Native woman to attend the university.

SEPTEMBER 16, 1949 The city moves to prosecute service stations selling gasoline on Sundays in contravention of the Lord's Day Act.

Nurses and nuns at St. Vincent's Hospital really had to scramble after World War II. The baby boom was on and extra cribs were set up in a makeshift nursery. Some of you baby boomers might be in this photo taken January 27, 1947. (VPL)

OCTOBER 15, 1949 Service stations win a Supreme Court decision allowing them to stay open beyond 7:00 p.m. on weekdays.

OCTOBER 21, 1949 A dogwood is planted in Queen Elizabeth Park to mark the beginning of Canada's only arboretum.

NOVEMBER 5, 1949 The bitter printers' strike at the *Vancouver Daily Province* ends. It lasted forty-one months.

NOVEMBER 15, 1949 The city's first underground parking lot opens on Hornby Street. Parking rates are set at fifteen cents per hour.

NOVEMBER 21, 1949 Nearly one quarter of Vancouver's 1889 population is on hand for a special Diamond Jubilee dinner at the Stanley Park Pavilion.

DECEMBER 1, 1949 The first section of the Grouse Mountain chair lift opens.

Indian Prime Minister Jawaharal Nehru visited Vancouver in early November 1949. One of his stops on a tour of the city was the Sikh Temple at 1866 West 2nd Avenue where he was given a tumultuous welcome. (VPL)

PART V

THE FIFTIES AND SIXTIES

JANUARY 8, 1950 Tom Alsbury is sworn in as mayor. He is the first Vancouver mayor to have been born in the twentieth century.

JANUARY 12, 1950 The first families move into the Fraserview housing development.

FEBRUARY 14, 1950 Nancy Hodges of Vancouver is the first woman in the British Empire to be named Speaker of the Legislature.

MARCH 13, 1950 Musical history is made in Vancouver when the Symposium of Canadian Music opens. The works of thirty-four Canadian composers are played over the four-day event.

AUGUST 20, 1950 The city's first atomic bomb shelter is built at an undisclosed location in the Shaughnessy District. The owner wishes to remain anonymous.

AUGUST 22, 1950 A national railway strike begins. It lasts nine days.

OCTOBER 3, 1950 The first section of Totem Park at UBC is open. The park will eventually represent works of every carving tribe in the province.

OCTOBER 8, 1950 Many of Canada's 5,000-strong Wong clan gather in Chinatown for a family reunion.

DECEMBER 11, 1950 Priceless art from China, Egypt, and the Haida Indian Band is donated to the Vancouver Museum by Elizabeth Rogers.

DECEMBER 13, 1950 Fred Hume, a former mayor of New Westminster, is elected mayor of Vancouver.

DECEMBER 27, 1950 Sprinter Percy Williams is named Canada's outstanding athlete of the half-century. Jimmy McLarnin is named outstanding boxer, and swimmer Irene Strong is a runner-up for the top woman athlete award.

JANUARY 8, 1951 Expert mountaineers and skiers form a rescue squad to deal with emergencies on the North Shore mountains.

JANUARY 10, 1951 The Vancouver Bar Association attracts over forty clients to its first free legal aid clinic.

JANUARY 18, 1951 The first Canadian casualty of the Korean War is Vancouver resident James Dean Wood.

JANUARY 31, 1951 Three inches of ice are blasted from the upper reaches of Burrard Inlet to allow barges to deliver fuel to the city.

This November 1950 advertising photograph for a kitchen cabinet design company clearly illustrates the modern lifestyle that emerged after World War II. An electric stove and refrigerator replaced the sawdust burner and icebox in Mom's dream kitchen. (VPL)

FEBRUARY 9, 1951 Dr. Gordon Shrum reveals that radioactive rain is falling in Vancouver, likely as a result of nuclear tests being conducted in Nevada.

FEBRUARY 12, 1951 Dr. Stewart Murray announces scarlet fever cases are reaching epidemic proportions.

FEBRUARY 28, 1951 An outbreak of influenza keeps over 7,000 students and many teachers from attending school.

FEBRUARY 28, 1951 The B.C. Packer's dock, at the foot of Campbell Street, is destroyed by fire.

MAY 2, 1951 Humorist Eric Nicol wins the Leacock Award for humor for his book *The Roving I.*

MAY 11, 1951 The "drunkometer," the latest weapon against impaired drivers, is demonstrated at the Hotel Vancouver.

JULY 1, 1951 Alderman Ann Sprott serves as acting mayor, the first woman to do so in the city's history. The post is rotated during the mayor's absence.

OCTOBER 20, 1951 Crowds are on hand everywhere to welcome Princess Elizabeth and Prince Philip to Vancouver during their first visit to Canada.

NOVEMBER 1, 1951 The announcement of a major oil discovery in the Peace District brings a flurry of activity to the Vancouver Stock Exchange.

The Delta Drive-In opened its gates to moviegoers in May 1953. Television and local weather conditions worked against the drive-in's success and by the 1970s weekend flea markets and swap meets brought in more people than did the films. The Delta Drive-In closed in February 1981. (VPL)

The height of 1953 interior design was beautifully reflected at the Del Mar Restaurant where sumptuous tropical flamingo murals somehow complemented the knotty pine wall board and furniture. (VPL)

NOVEMBER 15, 1951 The *Joe P. Martinez* sails into Vancouver, carrying 207 Canadian soldiers returning from the Korean War.

NOVEMBER 16, 1951 For the first time in over a decade two cases of leprosy are identified in the city. The victims are sent to the leper colony on Bentinck Island.

JANUARY 31, 1952 American singer and actor Paul Robeson, travelling to Vancouver for a performance, is refused entry to Canada at the Blaine border crossing. The U.S. government restricts Robeson's movements because of his suspected Communist sympathies.

MARCH 28, 1952 Retiring director Charles H. Scott officially opens the Vancouver Art School at Dunsmuir and Hamilton.

APRIL 16, 1952 Elizabeth Rogers presents *The Spanish Dancer* by painter John Phillips to the Vancouver Museum.

APRIL 23, 1952 The worst waterfront fire since the destruction of Pier D breaks out at 1:15 p.m., destroying the United Grain Growers' dock.

MAY 1, 1952 A British manufacturer signs a $3-million deal to produce an automatic telephone recorder invented by Vancouverites Allan McLean and John Fontaine.

MAY 19, 1952 An exhibition of Picasso works opens at the art gallery.

MAY 30, 1952 Canada's first cataract operation is performed at Vancouver General Hospital.

JUNE 23, 1952 Theatre Under the Stars reopens in the newly renovated Malkin Bowl. A gift from W.H. Malkin paid for half the renovations, including a larger stage.

JULY 15, 1952 H.D. Anderson, president of the B.C. Manufacturers Association, unveils a new Lumberman's Arch at Stanley Park.

AUGUST 2, 1952 Tilly Rolston, member for Point Grey, is named a minister without portfolio, and is the first woman in Canada to fill a Cabinet post.

Construction on the present Granville Street Bridge began in 1952 and continued through 1953. The official opening for the finished structure was February 4, 1954. The mid-span cantilevered out into thin air was one of 1953's most spectacular engineering sights. (VPL)

NOVEMBER 29, 1952 The Vancouver Little Theatre, in operation for thirty-two consecutive seasons, is said to be the oldest amateur theatrical organization in North America.

DECEMBER 1, 1952 A three-day celebration begins in Chinatown, marking the reopening of the headquarters of the Chinese Benevolent Association, damaged by fire eighteen months earlier.

DECEMBER 10, 1952 Fred Hume is reelected mayor.

JANUARY 8, 1953 The longest manhunt in the Lower Mainland ends with the arrest of Walter Pavlukoff in Toronto. He is charged with the August 25, 1947, murder of bank manager Sydney Petrie.

JANUARY 15, 1953 A parks board employee discovers two children's skeletons in Stanley Park. The case, known as the "Babes in the Woods" murders, has never been solved.

JANUARY 16, 1953 Police raid the Avon Theatre and arrest the cast of the Everyman Theatre Company for an allegedly indecent performance. The bill is Erskine Caldwell's *Tobacco Road*.

JANUARY 23, 1953 Erskine Caldwell testifies in the Everyman Theatre Company obscenity trial.

MARCH 10, 1953 Council passes a by-law outlawing Sunday burials.

APRIL 4, 1953 *Bwana Devil* plays at the Plaza—the first 3-D film to be shown in Vancouver.

APRIL 18, 1953 Canadian Pacific Ships resume service to Asia for the first time since the famous "White Empresses" were withdrawn from the route in 1941.

APRIL 18, 1953 The last streetcar run on Oak Street is made at 4:04 a.m. An official last run from Victory Square to Marpole is held the following day, with dignitaries riding in five streetcars.

JUNE 20, 1953 "Operation Beware" tests the new air raid warning system. Twenty-eight sirens sound at 9:30 a.m.

JULY 9, 1953 The Davis Cup Tournament opens at the Vancouver Lawn and Tennis Club. The club was chosen as host when the Japanese team insisted on playing on grass courts, and none were available in the U.S.

JULY 28, 1953 Wai Chan, the city's last Chinese pushcart peddler, retires.

AUGUST 30, 1953 Vancouver's Douglas Hepburn wins the world heavyweight weightlifting championship.

OCTOBER 10, 1953 A bill to allow serving liquor by the glass passes second reading in Victoria.

DECEMBER 9, 1953 The inaugural meeting of the Chinese Lions Club marks the formation of the first Chinese Lions Club in North America.

DECEMBER 16, 1953 CBC president A. Davidson Dunton pushes the button to put CBUT (Channel 2) on the air.

JANUARY 1, 1954 Changes to the liquor act allow music, radio, and television in pubs.

FEBRUARY 4, 1954 The new (and present) Granville Street Bridge is opened, replacing the structure built in 1909. By March 6 a million automobiles have used the bridge.

MARCH 2, 1954 The first edition of the *Chinese Free Press* is published. It is Canada's only bilingual (Chinese-English) newspaper.

This view south from downtown along the old Granville Street Bridge shows how the bridge looked in 1953, its last year of service before completion of its modern replacement located slightly to the west. The old bridge was built in 1909 and was similar to the Cambie Street Bridge in that both had central pivoting swing spans. (VPL)

The saddest moment of the 1954 British Empire Games occurred when English long distance runner Jim Peters entered Empire Stadium in first place position after having completed all but the final lap of a twenty-one-mile marathon. Dazed by fatigue he roamed aimlessly about the track looking for the finish line. He finally collapsed and was disqualified when his coach was forced to come to his aid. (VPL)

APRIL 22, 1954 Drinks by the glass are available in restaurants and hotels. Hotels are allowed to serve hard liquor but restaurants are restricted to serving only wine or beer with meals.

JUNE 1, 1954 The city acquires the McCleery farm, settled at the foot of Macdonald Street in 1862, for a golf course. The farmhouse (the second built on the farm) is demolished in 1956.

JUNE 23, 1954 A plebiscite for a six-day shopping week passes and Wednesday afternoon closing ceases.

JULY 2, 1954 Vancouver's first cocktail bar is opened on the main floor of the Sylvia Hotel.

JULY 21, 1954 A time capsule is buried beneath "Centuries Rock" in Queen Elizabeth Park. It is to be opened in 2054.

DECEMBER 8, 1954 Fred Hume is reelected mayor for a third term.

DECEMBER 29, 1954 City hall releases figures estimating Vancouver's population to be 396,016.

FEBRUARY 21, 1955 Mayor Fred Hume calls for "an all-out war" to clean up the city's drug problems.

MARCH 7, 1955 Margaret Jean Gee is the first woman of Chinese descent to be called to the British Columbia bar.

APRIL 14, 1955 An era in entertainment history ends with the demolition of the Palomar Ballroom, opened in 1937.

APRIL 30, 1955 Helen Stewart sets five new Canadian records at the B.C. Swimming Championships, held at Crystal Pool.

MAY 9, 1955 A by-law is passed allowing cabarets without liquor licences to remain open until 2:00 a.m., the same hours granted licensed cabarets.

MAY 10, 1955 The pivot pier of the old Granville Street Bridge is blasted out with dynamite. The bridge is sold as scrap.

JUNE 5, 1955 Mrs. S.H. Ramage, formerly Annie Sanders, one of the seven girls for whom the Seven Sisters grove of evergreens in Stanley Park was named, dies in New Westminster. Vancouver had only seven girls between the ages of ten and eighteen when the park

was dedicated and the clump of evergreens was their favorite playground.

AUGUST 22, 1955 The B.C. Lions defeat the Calgary Stampeders in a game at Empire Stadium played before 28,066 fans, the largest reported football crowd at a game in Canada.

OCTOBER 24, 1955 Walter Mulligan is fired as chief of police.

OCTOBER 31, 1955 In the wake of Chief Mulligan's departure, a royal commission is appointed to look into charges of graft and corruption in the police force.

NOVEMBER 22, 1955 A home for teenage boys is opened by Central City Mission.

NOVEMBER 26, 1955 The Edmonton Eskimos and the Montreal Alouettes play in Vancouver's first Grey Cup.

DECEMBER 9, 1955 The provincial government gives Locarno Beach to the city. The tuberculosis infirmary on the site is to be torn down.

Left: Car clubs for young men flourished in the 1950s. Here the "Igniters" really clean up at a club car wash, circa 1955. (VPL)

Facing page: The 1950s saw the death of the steam train and the rise of the diesel locomotive. This locomotive met its ignominious end April 12, 1955, when it plowed into some grain cars parked in the freight yards just below Clark Drive. (VPL)

JANUARY 1, 1956 George Archer is named chief of police. Sworn in two days later, he orders an immediate reorganization of the force.

JANUARY 11, 1956 Helen Stewart, age seventeen, is named B.C.'s Athlete of 1955. She holds twenty-three Canadian speed swimming records.

FEBRUARY 28, 1956 The Tupper royal commission on corruption in the police force makes its report. It finds four of fifteen charges to be true and reports that ex-chief Walter Mulligan is guilty of taking bribes from bookmakers.

APRIL 24, 1956 Premier W.A.C. Bennett announces the Homeowner's Grant. Each year all homeowners in the province will receive a grant of twenty-eight dollars.

APRIL 27, 1956 The Vancouver Mounties play the San Francisco Seals in the inaugural game of baseball's Pacific Coast League, played at Capilano Stadium.

JUNE 5, 1956 The number of aldermen is boosted from eight to ten, the first change since 1936 when the numbers dropped from twelve to eight.

JUNE 27, 1956 Bill Haley and the Comets give Vancouver's first rock and roll concert at Kerrisdale Arena.

AUGUST 31, 1956 Friday night shopping goes into effect for the first time outside the Christmas season.

Above: Television made its debut in Vancouver December 16, 1953, with the introduction of Canadian Broadcasting Corporation station CBUT. Before the days of national interconnect and satellites, most programming was either from film sources or local live events like this fashion show at the 1954 PNE. (VPL)

Left: Although the effectiveness of the first polio vaccines would later be questioned, the introduction of immunization programs in March 1955 tended to quell the fears of anxious parents who had seen the disease rise to epidemic proportions among children in the late 1940s and early 1950s. (VPL)

SEPTEMBER 21, 1956 A thirty-one-year-old man receives a six-month jail sentence for impaired driving—the longest sentence for such a crime ever imposed in British Columbia.

SEPTEMBER 24, 1956 Rock and roll performer Little Richard is mobbed by fans and a near riot occurs during his performance at the Kerrisdale Arena.

SEPTEMBER 25, 1956 Radio station CKWX opens new studios on Burrard Street.

OCTOBER 27, 1956 Helen Stewart sets a new world record in the 100-yard freestyle in a swim meet at Crystal Pool.

NOVEMBER 28, 1956 Mayor Fred Hume is returned to office by acclamation. He is the first mayor to go unchallenged since 1921, and the first to serve four consecutive terms. During his terms of office Hume gives his mayor's salary to charity.

In 1956 the eastern end of False Creek was jammed with squatters' shacks where the city's abject poor lived in a floating slum surrounded by industrial waste. (VPL)

The Chinese and East Indian communities were not given the right to vote in British Columbia until 1947 and it wasn't until 1957 that the first person of Chinese descent, Douglas Jung, was elected to public office. Jung, pictured here during his 1958 campaign, was re-elected MP for Vancouver Centre during the Diefenbaker Conservative's cross-country sweep. (VPL)

DECEMBER 5, 1956 The first Hungarian refugees arrive in Vancouver aboard CP Air's "Freedom Express."

DECEMBER 6, 1956 The PNE purchases Coleman E. Hall's interest in the Vancouver Canucks.

DECEMBER 15, 1956 A parade and reception welcome home the UBC rowing crews who won a medal in the recent Melbourne Olympics.

APRIL 15, 1957 Stan Leonard wins the Greensboro Open Golf Tournament. It is his first win on the American circuit.

JUNE 2, 1957 A gold-lacquered statue of Buddha is installed in a "shrine ceremony" at the Buddhist Church on Powell Street. It is the first ceremony of its kind in Vancouver since the outbreak of World War II.

JUNE 10, 1957 Douglas Jung becomes Canada's first MP of Chinese descent. He is the Conservative member for Vancouver Centre.

JUNE 15, 1957 The last edition of the *News-Herald* is published. The *Province* moves into the morning newspaper field.

JUNE 29, 1957 The Marpole swing bridge, built in 1890, is closed.

JULY 1, 1957 The Oak Street Bridge is officially opened. Merchants in the Marpole District to the west protest the effect of the Oak Street route on their business.

AUGUST 26, 1957 Midnight marks the switch to new one-way streets in the downtown core.

SEPTEMBER 21, 1957 Leon Koerner sets up a $1-million "Thea and Leon Koerner Foundation" in the largest private philanthropic gift in the city's history.

OCTOBER 10, 1957 Elsworth McAuley Searles is the first black man to be called to the B.C. bar.

DECEMBER 28, 1957 A new Fisherman's Wharf is opened at False Creek. Two years under construction, the dock cost $800,000.

MARCH 23, 1958 Jack Shadbolt wins the Canadian section of the biannual Guggenheim International Art Competition. His winning canvas is called *Medieval Town*.

MARCH 27, 1958 For the first time the Vancouver Foundation Fund exceeds the one-million-dollar mark.

The annual January First Polar Bear Swim in English Bay is one of Vancouver's oldest rituals. In 1957 these three swimmers, left to right, Juanita Brown, Doug Rivette, and Ami Brown, were the only three of fifty-three entries to stay in the freezing waters for the entire one-hour event. (VPL)

APRIL 28, 1958 A by-law approving Sunday sports is passed.

JUNE 17, 1958 The partially constructed Second Narrows Bridge collapses. Eighteen die in Vancouver's worst industrial accident in twenty-eight years.

JULY 19, 1958 Chief Mungo Martin is at Windsor Castle for the dedication of his totem pole presented to Queen Elizabeth to mark B.C.'s centennial. A replica of the 100-foot pole stands before the Maritime Museum.

JULY 19, 1958 After four years of planning, the first Vancouver International Festival gets underway. The opening ceremonies at the Orpheum feature contralto Maureen Forrester. Bruno Walter conducts the Festival Orchestra.

AUGUST 13, 1958 The parks board closes all of Vancouver's beaches due to pollution. Beaches do not reopen until June 1959.

DECEMBER 30, 1958 Mayor Fred Hume leaves office after serving as Vancouver's mayor since 1950.

MARCH 16, 1959 The first ship docks at the new Centennial Pier.

APRIL 6, 1959 Dr. H. Gobind Khorana gains world fame as he and a team at B.C. Research synthesize co-enzyme A, a complex molecule important in metabolism. For this and other work in genetics he wins the Nobel Prize for medicine in 1968.

When Elvis Presley performed at Empire Stadium August 31, 1957, he sang one song and then had to leave the stage as fans battled with police. After Colonel Parker pleaded with the crowd of 20,000 to settle down, Elvis reappeared and sang four more songs which couldn't be heard through the screams. (VPL)

146

MAY 11, 1959 The Salvation Army opens the Maywood Home for Unwed Mothers on Oak Street.

MAY 15, 1959 Harry Jerome breaks the record for the 220-yard dash previously held by Percy Norman. Jerome runs the distance in 21.9 seconds. The same year his sister, Valerie, ties the Canadian Open sixty-metre record for women.

JULY 15, 1959 Queen Elizabeth and Prince Philip spend a busy day in Vancouver. The Queen opens the new Deas Island Tunnel, attends a civic luncheon, visits Shaughnessy Hospital and Queen Elizabeth Park, attends a "Children's Salute to the Queen" at Empire Stadium, drops in at a TUTS performance, and then attends a special festival concert at the new auditorium, to which she lends her name.

SEPTEMBER 4, 1959 The Georgia Auditorium falls to the wrecker's ball.

OCTOBER 2, 1959 The first western news bureau in modern China is opened jointly by the *Vancouver Sun* and the *Globe & Mail.*

OCTOBER 24, 1959 The B.C. Lions are in the first Western Conference final of their career.

The beginning of another school year and it's decision time again, circa 1959. Which lunch bucket will be in this year? You have your Zorro and Matt Dillon themes, but what about the space race and a journey to the moon to take your mind off school? (VPL)

NOVEMBER 5, 1959 The Edmonton Eskimos defeat the B.C. Lions in the Western Conference final.

NOVEMBER 10, 1959 Leon Koerner donates money to construct a graduate student's centre at UBC in memory of his wife Thea.

MARCH 1, 1960 The 1960 World Figure Skating Championships open in Vancouver. Four local teams are among the skaters from fifteen countries.

MARCH 18, 1960 A spectacular fire, with flames leaping 300 feet in the air, destroys a city landmark. The block-long Stanley Park Armories, built fifty-two years earlier, burns to the ground.

APRIL 27, 1960 The Percy Norman Memorial Pool is dedicated. Records are set when fourteen-year-old Mary Stewart breaks the 100-metre women's freestyle and Ed Cazalet becomes one of the few men to crack the one-minute barrier in the men's 100-metre freestyle.

JUNE 11, 1960 Arthur Erickson designs a children's gallery at the Vancouver Art Gallery. Paintings are hung three and a half feet from the floor.

JUNE 14, 1960 The figurehead of the *Empress of Japan* is replaced with a fibreglass replica, carved by Andrew Zborovsky. The original, placed in Stanley Park in 1927, fell victim to dry rot, and in 1986 it is being slowly and lovingly restored.

JULY 3, 1960 The largest fire in the city's history, and its first five-alarm fire, wipes out the B.C. Forest Products mill and lumberyard.

JULY 15, 1960 Harry Jerome ties the world record in the 100-metre dash at Olympic trials in Saskatoon.

AUGUST 25, 1960 Premier W.A.C. Bennett opens the Second Narrows Bridge. The cantilevered span of the main arch, at 1,100 feet, is the second largest in Canada.

JANUARY 14, 1961 Gertrude Guerin is the first woman to be elected chief of the Musqueam Indian Band.

MAY 27, 1961 Indian canoes race to Kitsilano Showcase, where the canoeists present a concert as part of the city's seventy-fifth anniversary celebrations.

MAY 28, 1961 Native trees from New Zealand are planted in Stanley Park in memory of New Zealand airmen who trained in Canada and lost their lives in World War II.

JUNE 5, 1961 Direct distance dialing begins in Vancouver.

JUNE 25, 1961 The Haida section of UBC's Totem Park is opened. The Haida poles were salvaged from desolate Anthony Island in the Queen Charlottes.

AUGUST 1, 1961 Premier W.A.C. Bennett announces the takeover of B.C. Electric by the provincial government.

OCTOBER 13, 1961 Royal Canadian Mounted Police raid bookstores and libraries, seizing copies of Henry Miller's *Tropic of Cancer.*

OCTOBER 31, 1961 Vancouver's first private television station, CHAN-TV, begins broadcasting.

DECEMBER 10, 1961 A six-foot hickory staff, given by Queen Victoria to former Musqueam chief Thism-Lano, is presented to the band by the Department of Indian Affairs who had it in safekeeping for years at the request of the chief's family.

MARCH 13, 1962 "Jubilee," the first grizzly bear born in Stanley Park to grow to adulthood, dies. Born in 1936, he was named for the city's Golden Jubilee.

JUNE 18, 1962 Native Indians vote for the first time in a federal election.

JULY 31, 1962 The chief licence inspector, Milt Harrel, closes the Lenny Bruce show at the Cave after one performance.

OCTOBER 11, 1962 Hurricane Frieda, with winds of forty to fifty

The *St. Roch,* the RCMP ship that helped establish Canadian sovereignty in the Arctic by sailing the Northwest Passage in the early 1940s, was permanently beached at Kitsilano Point on April 9, 1958. A building was erected over it and the site established as Vancouver's first national historical monument. Later the Vancouver Maritime Museum was constructed alongside the *St. Roch.* (VPL)

miles per hour, gusting to ninety miles per hour, brings death and destruction to the Lower Mainland. Ten deaths are attributed to the storm, and trees in Stanley Park fall like matchsticks.

OCTOBER 22, 1962 Scuba divers recover the drive shaft of the SS *Beaver* lying near Prospect Point since the *Beaver* was wrecked in 1889.

DECEMBER 4, 1962 Residents are alarmed when they hear a loud noise at 3:55 p.m. It is the sound of an American military jet breaking the sound barrier.

DECEMBER 9, 1962 Bill Rathie is elected mayor. He is Vancouver's first native son to serve as mayor.

DECEMBER 17, 1962 Dr. Patrick McGeer wins a by-election in Point Grey for the Liberal Party. It is the first time in nine years that Social Credit has lost a by-election.

FEBRUARY 10, 1963 Gary Thomas defeats Chief Dan George in an election of the Burrard Indian Band, marking the first time in the history of the band that a member of the George family is not chief.

JUNE 8, 1963 The Agrodome, a domed exhibition hall, is opened at the PNE.

JULY 9, 1963 The parks board gives permission for a Speaker's Corner at Hallelujah Point in Stanley Park.

The Second Narrows of Burrard Inlet has seen more accidents than any other waterway in Canada. Most of these mishaps involved ships ramming the bridge used for rail traffic, but the worst disaster occurred June 17, 1958, when the highway bridge under construction collapsed, killing eighteen workers and a police diver. (VPL)

AUGUST 16, 1963 One of the city's oldest churches, the St. Michael's Roman Catholic Church on the Musqueam Indian Reserve, is destroyed by fire. It was built in 1902.

AUGUST 25, 1963 Movie theatres are allowed to open after 1:30 p.m. on Sundays.

JANUARY 1, 1964 The Hotel Vancouver is sold to the Hilton chain.

MARCH 28, 1964 The Most Reverend Martin Johnson is named Roman Catholic Archbishop of Vancouver.

MAY 30, 1964 The Vancouver Indian Centre Society opens a centre for Native youth on West Broadway. It is the first such establishment in Canada to have an all-Native board of directors.

AUGUST 13, 1964 The anchor of the SS *Beaver* is recovered off Prospect Point.

OCTOBER 3, 1964 Maisie Hurley, publisher of the *Native Voice*, and the only white on the board of directors of the Native Brotherhood of British Columbia, dies at age seventy-six.

OCTOBER 15, 1964 The UBC coxless rowing pairs win a gold medal at the Tokyo Olympics. Other city winners in the Olympics are rower George Hungerford and runner Harry Jerome.

OCTOBER 21, 1964 Vancouver's Doug Rogers becomes the first Canadian to win a medal (silver) for judo in the Olympics.

NOVEMBER 14, 1964 The Marco Polo, the first Chinese nightclub in Canada, opens.

DECEMBER 4, 1964 Professional baseball returns to Vancouver when the Vancouver Mounties are readmitted into the Pacific Coast League. They had been dropped from the league in 1962 because of financial difficulties.

DECEMBER 10, 1964 The Vancouver Stock Exchange is formally opened at 536 Howe Street by Premier W.A.C. Bennett. This is the seventh time the exchange has moved since it was established in 1907.

JANUARY 5, 1965 The H.R. MacMillan Family Fund is established. The fund promotes religious and cultural work.

JANUARY 11, 1965 Victor Odlum is named publisher of the

Vancouver Times, brought out to take advantage of a strike by the city's two dailies.

JANUARY 28, 1965 A $55-million exhibition of Egyptian art from the tomb of King Tutankhamen goes on display at the Vancouver Art Gallery.

FEBRUARY 11, 1965 A holdup at the Canadian Pacific Merchandising Service results in the theft of $1.2 million, mostly cancelled bills being returned to the Treasury Board. Two former police are among the four charged.

FEBRUARY 15, 1965 Canada's new Maple Leaf flag is to fly on all schools and ships by noon. Mayor Bill Rathie orders the flag raising at city hall three hours earlier.

FEBRUARY 26, 1965 A fireworks display in Chinatown marks the opening of Vancouver's first Spring Carnival, held at a time when most of Canada holds winter carnivals.

APRIL 27, 1965 Yokohama, Japan, becomes a sister city.

One of the zaniest ideas cooked up by UBC students was the Bed-Pushing Marathon that went along a course stretching from downtown Vancouver all the way to the U.S. border. (VPL)

AUGUST 6, 1965 The *Vancouver Times* suspends publication after eleven months.

AUGUST 16, 1965 Jockey Johnny Longden rides his 6,000th winner at Exhibition Park.

SEPTEMBER 10, 1965 Simon Fraser University, designed by Arthur Erickson, is officially opened. Premier W.A.C. Bennett and Lord Lovat of Scotland receive honorary degrees.

DECEMBER 2, 1965 Dr. Gordon Dower, of UBC, invents a polarcardiograph, a diagnostic tool for heart disease.

DECEMBER 11, 1965 Pacific Press, Ltd., begins a move to its new quarters on South Granville. The first editions of the *Sun* and *Province* are printed from the new premises on December 27.

FEBRUARY 2, 1966 The gondola is opened on Grouse Mountain.

FEBRUARY 11, 1966 Right Reverend James Francis Carney is the first Vancouver-born Roman Catholic to be named a bishop when he is consecrated as auxiliary bishop of Vancouver.

MARCH 24, 1966 Singer and songwriter Bob Dylan perfoms at the Agrodome.

MARCH 25, 1966 The first lots are sold in the Musqueam Heights subdivision. Sixty-nine lots are sold in ten days for prices ranging from $10 to $20,000.

APRIL 19, 1966 Top prizes in the courthouse fence painting contest go to abstract artists Steve Barrett and Shirley Coan. Over 200 works of art are painted on the fence panels while landscaping and other work goes on.

JULY 16, 1966 Elaine Tanner is named female swimmer of the year by the Canadian Amateur Swimming Association. She set fifteen Canadian and Open records during the year.

AUGUST 12, 1966 Elaine Tanner wins four golds, three silvers, and sets two world records at the British Empire Games in Jamaica.

SEPTEMBER 13, 1966 It is revealed that the anonymous donor of $1.5 million for a city planetarium is H.R. MacMillan. It is then named the MacMillan Planetarium.

SEPTEMBER 19, 1966 The Bunkhouse is the first restaurant in the city to introduce topless waitresses at lunch hour.

DECEMBER 3, 1966 College and university students stage a twelve-mile bed-pushing contest from SFU to the grounds of Vancouver City College.

DECEMBER 14, 1966 Thomas J. Campbell is elected mayor of Vancouver.

DECEMBER 14, 1966 The Vancouver Metropolitan Orchestra, comprised of amateurs who pay a fee to play, gives its first public performance.

FEBRUARY 22, 1967 Harry Jerome is named B.C.'s athlete of the year.

MARCH 3, 1967 Professor Harry Logan, the last of UBC's original faculty members, announces his retirement.

MARCH 26, 1967 Hippies hold an "Easter Be-In" in Stanley Park.

APRIL 6, 1967 A gigantic birthday cake is served at Courthouse Square, celebrating the city's eighty-first birthday.

Vancouver's first anti-nuclear march consisted of about 300 "Ban-The-Bombers" parading down Kingsway October 1, 1961. The event was organized by Michael Dean of White Rock, whom the newspaper described as a "beatnik." Two years later Prime Minister Diefenbaker went against the wishes of his party in refusing to have the Canadian military become a nuclear force. (VPL)

APRIL 8, 1967 It is reported that hippies are taking over 4th Avenue. Four stores and a coffee shop, run by hippies, have opened in the 2000 to 2300 blocks.

MAY 9, 1967 Approval is given to erect four sixty-foot pylons on Georgia Street to mark Canada's centennial.

JUNE 1, 1967 Vancouver businessman Harry Con publishes the first history of Canada written in Chinese.

JUNE 10, 1967 The first "Miles for Millions" walk attracts 2,500 participants and raises funds for India's poor.

JUNE 15, 1967 The "Arts of the Raven" exhibit opens at the Vancouver Art Gallery. The exhibition of 550 pieces of Native art is the largest and costliest exhibit undertaken by the gallery.

JUNE 19, 1967 Air chimes designed by Robert Swanson are placed atop of the B.C. Hydro Building. They play the first four notes of "O Canada" each noon.

The trendy Bolo-Bat reached the peak of its popularity in the early 1960s. Here at a Bolo-Bat contest in February 1962 we see everyone from the champion (far right) to the rank amateur (note the group of boys far left trying to unsnarl their rubber bands). (VPL)

JULY 4, 1967 A crowd of 32,000 is moved to silence when Chief Dan George recites "A Lament for Confederation" at Canada's birthday party, held at Empire Stadium. The lament mourns the passing of the Indian's way of life and communion with nature.

JULY 6, 1967 The Family, a statue by Jack Harmon, is unveiled at the Pacific Press building on South Granville. The work creates controversy because, while the parents are clothed, their son is naked.

AUGUST 5, 1967 Premier W.A.C. Bennett hosts a "strawberry social" in Stanley Park to mark the fifteenth anniversary of Social Credit rule.

OCTOBER 19, 1967 A parade is held on Pender Street to protest a proposed freeway through Chinatown.

DECEMBER 1, 1967 Powell Street Dugout opens as a day centre for homeless Skid Road men.

DECEMBER 12, 1967 Canada's largest braille library opens at UBC. The nucleus of the collection is the private library of Charles Crane, the first deaf and blind person in Canada to attend university, in 1915.

JANUARY 6, 1968 Prior to the Ice Capades a ceremony is held officially opening the Pacific Coliseum. Civic Chaplain George Turpin prays "Please God, bring us the NHL."

FEBRUARY 7, 1968 Two people are killed when a CP Air jet roars out of control during a landing in fog at the airport. The flight from Honolulu leaves a trail of wreckage and fire in its wake.

FEBRUARY 15, 1968 Skier Nancy Greene wins the gold in the Winter Olympics.

MARCH 12, 1968 The inaugural meeting of TEAM (The Elector's Action Movement) is held. They will soon become a major force in civic politics.

APRIL 1, 1968 Joachim Foikis is presented with a $3,500 Canada Council grant and becomes Vancouver's official "Town Fool." He dresses in cap and bells and appears at public functions.

JULY 8, 1968 Chief Dan George is awarded the role of Ol' Antoine in the Walt Disney film *Smith!* based on the book *Breaking Smith's Quarter Horse* by Vancouver author Paul St. Pierre.

AUGUST 2, 1968 A "Nat Bailey Night" honors him prior to a

Left: Upset over the jailing of congregation members in the Agassiz Prison, 400 miles from their homes, a group of 200 Freedomite Doukhobors trekked out to the coast and camped in Vancouver's Victory Square in January 1963 to bring public attention to their plight. (VPL)

Below: The West End began a transition from single-family homes to highrise apartment buildings in the early 1960s. In this 1963 aerial view a few highrises can be seen popping up but smaller homes and low-rises still dominate. (VPL)

baseball game at Capilano Stadium. Bailey has been instrumental in bringing professional PCL baseball to Vancouver.

SEPTEMBER 22, 1968 The Community Arts Council sponsors a walking tour to promote interest in preserving the Gastown area.

OCTOBER 23, 1968 Activist Jerry Rubin and the Students for a Democratic Society "liberate" UBC's faculty club. The two-day occupation results in $6,000 damages.

The giant Grey Cup, a replica of the biggest prize in Canadian football, is paraded about the field at Empire Stadium on November 21, 1963. The night of the big game, sports fans went berserk in downtown Vancouver and police had to make more than sixty arrests before peace returned to the streets of the city. (VPL)

OCTOBER 24, 1968 British Columbia's first kidney transplant is performed at Vancouver General Hospital.

NOVEMBER 1, 1968 Central Heat Distribution, Ltd., begins supplying steam heat to downtown offices through underground pipes.

JANUARY 8, 1969 The inauguration of the new city council is delayed when Art Phillips demands an aldermanic recount. Phillips wins a seat on January 27.

JANUARY 20, 1969 Harry Con is president of the newly formed Strathcona Property Owners and Ratepayers Association. The group is organized to oppose an urban renewal scheme in Chinatown.

FEBRUARY 1, 1969 The Nine O'Clock Gun vanishes from Stanley Park where it has stood for seventy-five years. The 1,500-pound gun is "kidnapped" by UBC engineering students who "ransom" it to raise funds for the Children's Hospital. It is returned on February 6.

MARCH 9, 1969 The city's first antique flea market opens on Water Street in Gastown.

MARCH 31, 1969 Vancouver is granted an up-to-date coat of arms. The lumberman and the fisherman, representing the largest industries on the coast, sport modern clothing and clean-shaven faces. The motto, thanks to a suggestion by Alderman Halford Wilson, now reads "By Sea, Land and Air We Prosper."

APRIL 27, 1969 Joachim Foikis, Vancouver's town fool, uses part of his Canada Council grant to throw a big Skid Road party.

MAY 10, 1969 William Wosk opens four off-track betting shops. He is immediately served with a cease and desist order by the Vancouver Jockey Club.

MAY 27, 1969 A fire in the stables of Exhibition Park kills several racehorses. Arson is suspected. Trainer Jack Russell suffers a fatal heart attack at the scene.

JUNE 13, 1969 Mayor Tom Campbell swims at Kitsilano Beach in an attempt to prove the beaches are safe and waters do not have a high coliform count.

JULY 14, 1969 Theatre at Malkin Bowl is revived with the opening night production of *Carousel* by Theatre in the Park.

JULY 29, 1969 Arthur Clarke is the first black to join the city's police force.

AUGUST 8, 1969 Prime Minister Pierre Trudeau abandons an attempt to address Vietnam War protestors outside Seaforth Armories when protestors drown him out. Three days later a demonstrator attempts to have charges laid against Trudeau for assault. The case is thrown out of court.

OCTOBER 1, 1969 Local university students join their counterparts in the U.S. in border-crossing protests against U.S. nuclear testing at Amchitka in the Aleutian Islands.

OCTOBER 1, 1969 A firebomb is hurled at the U.S. consulate in the Burrard Building in apparent retaliation for the Amchitka tests.

OCTOBER 22, 1969 The Vancouver Centennials of the Junior A Hockey League play their first game.

OCTOBER 24, 1969 Approximately twenty women picket the Engineers Club on Hornby Street to protest discrimination. Women are not allowed to become members of the club.

NOVEMBER 1, 1969 The X-Kalay foundation, a halfway house for rehabilitation of ex-convicts, seeks a licence to operate from 2025 West 16th.

NOVEMBER 14, 1969 A candlelight procession is held downtown in a quiet protest against the Vietnam War.

NOVEMBER 17, 1969 Three thousand join a protest march against the Vietnam War.

DECEMBER 1, 1969 Vancouver is awarded a National Hockey League franchise.

DECEMBER 31, 1969 Dr. R.L. Noble and Dr. C.T. Beer develop a new anti-cancer drug at UBC. Made from periwinkle leaves, the drug is hailed as one of the outstanding medical discoveries of the decade.

Facing page, far left: Siwash Rock, the subject of Indian legends, and a major tourist attraction, became the site of one of Stanley Park's most tragic events in June 1966. The parents of Robert Dennis Tribe stand with a plaque commemorating the death of their son who was killed when he dove from the rock at low tide. (VPL)

Facing page, left: Vancouver police count recovered loot on June 14, 1965. Four bandits held up the Canadian Pacific Merchandise office on Pender Street on February 11, 1965, and got away with over a million dollars in worthless defaced currency. Two of the robbers turned out to be former city police constables—one of them commited suicide before the jig was up. The money was discovered in a Victoria garage four months after the heist. (VPL)

Facing page, bottom: As the war in Vietnam escalated, scenes like this June 1965 anti-war picket of a U.S. Navy ship in the Vancouver harbor became a common sight around the world. Later anti-Vietnam War demonstrations in Vancouver in the early 1970s drew thousands of supporters, many of whom were American war resisters, living in exile in Canada. (VPL)

PART VI

THE SEVENTIES AND EIGHTIES

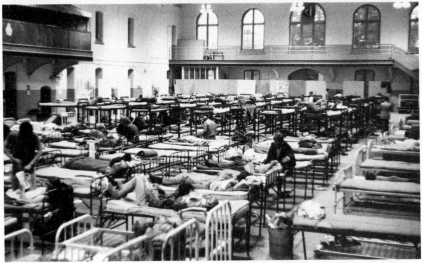

Preceding pages: Winter sunlight illuminates the highrises of the West End and the snowy peaks of the North Shore. This 1974 view graphically illustrates the dramatic changes that occurred in the West End since the 1950s. By the 1970s the West End was Canada's most densely packed neighborhood, having a population one and a half times that of the Yukon (over 35,000). (VPL)

Left, top: In the spring of 1971 Mayor Tom Campbell announced to the young people of Canada that they would not be welcome in his city. That June transient youths took over a vacant lot at the entrance to Stanley Park, turned it into a campground, and dubbed it All Seasons Park after the Four Seasons Hotel which owned the property. Once summer was over, All Seasons Park became history. Photo by Henri Robideau

Left, bottom: Canadian youths hit the road in record numbers during the summer of 1970. To alleviate the problem of homeless kids wandering the city streets, the federal government set up youth hostels in places like the Beatty Street Armory. Vancouver Mayor Tom Campbell, who felt that the hostel was nothing but a refuge for American draft-dodgers and young bums, tried unsuccessfully to have it shut down. Photo by Henri Robideau

FEBRUARY 4, 1970 The *Oronsay* sails. It was quarantined for twenty-one days after sixty-nine cases of typhoid among passengers and crew were confirmed. A contaminated water supply was to blame.

FEBRUARY 7, 1970 A third bombing occurs at UBC. The bombings, every second Friday between 7:00 and 7:30 p.m., damage Brock House, a wall of the mathematics building, and an office in the geology building.

FEBRUARY 15, 1970 A newspaper strike occurs at the *Sun* and *Province.* No daily papers are published for three months.

JUNE 12, 1970 A riot at English Bay precipitates a week of clashes between youth and riot police.

JUNE 27-28, 1970 "The Party," organized by the Vancouver

Liberation Movement, is held at Stanley Park, featuring free music, free food, and free dope. An estimated 4,000 hear revolutionary folksinger Phil Ochs in concert.

JULY 12, 1970 Police evict a noisy group of youths from council chambers' public gallery shortly after their spokesman read a list of demands to council which includes a call for the resignation of Mayor Tom Campbell.

AUGUST 27, 1970 Two armed bandits hold up a Loomis armored car at Burrard and Nelson and escape with $78,000.

OCTOBER 9, 1970 The Vancouver Canucks lose to Los Angeles (three to one) in their first game, which is played at the Pacific Coliseum.

OCTOBER 24, 1970 Seven people are taken into custody when they are found distributing FLQ literature. It is believed to be the first time in Vancouver that provisions of the War Measures Act are enforced. The FLQ is a radical group fighting for Quebec independence.

Chief Dan George achieved prominence as a Native leader and an internationally recognized actor. Photo by Peter Hulbert. Courtesy, Vancouver *Province*

DECEMBER 29, 1970 Chief Dan George is named best supporting actor by New York film critics for his role in *Little Big Man.*

JANUARY 1, 1971 Eagle Keys is named coach of the B.C. Lions.

JANUARY 6, 1971 The doors open at Vancouver Free University, which offers free courses in everything ranging from the academic to "creative lovemaking."

MARCH 2, 1971 Haida artist Bob Davidson opens his first one-man showing at the Centennial Museum.

MARCH 5, 1971 Prime Minister Pierre Elliot Trudeau, fifty-seven, weds twenty-two-year-old Margaret Sinclair in a secret ceremony in West Vancouver.

MARCH 26, 1971 A $10,000 statue by Rodin is found missing from the Vancouver Art Gallery. It is mysteriously returned by mail three days later in an old brown satchel bearing a six-cent stamp.

MAY 29, 1971 Youths tear down a fence to "occupy" the site of Four Seasons Hotel at the entrance to Stanley Park. They rechristen the area "All Seasons Park" and erect temporary shelters.

JUNE 22, 1971 Wrought iron security gates are installed at the

Playing the ponies at Exhibition Park Race-track was the only form of legalized gambling available to Vancouverites until recent government-sponsored lotteries. Here a couple of racing enthusiasts check out the tip sheets for the best bets on a June afternoon in 1972. Photo by Fred Rosenberg (VPL)

entrance to city hall's visitors' gallery on orders from Mayor Campbell.

AUGUST 5, 1971 A report released by Robert Collier of UBC identifies the West End (population 35,000) as the most densely populated square mile in Canada.

AUGUST 7, 1971 A riot ensues in Gastown as police arrive to break up a hippie "smoke-in" at Maple Square. Charges of police brutality ensue.

AUGUST 14, 1971 Gastown merchants sponsor a peace party and invite the police and civic officials to meet the city's youth.

SEPTEMBER 17, 1971 Mayor Tom Campbell leads a delegation on a visit to Vancouver's sister city, Odessa, USSR.

OCTOBER 6, 1971 An estimated 10,000 local high school students gather outside the U.S. consulate to protest the nuclear testing at Amchitka.

OCTOBER 22, 1971 Alexei Kosygin, Soviet premier, makes a forty-two-hour visit. Extra policing costs $37,000.

DECEMBER 9, 1971 Tom Campbell is reelected mayor.

The Hare Krishna sect was a new phenomenon appearing in airport waiting rooms and intersections of major thoroughfares in the 1970s. The Hare Krishna showed up at almost all counter-culture events, like the 1973 Stanley Park Love-In, where they played their music and served paper plates full of cream of wheat and curried lentils. Photo by Henri Robideau

DECEMBER 31, 1971 At the close of B.C.'s centennial year, *Vancouver Province* publisher Fred Auger buries a time capsule near the reception desk in the editorial department. It is to be opened by the *Province* publisher on B.C.'s 200th birthday in 2071.

JANUARY 9, 1972 Demonstrators kick and spit at Mayor Tom Campbell's limousine, the first car through the new Georgia Viaduct. The $1.2-million viaduct is viewed as a link to the unwanted east-west freeway proposed to run through Chinatown.

FEBRUARY 19, 1972 As Vancouver College celebrates its fiftieth anniversary it becomes co-educational.

MARCII 22, 1972 Jail sentences are given to two men found guilty of arranging "marriages of convenience" between East Indian men and Canadian women in an attempt to circumvent immigration laws.

APRIL 20, 1972 Bulldozers demolish the huts at "All Seasons Park" at the entrance to Stanley Park. The transients move to Jericho Beach.

APRIL 27, 1972 A strike of civic workers shuts down all but essential services. It lasts seven weeks.

MAY 24, 1972 Percy Williams is named Canada's outstanding all-time Olympic competitor at a ceremony held before the opening of the Montreal Olympics.

JUNE 2, 1972 Twenty-one police are injured when a disturbance breaks out outside the Pacific Coliseum during a performance by the Rolling Stones.

JUNE 10, 1972 Council decides to remove the benches at Pioneer Square (informally known as Pigeon Park) in an attempt to rid the area of derelicts.

JUNE 12, 1972 Vancouver People's Law School, funded by a federal Opportunities for Youth grant, offers its first free course on legal problems.

JUNE 16, 1972 Explosive experts are called to remove a cache of dynamite found at a rear entrance of city hall.

AUGUST 6, 1972 A crowd estimated at 1,500 gathers in Stanley Park to mark the twenty-seventh anniversary of the bombing of Hiroshima.

Left: New Democratic Party members stare in joyful disbelief as provincial election results come in over the TV on August 30, 1972. After twenty years of Social Credit rule, the NDP gained control of the government, sweeping a majority of seats in Vancouver and the Lower Mainland. Photo by Fred Rosenberg (VPL)

Below: Much to the chagrin of the parks board, the Easter Love-In, first held in 1970, became an annual event at Lumberman's Arch in Stanley Park. Photo by Henri Robideau

The giant hand and loaf was erected atop the McGavin Bakery at Broadway and Arbutus streets in December 1947. The shirt cuff fell off in a wind storm, and by 1973, when this photo was taken, the sign was in such bad shape that it was scrapped. Photo by Henri Robideau

AUGUST 23, 1972 Fran Cannon is the first woman to successfully swim Georgia Strait.

SEPTEMBER 4, 1972 Donna Marie Gurr wins a bronze medal in swimming at the Olympics in Munich.

SEPTEMBER 16, 1972 De Cosmos Village, the city's first co-op housing development, opens at 49th and Boundary.

OCTOBER 4, 1972 Art Phillips wins the mayoralty nomination for TEAM.

DECEMBER 13, 1972 The thirty-five-year domination of the Non-Partisan Association on council is shattered when TEAM wins eight aldermanic seats. Art Phillips is elected mayor.

DECEMBER 29, 1972 Tom Campbell, in his last official act as mayor, cuts the ribbon to open the Vancouver City Archives in the Major Matthews Building in Vanier Park.

JANUARY 10, 1973 Mayor Art Phillips shatters tradition by not wearing the mayor's chain of office in council chambers.

JANUARY 12, 1973 MP Ron Basford announces that Central Mortgage and Housing Corporation has acquired Granville Island and redevelopment will commence immediately.

JANUARY 18, 1973 An old brewery built on Granville Island in

1912 is renovated. The Creekhouse is the first building on the island to be converted from purely industrial use.

FEBRUARY 3, 1973 Hippies stage the first annual Kitsilano Winter Garden Street Festival.

APRIL 1, 1973 The city acquires seventy-two acres of Jericho defence lands from the federal government for the sum of one dollar. In November the remaining thirty-eight acres are purchased for $388,000 under an agreement that the lands will be retained for recreational purposes.

MAY 11, 1973 Businessman Jimmy Pattison purchases the Philadelphia Blazers and moves the team, renamed the Vancouver Blazers, to Vancouver.

MAY 20, 1973 Baseball returns to Vancouver after a four-year absence when the newly formed Metropolitan League plays its first game.

JUNE 23, 1973 The opening of False Creek Park marks the official start to redeveloping False Creek.

JUNE 23, 1973 Indira Gandhi addresses about 2,000 East Indians at Queen Elizabeth Theatre, while demonstrators mill outside. Gandhi is presented with a painting by Raymond Chow depicting scenes of East Indian life in B.C.

SEPTEMBER 8, 1973 David Miller wins Canada's first Olympic medal in yachting in forty years.

SEPTEMBER 23, 1973 Two freighters, the *Sun Diamond* and the *Erawan,* collide off Point Grey resulting in an oil spill which spreads from Ambleside Park to Horseshoe Bay.

JANUARY 15, 1974 The new Knight Street Bridge is officially opened by highways minister Graham Lea.

JANUARY 30, 1974 Wendy Cook wins a gold medal in the 100-metre backstroke at the Commonwealth Games in Christchurch. She is two-fifths of a second off tying the world record.

FEBRUARY 1, 1974 Fraser Street Bridge is closed and scheduled for demolition.

MARCH 8, 1974 The Dover Arms, Vancouver's first neighborhood pub, opens in the West End.

MAY 3, 1974 The Aquatic Centre, built at a cost of 2.4 million dollars to replace Crystal Pool, is officially opened. It opens to swimmers on May 6.

MAY 4, 1974 Professional soccer comes to town as the Vancouver Whitecaps play their opening game at Empire Stadium against the San Jose Earthquakes.

JUNE 21, 1974 The *Royal Hudson* makes its inaugural run to Squamish. The big locomotive is an instant hit, taking sightseers along the water all summer.

JULY 1, 1974 John Fisk retires as chief of police, and Don Winterton, appointed earlier in the year, takes over.

AUGUST 22, 1974 A three-day festival, featuring bands, theatre, and music, marks the opening of the Granville Street Mall.

SEPTEMBER 10, 1974 Ethnomusicologist Dr. Ida Halpern releases a two-recording set of Nootka songs, sequel to her earlier recordings of Kwakuitl music.

The Birks Building was built between 1912 and 1913 and was regarded by most Vancouverites as the loveliest terra-cotta-faced office building in the city. When the owners of the property announced plans for a new office tower on the spot, heritage groups tried in vain to stop it. Demolition commenced in November 1974 and little was left of the Birks Building by January 1975. Photo by Henri Robideau

NOVEMBER 13, 1974 Arbutus Village Square opens. The architect is Zoltan Kiss.

NOVEMBER 20, 1974 Art Phillips is reelected mayor, defeating challengers George Puil, Brian Campbell, and Mr. Peanut (Vincent Trasov). Mr. Peanut campaigns in a peanut-shell suit and never speaks.

APRIL 6, 1975 Sixty-one orphans from Vietnam arrive at the airport. Seven are adopted by B.C. families.

APRIL 14, 1975 Vancouver Co-operative Radio, CFRO-FM, is on the air.

MAY 7, 1975 The Vancouver Blazers of the WHL are moved to Calgary.

AUGUST 7, 1975 Gaslight Square is officially opened.

AUGUST 27, 1975 The Arthur Laing Bridge opens to traffic.

SEPTEMBER 20, 1975 The first annual Gastown Days are held, marking the completion of the Gastown beautification project.

SEPTEMBER 21, 1975 Fire destroys the grandstand at Brockton Oval.

SEPTEMBER 30, 1975 Six hundred and fifty residents of the Collingwood District, some coming from as far as Hawaii, gather at Champlain Mall for a district reunion.

DECEMBER 1, 1975 The new Vanterm container terminal is in operation.

FEBRUARY 9, 1976 Prime Minister Pierre Trudeau officially commissions the TRIUMF nuclear accelerator at UBC.

APRIL 1, 1976 Vancouver's first Rain Festival is held. Festivities include a landlubber's bathtub race in Gastown.

APRIL 23, 1976 The Four Seasons Hotel officially opens with a benefit function to raise funds for the Vancouver Symphony Orchestra.

MAY 27, 1976 Habitat Forum opens in the hangars of the former Jericho Air Base. The forum, spearheaded by Alan Clapp, is designed to give a voice to ordinary citizens during the time the formal UN Conference on Human Settlements meets in Vancouver.

JUNE 7, 1976 Filipinos demonstrate outside the Queen Elizabeth Theatre when Phillipines first lady Imelda Marcos addresses the UN Habitat Conference.

JUNE 11, 1976 The UN Conference on Human Settlements closes. Canada abstains from a motion, presented by Cuba, proposing Zionism be equated with racism and Israel be condemned for its occupation policies. The motion passes seventy-seven to eight.

JUNE 27, 1976 The first Greek Days Festival is held on West Broadway, sponsored by the Hellenic Community Association.

JUNE 29, 1976 The first report of the city's property endowment fund board discloses the city owns about $125 million in land and buildings.

JULY 17, 1976 Peter Colistro wins the first annual Sea Festival wheelchair marathon.

AUGUST 26, 1976 Two Russian destroyers visit Vancouver on a goodwill mission. It is the first visit of Soviet military vessels to Canada since 1944.

SEPTEMBER 7, 1976 B.C. Telephone inaugurates direct distance dialling overseas. The first call is placed by Mayor Art Phillips to the mayor of Kings Lynn, Norfolk, England, the birthplace of Captain George Vancouver.

The most famous locomotive in Canadian history, old Number 374 was the engine that pulled the first transcontinental into Vancouver in 1887. It was later salvaged and resurrected at Kitsilano Beach as a monument, where it served for many years in a playground. It's pictured here in April 1981 as the starting point for the annual Peace March. It was moved in 1984 to be fixed up as an attraction for Expo 86. Photo by Henri Robideau

In June 1976 Vancouver played host to the United Nation's International Conference On Human Habitation, known as Habitat. The main sites for the conference were the old seaplane hangars at Jericho which were converted into indoor amphitheatres and display areas like the one shown here. Downtown in front of the old courthouse was a reception pavilion made of papier-mache painted by Vancouver schoolchildren. Photo by Henri Robideau

SEPTEMBER 10, 1976 Preliminary census figures reveal the city's population has dropped nearly 30,000 since 1971. The population of the city's suburbs is climbing rapidly.

SEPTEMBER 21, 1976 Following years of controversy council votes to retain the land at the entrance to Stanley Park and to scrap any idea of leasing the land to developers.

OCTOBER 21, 1976 Jack Short, the voice of horse racing, retires after forty-three years as the announcer at Exhibition Park.

NOVEMBER 17, 1976 Jack Volrich is elected mayor of Vancouver.

NOVEMBER 30, 1976 Virginia Briant and Elspeth Alley are ordained as women priests at Christ Church Cathedral.

FEBRUARY 16, 1977 Marjorie Cantryn is one of the first two women to be made judges of the citizenship court. She is also the court's first Native judge.

APRIL 2, 1977 A gala performance by the Vancouver Symphony Orchestra marks the official opening of the refurbished Orpheum Theatre.

APRIL 6, 1977 Popular *Sun* columnist Jack Wasserman collapses and dies in the middle of an address at a roast at the Hotel Vancouver for Gordon Gibson, Sr.

JUNE 8, 1977 Vancouver Centre is officially opened. The tower stands 651 feet above sea level, making it the tallest structure in the city.

JULY 25, 1977 Human resources minister Bill Vander Zalm says he is unimpressed by the 2,000 who turned out at the Orpheum on Sunday to protest the closure of the Vancouver Resources Board.

AUGUST 7, 1977 Five Vancouver residents are arrested in Bangor, Washington, during protests against construction of the Trident nuclear base.

AUGUST 12, 1977 A plaque designed by artist Stjepan Pticek dedicates a section of Hornby Street as "Wasserman's Beat" in memory of the late *Sun* columnist.

DECEMBER 8, 1977 Free downtown bus service for shoppers is inaugurated.

FEBRUARY 3, 1978 The Italian community stages its first Carnevale Italiano in the newly opened Italian Cultural Centre.

FEBRUARY 12, 1978 The Variety Club Telethon raises $1,152,000, a record for any telethon sponsored by Variety.

FEBRUARY 14, 1978 Harry Ornest announces the new Pacific Coast League baseball team will be called the Vancouver Canadians.

MARCH 1, 1978 Capilano Stadium is renamed Nat Bailey Stadium.

MARCH 5, 1978 The Brier curling championships are held in Vancouver for the first time since 1950.

APRIL 30, 1978 The Labor Memorial Committee erects a tombstone at the unmarked grave of pioneer labor organizer Frank Rogers. Rogers was shot and killed, allegedly by a professional strikebreaker, during a 1903 CPR strike in Vancouver.

MAY 29, 1978 A Vancouver International Children's Festival is held in Vanier Park, in conjunction with the Heritage Festival. The big colorful tents in which performances are held will become an annual tradition.

SEPTEMBER 2, 1978 Eleven die when an Airwest float plane crashes into Coal Harbor. Most are vacationing Japanese.

SEPTEMBER 17, 1978 A Festival for Life is held in Stanley Park, sponsored by a coalition of twenty anti-nuclear organizations.

SEPTEMBER 30, 1978 A dance marathon is held at UBC's Memorial Gymnasium. Sponsored by Miles for Millions, it raises funds for medical relief in Third World countries.

NOVEMBER 1, 1978 Clark Davey is named publisher of the *Vancouver Sun*, succeeding Stuart Keate. On the same day a strike-lockout commences at Pacific Press, leaving the city without major daily newspapers for eight months.

NOVEMBER 30, 1978 Actors, musicians, and writers protest at the courthouse over planned cutbacks in arts funding.

FEBRUARY 23, 1979 W.A.C. Bennett, B.C.'s longest serving premier, dies.

MAY 6, 1979 The Vancouver International Marathon is run. It is the first marathon held in Vancouver since the 1954 British Empire Games.

JUNE 30, 1979 Houseboats are evicted from Coal Harbor to make way for an expansion of the Bayshore Inn.

More than 40,000 public and private sector workers held a mass rally at Empire Stadium August 10, 1983, to protest the Social Credit government's firing of 5,000 teachers and public sector workers, elimination of the Human Rights Branch, dismantling of rape relief centres, and massive cuts to education and health care. The rally was organized by a broad base of labor and community groups which banded together and called itself Operation Solidarity. Photo by Henri Robideau

JULY 4, 1979 The *Vancouver Courier* enters the newspaper market as a daily publication.

JULY 4, 1979 Banners designed by local children are hung on Burrard Bridge to celebrate the UN's International Year of the child.

JULY 13, 1979 Police raids on Chinese social clubs result in thirty-three persons being charged with keeping a common gaming house.

JULY 26, 1979 The fishermen's market in Gastown closes after two years in operation.

AUGUST 12, 1979 The first edition of the Sunday *Province* is published.

SEPTEMBER 8, 1979 The Vancouver Whitecaps win the NASL championship, defeating the Tampa Bay Rowdies two to one.

DECEMBER 19, 1979 Michael Robitaille wins $374,840 in damages from the Vancouver Canucks, who he claimed ordered him to play hockey with a spinal injury.

FEBRUARY 16, 1980 Noel Coward's *Private Lives,* running at the Arts Club, sets a record as Vancouver's longest-running show.

MAY 27, 1980 The first major eruption of Mount St. Helen's volcano in Washington scatters some ash in Vancouver.

JUNE 10, 1980 Beer is sold for the first time at Empire Stadium.

AUGUST 16, 1980 Vancouver's Lois Wilson is the first woman named moderator of the United Church of Canada.

AUGUST 27, 1980 Southam, Inc., acquires ownership of the *Vancouver Sun* and purchases Thomson Newspaper's 50 percent interest in Pacific Press, Ltd.

SEPTEMBER 14, 1980 The first phase of the Chinese Cultural Centre is opened. It was built at a cost of $900,000.

OCTOBER 14, 1980 Some 700 Native Indians gather outside Grace McCarthy's residence to protest the Ministry of Human Resource's policy of placing Native children in white foster homes.

NOVEMBER 30, 1980 Right Reverend Douglas Hambridge is installed as the seventh bishop of New Westminster at ceremonies held at Christ Church Cathedral.

DECEMBER 11, 1980 Most schools in the Lower Mainland are closed as teachers hold a day of protest in a campaign for fully indexed pensions.

JANUARY 11, 1981 A huge Sunday sale is held by Gastown merchants protesting the government's failure to exempt the area from Sunday shopping hours. An estimated 60,000 shoppers jam the area.

FEBRUARY 1, 1981 A Vancouver landmark, Englesea Lodge, is destroyed by fire.

MARCH 15, 1981 Angered by a prolonged civic strike, residents deposit garbage on the grounds of city hall.

MAY 2, 1981 Two die and eight are injured when the diving charter vessel *Huntress* explodes in Coal Harbor.

AUGUST 1, 1981 "Gay Week" is proclaimed by Mayor Mike Harcourt.

AUGUST 18, 1981 Delegates from Vancouver's sister city, Odessa, USSR, visit Vancouver.

The annual March for Peace has been held every April since 1981. In recent years more than 50,000 people have attended the walk which runs from Kitsilano Beach, across the Burrard Bridge, through downtown, and ends up at Sunset Beach where a rally is held. The walk attracts people from the entire political spectrum whose common interest is world peace. Photo by Henri Robideau

AUGUST 30, 1981 The Vancouver Detoxification Centre is opened on Great Northern Way.

OCTOBER 17, 1981 An anti-racist rally erupts in a battle between the People's Front and members of the B.C. Organization to Fight Racism. They clash at South Memorial Park.

OCTOBER 17, 1981 Police are called to break up a Ku Klux Klan rally celebrating the death of Egypt's Anwar Sadat. A cross-burning ceremony held at Marina Drive at the foot of Angus is the first such Klan activity in the city for nearly half a century.

DECEMBER 21, 1981 Ten days after Poland declares martial law, twenty-seven seamen from a visiting Polish fishing vessel inquire about political asylum. When the ship sails on December 23 only five choose to remain behind.

JANUARY 12, 1982 The mayor's salary is raised to $56,800.

JANUARY 14, 1982 Mass killer Clifford Robert Olson pleads guilty to the murder of eleven Vancouver-area children and is sentenced to life imprisonment. Controversy rages over a $100,000 payoff made to Olson's family for leading police to the bodies of his victims.

JANUARY 16, 1982 Fire damages Malkin Bowl in Stanley Park.

MARCH 3, 1982 CROWE (Concerned Residents of the West End) is formed to rid the West End of street prostitution.

Haida Indians celebrate outside the Vancouver courthouse on December 6, 1985. Nine Haidas had just received suspended sentences after being charged with contempt of court for blocking a logging road on their land. The Haidas wanted to stop the logging until their aboriginal land claims were settled as they had never surrendered title to their land by treaty. Photo by Henri Robideau

APRIL 2, 1982 Premier Bill Bennett announces that Vancouver will host Expo 86 and that a trade and convention centre will be built in the city.

APRIL 24, 1982 About 30,000 join in a peaceful "End the Arms Race" march in Vancouver.

MAY 16, 1982 The New York Islanders win the Stanley Cup, defeating the Vancouver Canucks in four straight games, despite Canuck fans' "white towel power" support. Inspired by coach Roger Neilson's ironic waving of a white towel to indicate "surrender" to referees' decisions, fans buy towels by the thousands and wave them during games.

MAY 19, 1982 Vancouver gives a rousing reception to the defeated Canucks upon their arrival home. May 18 to 25 is proclaimed Canuck Week by the mayor.

NOVEMBER 6, 1982 The B.C. Lions are victorious over the Montreal Alouettes in their final game played at Empire Stadium.

NOVEMBER 9, 1982 Vic Rapp is fired as head coach of the B.C. Lions.

NOVEMBER 14, 1982 The teflon roof on B.C. Place Stadium is inflated in just under one hour.

NOVEMBER 20, 1982 Vancouver is declared a nuclear free zone in a plebiscite. Voters also okay Sunday shopping and a ward system, but the latter is not approved by the provincial government, which has control over the city's charter.

NOVEMBER 20, 1982 The UBC Thunderbirds win the Vanier Cup, defeating the University of Western Ontario football club thirty-nine to fourteen.

NOVEMBER 21, 1982 Michael Harcourt is reelected mayor.

DECEMBER 7, 1982 A Hong Kong bank opens a branch in Chinatown, operating in both English and Chinese.

JANUARY 4, 1983 Don Matthews is named head coach of the B.C. Lions.

MARCH 9, 1983 The Royal yacht *Britannia* sails into Vancouver, bringing the Queen and Prince Philip to the city. The Queen opens the Graham Amazon Gallery at the aquarium and watches the whale show. At B.C. Place she appears on a special satellite hookup and invites the world to Expo.

APRIL 23, 1983 A peace march in downtown Vancouver attracts 6,000.

MAY 24, 1983 A two-week festival of peace, devoted to nuclear disarmament, gets underway at the Vancouver East Cultural Centre.

JUNE 1, 1983 Vancouver's first civic flag is unveiled.

JUNE 12, 1983 The last professional sports event at Empire Stadium is an international soccer series.

JUNE 19, 1983 Premier Bill Bennett opens the 60,000-seat B.C. Place Stadium. It is Canada's first domed stadium.

JUNE 20, 1983 The Vancouver Whitecaps defeat the Seattle Sounders in the first event held at the stadium.

JULY 11, 1983 The formation of "Operation Solidarity" is announced by B.C. Federation of Labor president Art Kube. It is an amalgamation of labor groups and others protesting provincial government cutbacks in social services.

AUGUST 10, 1983 A massive rally, drawing an estimated 40,000, is held at Empire Stadium to protest the government's restraint program.

SEPTEMBER 14, 1983 A parks board employee discovers an ivy-covered totem pole behind the bear pits in Stanley Park. It is learned that the pole was placed in the park in 1903.

SEPTEMBER 16, 1983 Approximately eighty people occupy the government offices in Robson Square as protests continue against restraint.

NOVEMBER 2, 1983 The B.C. Lions lose eighteen to seventeen to the Toronto Argonauts in the first Grey Cup played at B.C. Place.

NOVEMBER 28, 1983 Government workers, supported by many teachers, stage a walkout across British Columbia.

JANUARY 21, 1984 Chinese Premier Zhao Ziyang pays his first visit to Vancouver.

FEBRUARY 22, 1984 Protestors clash with police outside the $150-

a-plate dinner addressed by Henry Kissinger and sponsored by the Junior League and the Arts and Science Technology Centre.

MARCH 28, 1984 A strike at the *Sun* and *Province* lasts until May 24.

APRIL 28, 1984 A peace rally draws 100,000.

MAY 2, 1984 The Mandarin International Hotel of Hong Kong opens its first hotel outside Southeast Asia in downtown Vancouver. It cost forty-one million dollars to construct.

MAY 25, 1984 A "Shame the Johns" operation begins in an attempt to drive prostitutes' clients from the West End. Participants taunt men cruising in cars, write down licence numbers, and threaten to publish names.

JUNE 15, 1984 A bus strike begins in Vancouver and lasts until September 17.

JULY 4, 1984 Prostitutes move from the West End to Seymour Street and east.

AUGUST 13, 1984 Stephen Hinton and Nicola Kozaklewicz start a company called Streetworks to adorn bleak street corners with murals. The first is painted on the South Vancouver neighborhood house at 49th and Victoria Drive.

SEPTEMBER 18, 1984 Pope John Paul II makes the first papal visit ever to Vancouver. He arrives at Vanier Park by helicopter from a Mass at Abbotsford and attends a ceremony at B.C. Place.

OCTOBER 18, 1984 A team of Canadian chefs wins the Culinary Olympics in Frankfurt, Germany. Four of the teams are from the Lower Mainland.

NOVEMBER 1, 1984 The Supreme Court of Canada upholds an award for a $10-million damage action to the Musqueam Indian Band over the leasing of land for the Shaughnessy Golf Club in 1957.

NOVEMBER 16, 1984 Pop star Michael Jackson performs the first of three shows at B.C. Place. It is the most successful entertainment event in the city's history, grossing nearly five million dollars.

NOVEMBER 18, 1984 The Connaught (Cambie Street) Bridge is closed. A replacement will be built before the opening of Expo 86.

NOVEMBER 19, 1984 Mike Harcourt is reelected for his third term as mayor, defeating Bill Vander Zalm. He is the fourth mayor in the city's history to win a third term.

DECEMBER 23, 1984 Demonstrators stage a "Scrooge McCarthy" party on the lawn of Grace McCarthy's West End residence. As minister of human resources, she is responsible for administering cutbacks in social services.

FEBRUARY 1, 1985 Black History Month, celebrated annually in the United States, is commemorated in Vancouver for the first time.

FEBRUARY 3, 1985 A "Concert for Life" given at the Queen Elizabeth Theatre raises money for African famine relief.

MAY 7, 1985 Allan Stables becomes a one-man school board when the elected board of Vancouver trustees is ousted by the provincial government for refusing to accept budget cutbacks.

JUNE 1, 1985 Bus fares rise to one dollar.

JUNE 11, 1985 Nearly three million gallons of raw sewage is dumped in the Fraser River while pipes are relocated during the construction of the Annacis Island Bridge. Mayor Harcourt and his son, Justen, swim at Jericho Beach on July 17 in an attempt to prove the waters are safe.

JUNE 12, 1985 Council establishes an AIDS co-ordinating office, as Acquired Immune Deficiency Syndrome continues to escalate in the city.

JUNE 27, 1985 Guangzhou, China, formerly called Canton, becomes a sister city.

JUNE 28, 1985 Women occupy the Transition House after the facility for battered women is closed by the Ministry of Human Resources.

JULY 6, 1985 Mayor Harcourt's campaign for famine relief in Africa surpasses 1.2 million dollars.

SEPTEMBER 30, 1985 Six residents from the Mount Pleasant District sleep in city hall, protesting the presence of prostitutes in their district.

OCTOBER 8, 1985 Council approves plans to force prostitutes to move from Mount Pleasant to a nearby industrial area.

Preceding page: The annual Japanese Festival is held each summer at Oppenheimer Park on Powell Street in "Japan Town." The festival features performances, displays, and of course many excellent food stands.
Photo by Ken Straiton

Below: Expo 86 was originally planned as an $85-million class "B" trade fair on the theme of transportation and communication to celebrate the Vancouver Centennial. However, by 1985 the B.C. provincial government had turned it into a world's fair.
Photo by Henri Robideau

Left: Vanterm, the new cargo container facility, is located on the spot once occupied by the old Hastings Mill. Photo by Ken Straiton

Below: The Children's Festival, held each spring in Vanier Park, offers a week-long series of concerts and performances as well as free attractions on four stages. Performers are brought in from all around the world, making the Children's Festival an international event. Photo by Henri Robideau

Below: This view of English Bay and the West End was taken from the top of the Scotia Tower at the very centre of the city. Photo by Henri Robideau

Facing page, top: A massive wood sculpture at the foot of Granville Street makes a great lunch-hour sunning spot for office workers and bicycle couriers. Photo by Ken Straiton

Below: This 1979 view of False Creek shows the transition from industrial to residential district at about the halfway point. Granville Island to the left and the north side of the creek still has factories, while the foreground is occupied by the first of the housing units to go in on the south shore. Photo by Ken Straiton

Facing page: A residential street basks in the glow of fall. Foggy mornings give way to brilliantly clear days during autumn in Vancouver. Photo by Ken Straiton

Left: B.C. Place Stadium is framed by autumn leaves in this 1984 view. Photo by Ken Straiton

Below: The Medical-Dental Building at Georgia and Hornby streets is a classic 1930s structure—functional in overall design and sparingly embellished with ornate deco stonework. Photo by Henri Robideau

This sculpture titled *Northwest Passage* is located in Vanier Park between the Centennial Museum and the Maritime Museum. It is symbolic of seemingly unbreakable North Arctic ice packs with a cut through the bottom as if made by an ice breaker. Photo by Henri Robideau

Left: Since the departure of heavy industry from its shores in the late 1970s, False Creek has become a haven for pleasure boaters. The space once occupied by long strings of log booms now serves as moorage for hundreds of yachts. Photo by Ken Straiton

Below: During the 1970s the federal government undertook the transformation of Granville Island from heavy industrial use into a concentrated public space. The Granville Market, Emily Carr College of Art, and the Arts Club Theatre are just a few of the many cultural and community centres now situated on the island. Photo by Ken Straiton

The Vancouver Centennial Museum, located in Vanier Park, Kitsilano Point, is the home of the city's museum and planetarium. Opened in 1968, it replaced the City Museum which had been housed on the top floor of the old Carnegie Library at Main and Hastings streets. The crab sculpture fountain, made of stainless steel, is the work of artist George Norris. Photo by Henri Robideau

Left: Looking east from the centre of downtown, a bright channel of streetlights marks Hastings Street as it stretches to the neighboring municipality of Burnaby. Photo by Henri Robideau

Below: Grouse Mountain looms large above the shallow torpid waters off Spanish Banks. Ships anchor here while awaiting entry to the main harbor to divulge their cargos upon the docks or to take on huge heaps of wheat, sulphur, or lumber. Photo by Henri Robideau

English Bay is a favorite aquatic playground for windsurfing and small sailboats. Photo by Ken Straiton

The Kitsilano Pool is a great place for a swim, a slide, or just to tan your hide. Photo by Ken Straiton

Above: The lofty office towers of Vancouver's business and financial district are reflected in the calm waters of Coal Harbor. Photo by Ken Straiton

Left: This unusual telephoto view of the downtown skyline was taken from North Vancouver. The mountains which appear to the south of the city are actually seventy-five miles away on the Olympic Peninsula of Washington. Photo by Ken Straiton

Facing page, top:
The Lions Gate
Bridge connects West
Vancouver with the
downtown peninsula.
Known as the First
Narrows, this is the
gateway to the Burrard
Inlet and the city's
busy waterfront. Photo
by Ken Straiton

Facing page, bottom:
The wind-blown tidal
mud flats off Locarno
Beach provide a splen-
did view of English
Bay, the downtown
peninsula, and the
north shore moun-
tains. Photo by Henri
Robideau

Above: The Chinese
community in Vancou-
ver is the second larg-
est in North America
(after San Francisco).
Pender Street runs
through the heart of
Chinatown. Photo by
Ken Straiton

Above: Robson Square, Vancouver Art Gallery, and the courthouse complex, designed by architect Arthur Erickson, provide an open space in the core of the city's skyscrapers. Photo by Ken Straiton

Left: The flower gardens of Little Mountain are a favorite Saturday afternoon location for wedding photography. Originally, a stone quarry, nowadays the garden is part of Queen Elizabeth Park and home of the Bloedel Botanical Conservatory. Photo by Ken Straiton

Left: The Vancouver Public Aquarium, located in Stanley Park, is visited by one million people a year. The entrance to the aquarium is graced by a bronze killer whale sculpture, created by artist Bill Reid. Photo by Ken Straiton

Facing page, top: Construction of B.C. Place Stadium, Canada's first covered stadium, began in spring of 1981 and was completed early in 1983. It is the home of the B.C. Lions football club and for a short time served as the headquarters for the now-defunct Vancouver Whitecaps soccer team. Photo by Ken Straiton

Facing page, bottom: An incredible range of exotic fruits and vegetables can be found in the markets of Vancouver's Chinatown. Most of the fresh green produce—like Bok Choi and Sui Choi—are grown locally in the rich soil along the shores of the Fraser River in southern Vancouver. Photo by Ken Straiton

Above: The outdoor cafe and restaurant tables on Granville Island are always jammed on sunny days as people gather to pleasantly banter away the afternoon. Photo by Ken Straiton

Left: The Expo 86 Display Centre is known locally as the "Giant Golf Ball." Inside this ten-storey-high bubble is an Omnimax panoramic movie theatre. Photo by Henri Robideau

PART VII

PARTNERS IN PROGRESS

The stories of Vancouver's partners in progress are only some of the tales that could be told of the many thousands of men and women whose energy and enthusiasm, ideas, and industry built the city of Vancouver.

The evolution from small mill town to major metropolitan city in 100 years does not happen by mere chance. For a community to progress it needs nurturing; it needs people, who in turn need to make or find opportunities for employment. It also needs a sense of community and the promise of sufficient civic income to provide the amenities and services that make an acceptable quality of life.

For every pioneer who arrived in Vancouver with money to invest, there were legions who arrived with only the clothes on their backs and a determination to succeed. The setbacks they encountered, and the trials they endured, tend to be glossed over by the survivors, but they should not be overlooked by those who enjoy the Vancouver those pioneers worked to build. The stories told here record only those who succeeded—those who are here to celebrate Vancouver's centennial.

This chapter is dedicated to Vancouver's partners in progress—those whom we know and whose modest beginnings, hard work, and struggles we can read about. It is also dedicated to the thousands of nameless and faceless pioneers who came with a spirit of entrepreneurship and made their contribution to the city of Vancouver.

Some of the companies are new, others have been active on the business scene since the city's infancy. For each of them Vancouver has presented a challenge and an opportunity that have been embraced knowingly and willingly.

The progress that brought Vancouver from mill town to graceful centenarian is not a finite process—it is ongoing. Those who are struggling now may, perhaps, see this chapter as a blueprint and an encouragement.

For many of the businesses mentioned in the following chapter, Vancouver has served as a gateway to the north and a gateway to the Pacific Rim, but as the city embarks on its second century, it is, without doubt, a gateway to the world. The crest of the city of Vancouver says "By land, sea and air we prosper"—not just a trite motto but a statement and a promise.

The organizations whose stories are detailed on the following pages have chosen to support this important literary and civic project. They illustrate the variety of ways in which individuals and their businesses have contributed to the city's growth and development. The civic involvement of Vancouver's businesses, institutions of learning, and local government, in cooperation with its citizens, has made the community an excellent place to live and work.

Facing page: This oil painting of the Vancouver waterfront in 1930 is by artist Charles H. Scott, after whom the art gallery at the Emily Carr College of Art and Design is now named. Courtesy, Vancouver Maritime Museum

THE VANCOUVER BOARD OF TRADE
WORLD TRADE CENTRE VANCOUVER

After the disastrous fire of June 13, 1886, the first question was how to rebuild the young city of Vancouver. A group of area businessmen held a series of meetings to discuss the need for some kind of formal organization to help in that work. On September 22, 1887, at a meeting chaired by Alderman R. Clark, a decision was made to form a board of trade. Realtor John Devine was chosen as temporary secretary.

Later that year a charter gave the new organization the official name of The Vancouver Board of Trade. Today a copy of that charter hangs in The Board's offices. It records the names of the Vancouver businessmen who were the organization's founding members. Some of their names are still familiar a century later: realtor Ceperley in Ceperley Park, Hastings Saw Mill manager R.H. Alexander, and real estate broker M.A. McLean.

The first president of The Vancouver Board of Trade was David Oppenheimer, who had come as a pioneer to British Columbia a few years earlier. He was subsequently elected mayor in 1888, a position he held for four years.

The Board's first small offices were in the Gilmour & Clark's Block—the exact address is not known. From a formidable list of thirty-three applicants, H.B. McGowan was hired as full-time secretary at a salary of fifty dollars per month. Members agreed on an entrance fee of twenty dollars and an annual subscription of twelve dollars, payable quarterly in advance. The organization also opened an account with the Bank of British North America.

Only a month after receiving its charter The Board made its first representations to the provincial government through the Provincial Secretary, John Robson. Board records show that the concerns addressed included the abolition of dual direct taxation (city and provincial) on per-

The Vancouver Board of Trade was located at 605 West Hastings Street in the late 1890s. The board had been active promoting Vancouver as the outfitting point for miners going to the gold rush country.

sonal property in Vancouver; the amendment of the law of lien to protect artisans and laborers engaged in construction work; the need for a land registry office, a courthouse, and a resident judge in Vancouver; school improvements; a request that the government set aside fifty acres of land at Hastings townsite for a public park; the need for a bridge across the north arm of the Fraser River, a road to the city to transport produce to Vancouver, and the diking and reclaiming of wastelands on Lulu Island and the Fraser River delta; and encouragement to developing mines.

To the federal government The Board expressed the need for a post office department and regular mail routes in some districts.

The Board's president in 1889, R.H. Alexander, brought about the formation of the B.C. Tree Fruit

Growers Association. Through that organization British Columbians were made aware of the climate's suitability for fruit growing.

In 1891 the organization began pressing for a submarine cable so that residents of Western Canada could communicate with Australia. It took a long time but in 1902, to the immense satisfaction of The Board,

the first cable was laid from Vancouver Island to Fanning Island, south of Hawaii. From there the cable went to Suva, to Auckland, and finally to Sydney.

The Vancouver economy ran out of steam in 1891, but by 1896 it began to recover. In response to a request from The Board, the dominion government announced the start of salmon hatcheries on the Skeena and Fraser rivers. In 1896 trade value of a year's salmon catch in British Columbia was more than three million dollars.

The discovery of gold in the Yukon in 1897 established Vancouver as the "Gateway to the North." The Board then mounted a successful advertising campaign promoting Vancouver as an outfitting point for miners rushing to the Yukon. In response to Board requests, a government assay office was opened in 1899.

The Vancouver waterfront when the new P&O Spirit of London *made her maiden visit on June 18, 1973. The Board's office at 1177 West Hastings Street shows clearly to the right. The site of the current office at Canada Place is still occupied by Piers B and C, on the left. Keen eyes will note the construction of the Holiday Inn, the presence of the old Customs House, and the absence of the Daon Building.*

A Dominion Day procession along Cordova Street on July 1, 1890. Courtesy, Vancouver Public Library

---

Other Board undertakings as the century drew to a close included helping to establish manual training schools, promoting the establishment of a Canadian Mint in Vancouver, and pushing for a dominion bankruptcy law, the provision of a fireboat, and the supply of badly needed laborers for the area.

By 1901 five-day steamer service from Seattle to Skagway via Vancouver had been inaugurated as a result of Board pressure. The organization also played a key role in recommending a steamship service to promote trade and open up the North. It also applied to the dominion government for a railway through the Crows Nest Pass to open up the Kootenays—a development that later played a major role in stimulating the economy of the province.

In 1906 The Board called for the abolition of the ward system in Vancouver. It also began the fight for grain elevators in the city. Vancouver was growing rapidly, and Board members were starting to visualize the city as it could become and were working toward that end.

By 1908 the Vancouver Board of Trade's membership stood at 151. Among its concerns was the British Columbia lumber industry, which was suffering unfair competition from

rough lumber coming into Canada duty free. The organization also supported the Vancouver Shipmasters' Association in its efforts to make the dominion government aware of the necessity of dredging First Narrows and appropriating $25,000 to remove the Parthia Shoal.

In 1909 The Board pushed for a new city hall and a dominion post office. Four years later the organization successfully asked for the establishment of Daylight Savings Time in Vancouver. The outbreak of war saw Board members heading Victory Bond drives. Many of the causes and projects that the organization promoted were achieved because they were endorsed by the people of Vancouver.

In 1924 B.C. Electric gave land for Capilano Park to The Board, which later turned it over to the Vancouver Parks Board. In 1926 the organization helped establish the Department of Commerce at U.B.C., and later was instrumental in the formation of the Canadian Chamber of Commerce. The Board was also involved in the development of the Community Chest, predecessor of the United Way, and in the establishment of the

B.C. Cancer Society.

Times continued to change, bringing new problems and new projects for The Vancouver Board of Trade. In 1948 the problem was raising $2.3 million for the B.C. Flood Emergency Fund. Twenty years later the association was working closely with the Vancouver School Board and was sponsoring a Business Administration program at Vancouver City College—a sponsorship it has maintained.

For years The Board had promoted tourism as a vital part of the city's economy and had acted as a tourist bureau. During the 1930s, however, the tourism division was separated from The Board and became what is now the Greater Vancouver Convention and Visitors Bureau.

The Board had moved its offices to Melville Street at Bute, but by 1968 it had outgrown those premises. It then became the first tenant in the newly constructed Board of Trade Tower at 1177 West Hastings Street. There, on the fifth floor, it moved into spacious new quarters and opened the VBT Club. The club, consisting of a dining room, a cocktail lounge, and meeting rooms, served thousands of Board members and their guests over the years. Its superb location on the fifth floor afforded magnificent views of the harbor and the north shore. The club was an extremely popular meeting place for area residents and out-of-town visitors.

During the 1970s board members took a close look at their organization. The long-range planning task

Canada Place, 1986—the new home of The Vancouver Board of Trade/World Trade Centre Vancouver.

force recommendations reflected changing conditions in the business community. No longer could voluntary presidents devote most of their year in office to Board activities. The organization's bylaws were revised to appoint a full-time president and chief executive officer, and for an executive and board of directors to be led by an elected chairman. Changes were also made to the committee structure, and the use of task forces was adopted.

Among the Vancouver Board of Trade's projects in the 1970s were two well-received publications: a study on critical trade skills and a response to the national energy policy. The organization's statement on national unity was read into the records of the House of Commons.

The 1980s saw the introduction of high technology to The Vancouver Board of Trade when an integrated office system was installed. It provided word-processing and accounting capabilities, as well as in-house typesetting.

The Board had become interested in the World Trade Centres Association knowing that even without membership it was performing as a World Trade Centre. At the WTCA General Assembly in Melbourne in 1983, The Vancouver Board of Trade was voted into membership—and immediately bid to host the General Assembly during 1986, the year of Expo.

The Vancouver Board of Trade continued in its role of promoting a better community but, realizing the role that international trade would play in enhancing the civic economy, also enlarged its international trade activities. This and additional services, such as a professionally managed library, soon presented yet another space problem.

The development of Piers B and C into Canada Place provided an opportunity for The Board/Centre to relocate. The complex includes the Canada Pavilion for Expo 86 (eventually to be the Vancouver Trade and Convention Centre), a cruise ship facility, a hotel, and an office building. The Vancouver Board of Trade/World Trade Centre Vancouver was the first tenant to move into the World Trade Centre Office early in 1986.

The new facilities allow the organization to expand both its domestic and international operations. The introduction of the WTCA NETWORK puts it in immediate contact with other trade centres around the world. Data research "retrieval" allows The Board to tap numerous sources of information across North America.

The new premises consist of offices and meeting rooms. The Centre-Board Club is operated by the adjacent Pan Pacific Vancouver Hotel for midday use by Board of Trade members.

Much has changed in the ninety-nine years since The Vancouver Board of Trade was officially chartered. The organization has seen good times and bad, war and peace. It has met problems, found solutions, and seen opportunities for Vancouver and worked to make them realities. The Board has an impressive record of service to the City of Vancouver and, as it shares in Vancouver's centennial celebration, pledges itself to another century of service.

FOUR SEASONS HOTELS LIMITED

The Four Seasons story began in 1954 when Isadore Sharp, an honors architecture graduate, became fascinated by the hotel business and its prospects. He tried to find financing to build his first hotel, but the banks were not interested. The young man persisted for seven years, and—with financing from two close friends—opened the Four Seasons Motor Hotel in Toronto in 1961.

The success of this venture encouraged Sharp to invest in a more luxurious establishment. He purchased sixteen acres in Don Mills, a Toronto suburb, and in 1963 opened The Inn on the Park—an urban resort lodge in a park setting. Exemplifying Sharp's dedication to quality, it is now one of eighteen facilities operated by Four Seasons Hotels Limited and five currently under construction.

The Four Seasons Hotel in Vancouver opened in 1976 and has maintained an enviable level of occupancy ever since. In 1984 extensive renovations and refurbishing were

The motor entrance of the Four Seasons Hotel in Vancouver.

undertaken, and the number of rooms has been reduced to 385 in order to develop new suites. Unable to control what surrounded the hotel, the organization designed its establishment with an inner garden for viewing and utilization.

Isadore Sharp is determined that quality should be the norm for his hotels. "Quality," he emphasizes, "is not luxury. It isn't extravagance or indulgence. Quality is a combination of performance and price, which adds up to value. Quality is enduring, not transient."

Employees of Four Seasons hotels everywhere are asked to adopt this philosophy of providing service, while management continually refines and makes changes in response to what it learns from its customers. Most of the hotels' guests are business people, politicians, and celebrities: They are demanding clients and expect value.

Four Seasons Hotels Limited expanded its operations into England with the Inn on the Park, erected in London in 1970. The firm also has facilities in major U.S. cities, including The Pierre in New York and The Clift in San Francisco. Four Seasons hotels appear six times in the first forty of a 1985 list of the world's best, and operate five of the top eleven hotels in the United States and Canada.

In planning new establishments the company always works with leading developers. A recent joint venture with Kuo Investments Limited of Singapore will initially seek opportunities in the Far East and Western Europe.

The corporation weathered the recession and now looks forward with confidence. That confidence, however, the founder warns, will only be justified if all the Four Seasons hotels continue to meet—and exceed—customers' expectations. Sharp sums it all up by stating, "We want to be the finest hotel in whatever city we are located."

Patrons are surrounded by a lush, tropical background in the beautiful Garden Lounge.

BC SUGAR

The year was 1890 and Benjamin Tingley Rogers was twenty-four years old. His youth had been spent in the sugar business in New York and he wanted to build a refinery in Vancouver. There was no such facility in Western Canada to serve the rapidly growing population of the Vancouver area, and the community needed secondary manufacturing to break its dependence on the primary resource industries. It had good port facilities to handle raw cane sugar from the producing countries of the Orient.

The city fathers of Vancouver listened to Rogers and deliberated—but not for long! Mayor David Oppenheimer granted Rogers a bonus of $30,000 in the form of a free graded site, free water for ten years, and no taxes for fifteen years if a 100-barrel-per-day refinery was built in eight months.

Cornelius van Horne's railroad, the Canadian Pacific, had just joined Vancouver to the rest of Canada. He

was anxious to see industrial activity develop in the West, so, with some of his associates, he joined Rogers in raising an astounding $25,000. The British Columbia Sugar Refining Company was organized, and the refinery was built: a *solid red brick building* as Rogers had promised.

The *Vancouver News Advertiser,* on August 31, 1890, stated: "The manner in which the Refinery Company is pushing its enterprise must be a matter of satisfaction to every citi-

The BC Sugar refinery, showing its location in Vancouver Harbor. Sugar leaving the ships is conveyed to the low raw-sugar warehouse, to the adjacent Melt House, to the taller Filter House and Pan House (top left of site), and is stored in the warehouse along the railroad tracks. Photo by Allen Aerial Photos Ltd.

zen and it is worthy of note that young as Vancouver is, she already possesses a trading company with connections with the Orient . . . ."

In 1891 the refinery produced 150 barrels of sugar a day at wholesale prices of seven and a quarter cents per pound for granulated and six and three-eighth cents for yellow. Rogers estimated the province's annual requirement to be nearly 4,000 tons.

The first president, J.M. Browning, the Vancouver representative of the CPR, resigned in 1891, and Rogers ran the refinery until his death in 1918. These years had been turbulent. Competition had come briefly from a short-lived beet-sugar factory in Alberta and from Hong Kong sugar sold on Vancouver Island. World War I had been difficult—shipping schedules were stringent and world supplies of sugar very low. Raw sugar was purchased from Java and from a plantation in Fiji that the company

BC Sugar in 1893. The Canadian Pacific Railway single-line track is inside the gate, and Powell Street is in the foreground. The building on the left is the office. The refinery entrance is on Raymur Street.

A ship discharging sugar at the BC Sugar refinery dock.

Sugar boilers in the Pan Room, 1916.

operated from 1905 to 1922.

The founder's eldest son, Blythe Dupuy Rogers, served as president from 1918 to 1920, then was succeeded by Fordham Johnson, who retired in 1930.

Ernest Rogers, Benjamin's second son, assumed the presidency in 1930. That decade saw the firm expand into Alberta through the purchase of a factory in Raymond from American owners and the construction of a second beet-sugar plant at Picture Butte. A company doctor and pension plan were introduced. Pensioner Bill Blankenbach said in 1981 that, even during the worst days of the Depression, the well-loved Ernest Rogers refused to lay off any employee.

The year 1939 brought the war and a new corporate head, P.T. Rogers, Benjamin's third son. He faced a wartime Sugar Administration Board, which set prices and quotas and,

eventually, rationed consumers. One raw sugar shipment was lost at sea when the S.S. *Donerail* was torpedoed near Hawaii on December 7, 1941.

In 1947 BC Sugar started construction of a new beet-sugar plant at Taber, Alberta. (Since 1978 it has absorbed the production from Picture Butte.) A cane-sugar plantation was operated in the Dominican Republic from 1944 to 1955; and the Manitoba Sugar Company was acquired in 1955.

Forrest Rogers, following his older brothers, was president from 1953 until his retirement in 1973 when he was succeeded by another family member, Peter Cherniavsky. The past thirty years have seen extensive alterations, refitting, and construction of facilities at the foot of Rogers Street. The dock now berths ships carrying 20,000 tons of sugar. The original plant was pulled down; a new warehouse, Pan House, Melt House, and shipping shed were erected. Having been rebuilt and re-equipped, BC Sugar is now a very modern refinery.

An impressive number of longtime employees, many with more than forty years' service, are on corporate records that show two or three generations of various families. Brothers,

sisters, and other relatives appear so often on the payroll that the enterprise must be considered a real family operation—from its leadership to the youngest employee. This loyalty and longevity are appreciated by the organization and reflect well on its management.

BC Sugar is a household name in Western Canada. The general citizenry recognizes the "Rogers" name and the firm's diamond logo on its products: granulated, berry, icing, cube, demerara, golden yellow, and best brown sugars. Pancake and cereal lovers, as well as serious cooks, know the Rogers Golden Syrup and Rogers pancake syrups. Oldtimers remember the cotton sacks of sugar and, some, even the barrels. Others recall the cardboard packages of sugar, partly replaced by paper and plastic bags. The cans of syrup are gone as progress replaced them with easy-opening glass bottles.

BC Sugar has matured alongside its community. The contribution to the lives of Western Canadians amply justifies and repays the foresight and confidence of the first city fathers of Vancouver.

JONES TENT & AWNING LTD.

The story of Jones Tent & Awning is the story of Vancouver. As the city grew and prospered, so did the company. As the city diversified, so did the company. But both started in a small way, Vancouver as a mill town and Jones as a sailmaker.

In Saint John, English immigrant Charles Jones hand-made sails for the ships that put into New Brunswick's harbours. Stories about the exciting West Coast encouraged him to

Charles H. Jones, founder.

weigh anchor and set course for Vancouver.

At Birtle, Manitoba, Jones homesteaded until the railway line to the coast was completed. He found plenty of extra work making canvas goods for the wagons and travellers heading west. The widower Charles, with his small sons, Fred and Charlie, and daughter Maude, arrived in Vancouver in 1887 on the first through C.P.R. train from Montreal, pulled by Engine 374.

Fire had destroyed Vancouver in 1886 and Jones found people living in shacks or sheltering under tarpaulins and tents. He immediately set up a workshop in a shack on the wharf in the Gastown area. Family tradition says that Charles Jones made the tent under which the first city council met after its inauguration in 1886. Since many of Jones' goods preceded him from the Prairies, there is little reason to doubt it!

Vancouver was bustling with pros-

pectors outfitting themselves and loggers gathering supplies and equipment. The tall sailing ships in the harbour required provisions and sails. There was a desperate need for an experienced canvas worker, and Jones used all his ingenuity to produce anything that could be fashioned from canvas.

The Klondike Gold Rush of 1898 brought thousands of sourdoughs to Vancouver on their way north to Skagway and the Yukon Trail. Fred had joined his father in the business, and C.H. Jones & Son struck its own gold supplying the prospectors. The first city directory, dated June 1899, lists "C.H. Jones Tent Factory and Sail Maker, No. 9-13 Water Street." The company had several employees and canvas was now sewn by machine.

By 1912 C.H. Jones & Son Ltd., with Fred in charge, had larger prem-

Charles H. Jones made the tent under which the first city council meeting was held after the Great Fire. The meeting took place on June 14, 1886.

In 1911 C.H. Jones & Son Ltd. moved to this facility at 110 Alexander Street.

ises at 110 Alexander Street. The tempo and life of Vancouver were changing, and British Columbia had a world reputation for big game hunting. Contemporary accounts acknowledge Jones as the foremost supplier of outdoor equipment to the visiting sportsmen. The firm's "Pioneer" brand name was developed.

Many Canadian troops in World War I carried Pioneer knapsacks and rallied under banners made by C.H. Jones & Son. During the 1920s the third generation, Fred's son, Ira, joined the business. He is currently chairman of the board. Ira quickly gained a reputation as an outdoorsman and a keen hunter, and his interest and experience brought new ideas and products to the company. In 1924 the firm bought the manufacturing rights to the popular Trapper Nelson packboard, which is still made today for serious outdoorsmen. During Prohibition, Vancouver had its share of rum-running smugglers, and corporate records reveal that some of them were also customers!

The days of the magnificent sailing ships were dwindling: Fewer and fewer ships came to Jones for canvas sails. Company president Ken Jones says that one of the firm's last sets of sails was produced in 1945 for the training ship *Pamir,* later lost at sea in a hurricane. His father, Ira Jones, recalls the Fraser River salmon fishers

who used dories powered by an oar and a single sail. They, too, have passed into history.

When World War II broke out, Jones Tent & Awning was producing a full range of canvas goods for outdoor use. Production was converted for the armed services, and military goods added to the ever-expanding range of products.

In 1918, after World War I, the business was located at 28 Water Street. In 1930 it relocated to 43 West Hastings Street but operated a separate waterproofing plant at Twenty-fifth and Kingsway. New and spacious premises at 2034 West Eleventh Avenue were acquired in 1956.

With the death of Fred Jones in

December 1949, his son, Ira, became company president. Ira's three sons, Bill, Ken, and Ron, later joined the firm, and now, just one year short of its centennial, Ira is chairman of the board and son Ken is president. Members of the fifth generation have joined Jones Tent & Awning after completing their formal education.

Since the 1950s Canadians have increased their enjoyment of the outdoors. More leisure hours have brought new recreational pursuits: more family camping, sailing, hiking, and skiing. Each new trend and development has been translated by Jones Tent & Awning into a potential market. Company production now includes high-fashion ski wear, rain wear, shell garments, down jackets, sleeping bags, tents, and camping equipment. An export market is being developed and Pioneer goods can now be seen in many faraway places.

Jones Tent & Awning Ltd. is a family affair—a business passed from the first to the fourth generation and probably on to the succeeding generations. It is a business that truly is a "Pioneer"—one that has grown with Vancouver, helping her and being helped by her, sharing the city's pride and being part of it.

Jones Tent & Awning Ltd. still occupies this building at 2034 West Eleventh Avenue, which was acquired in 1956.

THE NORTH AMERICAN GROUP

The 1890 sketch map of Vancouver on the office wall is the only backwards glance that this group allows itself. "Everything else," says its president, John Windsor, "is thinking ahead and using tomorrow's technology today."

The North American Group is comprised of two companies: North American Land Corporation (agency work and property management) and North American Property Corporation (property ownership and development).

North American Land Corporation concentrates its agency activity in the lower mainland area of British Columbia. Clients, both domestic and offshore, are helped in the assembly, acquisition, and sale of real estate. Experienced personnel, using the most sophisticated technology, analyze the holdings for their full investment potential—emphasizing possible tax efficiency. They work to ensure that investors are well advised and that the project itself achieves its maximum return.

The property management division controls holdings owned by clients and by North American Property Corporation. Local on-site managers' reports from the various apartments, hotels, retail premises, and office buildings are collated by the company computer. Its unique and specially designed software is used to prepare accurate, up-to-date reports that are

The 669-suite Lougheed Garden Estates project in Burnaby, British Columbia, is one of North American Land Corporation's management and marketing responsibilities.

easily assimilated.

North American Property Corporation secures realties for itself and in co-ventures with others. Its long-term focus is the acquisition of commercial warehouses in growth areas of the United States. Residential properties are purchased when worth can be improved through innovative management, upgrading, or other means of creating value.

The properties assembled, purchased, and sold by the group are residential and commercial: hotels, shopping centres, office buildings, apartment blocks, and warehouses. The company believes that, in every transaction, both the vendor and the purchaser must be satisfied. The North American Group has a track record of creating new and imaginative forms of financing where necessary or desirable. "We are attracted to difficult and complicated deals," avers Windsor with appreciation for the challenge.

The background for the organization began in 1970, when John Windsor visited Vancouver from his native England. Cashing in the return half of his ticket, he decided to stay and use his professional training as a chartered surveyor. His skills were applied in another Vancouver agency until he established The North American Group in 1978, which now employs twenty people—all carefully chosen for their skills in the property field or in the necessary support services.

In just one decade the housing and property industry has seen many changes in provincial and federal legislation—with rent controls, MURBS, and a host of other acronyms. During the early 1980s there was also a recession from which only the strongest and most pragmatic survived. The North American Group looks ahead with confidence, determined to meet the challenges of a continually changing real estate market.

BANK OF BRITISH COLUMBIA

The original Bank of British Columbia received its charter from Queen Victoria in 1862, and raised capital through the sale of 12,500 shares at $100 each. An early report describes service at the Quesnel branch:

"A log house with bearskins tacked on the outside to dry. . . . We treated our customers well, had a good fire, and furnished a plug of tobacco free, with a sharpened axe head and a board to cut it on."

Service notwithstanding, the bank faced stiff competition and was acquired by the Canadian Bank of Commerce in 1902.

In 1964 Premier W.A.C. Bennett proposed a new bank to service the needs of British Columbians. As the province's intention to take an equity position in the new bank violated federal legislation, the Bank of British Columbia was chartered in 1967 as a public company—with $128 million in funding from its shareholders. When it began operations a year later, it had an unusual problem: There was no Canadian alive who had started a bank!

An experienced banker, Albert E. Hall, was appointed chief executive officer. His mandate was to establish a financial centre in British Columbia to fulfill the banking needs of the small and middle-size business community. The institution was to support industrial development within the province and encourage foreign trade, particularly in the Pacific Rim.

The bank opened its first branch in Vancouver on July 18, 1968, and within three days more than 7,000 customers had deposited almost four million dollars. Today the bank has thirty-nine branches in British Columbia and two in Alberta.

In September 1984 Edgar F. Kaiser, Jr., was appointed chairman, and in 1986 the president of Canadian banking operations, Dale Parker, became president and chief executive officer. Under Kaiser's dynamic leadership, and as a result of actions taken by management, it is today one of the best capitalized major banks in Canada. Other recent changes include conversion of all branches to an on-line automated banking system and link-up with the Exchange ABM network.

An impressive Bank of British Columbia office building in downtown Vancouver will be completed in late 1986 and will house the bank's head office operations and the Vancouver main branch.

The Bank of British Columbia is an innovator in Canadian banking. It builds "friendly" branch premises, not the cold marble halls of old, and each manager is encouraged to settle in and become part of the local community. The organization introduced the first "all service, one charge" account and a Pioneer service plan for those aged fifty-five years and older.

The Bank of British Columbia proudly describes itself as "Canada's Western Bank," serving the people it knows and understands. Chairman Edgar F. Kaiser, Jr., states, "We are committed to being the best—to serving the West more effectively than any other bank."

This artist's rendering shows the Bank of British Columbia Building on Georgia Street. It is currently under construction and scheduled to be completed in late 1986.

MILONI FOOD IMPORTERS LTD.

A walk through the warehouse of Miloni Food Importers is a stroll through a "supermarket" of the world. Throughout the building there are staples, gourmet foods, and special delicacies—in boxes, cartons, bottles, and cold storage—which have been brought from places as far apart as Britain and Brazil, Italy and New Zealand. They have arrived from literally everywhere and anywhere in the world that Frank Miloni can find a quality product that he believes Canadians will want to taste.

The organization has evolved from a small business established in 1956 in Vancouver's "Little Italy" to bring

A family concern—president B. Frank Miloni (seated) is flanked by wife Anne (right), daughter Darlene Graham (left), and son Jerry (standing). All are actively involved in the business.

The Milonis present some of the tremendous range of products handled by the company.

to Italian-Canadians, and the newly arrived Italian immigrants, the ethnic foods they were missing. Branko "Frank" Miloni, a recent immigrant from Europe, had seen a potential market; and with capital of $2,500 and the support of his wife, Anne, Frank started his food-importing enterprise.

From that modest beginning the company has grown until today it employs twenty-six people. It is still very much a family concern, as the Milonis have been joined by a son, Jerry, and a daughter, Darlene.

The firm's first location, a 2,000-square-foot site, was close to its market in East Vancouver; however, business expansion made a move necessary. Since 1968 Miloni Food Importers has occupied premises on Gilley Avenue in Burnaby that it once considered spacious, but are now literally bursting at the seams. The two-acre complex has over 25,000 square feet of warehouse and office space.

The company's private rail spur line brings products from Eastern Canada in railcars whose capacity can reach 110,000 pounds. At least three of these railcars arrive each month, and they are supplemented by others from the San Joaquin Valley, California.

In the yards alongside the warehouses, huge containers from around the world arrive on flatbed trucks from the terminals in the Port of Vancouver. These goods are rapidly unloaded by warehouse staff, and are placed ready for immediate shipment or stacked for repacking before shipment or delivery.

Over the past thirty years Canada has experienced an era of intense immigration. Each new wave of immigrants has added to the nation's multiculturalism. It has exposed the countrymen to new tastes and dishes in the many ethnic restaurants, and to an ever-widening range of novel foods and drinks in the store.

Frank Miloni not only takes an active part in meeting this new demand, he was part of the initial impetus and continues to be a considerable factor in its encouragement. The entrepreneur is an energetic man who has learned several languages so that when abroad, it is easier to find and purchase the foods that he wants. In describing the imports he says, "We like to specialize in staple foods while carrying gourmet and specialty items as well, to round off our product lines."

The warehouses and showroom demonstrate this every day. There are tons of pasta, made by Primo in Eastern Canada and distributed by Miloni. There are all the essential ingredients for the sauces—olive oils, tomatoes, tomato pastes, olives, peppers, canned meat and fish, an-

chovies, and garlic products—from countries including Italy, Brazil, Turkey, Greece, and the United States. It seems that Canadian consumption of pasta, per capita, ranks third worldwide—after Italy and Argentina.

For those with a sweet tooth, there are fine cookies and cakes, and chocolates and candies from Italy, West Germany, and Yugoslavia. (Miloni says that the annual bill for chocolates alone in Canada is one billion dollars!) There are bottles of mineral water from Italy and Yugoslavia. The cold-storage areas chill New Zealand, German, Danish, Finnish, Dutch, and Swiss cheeses, cured meats, and filo for Greek pastry and strudels. The warehouse inventory seems endless, but it is never static. It varies as prices and quality fluctuate around the world and as additional items and suppliers are discovered. It will increase as Canadians expand their taste horizons and appetites.

The company distributes products under both the manufacturers' names and its own special brand names, **Adria, Caprie,** and **Albatross,** among others. They are delivered in the Vancouver area, where four trucks load up every day at the warehouses, and most of British Columbia. The company also ships its products into major centres in Alberta,

Saskatchewan, Manitoba, and as far east as Ontario and Quebec. Some private brand lines are shipped in containers direct to distributors in Toronto and Montreal.

Miloni Food Importers is also an exporter, and vigorous merchandising has opened up a market in the United States. San Francisco and Los Angeles both receive regular deliveries of the twenty-ton-truck shipments, and cargo ships en route for Vancouver "drop off" containers.

"Canadians manufacture many excellent products that only need to be introduced on the world market to become sought after," notes Jerry Miloni, who handles the export sales. He is making those introductions!

The firm's founder does not forget the community in which he lives, showing his concern and interest in various ways. A sponsor of two collegiate soccer teams and an Atlantic Formula racing car, Frank Miloni is also an active member of The Vancouver Board of Trade, the Canadian Chamber of Commerce, the Canadian Importers' Association, and Vancouver's Opera and Symphony societies.

The successful businessman is dedicated to finding quality foods, and, in his pursuit of just the "right thing," he is ready to "shop the world."

Miloni Food Importers Ltd.'s headquarters, warehouse, and storage area. Not visible is a private rail siding to facilitate shipping and receiving.

BRITISH COLUMBIA FOREST PRODUCTS LIMITED

A May 1963 aerial view of the construction of the firm's first newsprint mill (far left) at the Crofton Pulp Mill on Vancouver Island, with chip storage piles in the background and loading docks of Stuart Channel Wharves (upper right).

In just four decades British Columbia Forest Products Limited has grown from a brainchild of industrialist E.P. Taylor to one of Canada's largest integrated forest-products companies.

Originally a private enterprise held by Taylor and some Argus associates, the firm changed its name to British Columbia Forest Products Limited (BCFP) and went public in May 1946. Shares were offered at five dollars apiece and some mortgage bonds were sold.

The new venture immediately acquired some timber rights and operating sawmills: Cameron Lumber Company of Victoria, the Hammond Cedar Company on the Fraser, and Industrial Timber Mills on Vancouver Island. For just under nine million dollars, BCFP became an operating forest-products company. A contract with the H.R. MacMillan Export Company provided both experienced management and sales outlets, an arrangement that worked well for many years.

The first decade was one of consolidation, expansion, and modernization.

Taylor and Argus controlled the company until 1955 when Scott Paper Company bought 29 percent of the stock, thereby providing some funding for the new pulp mill at Crofton and a market for the pulp. This also signalled the first change in ownership. Major changes in shareholders also occurred in 1969 and 1981. Ownership today consists of 26 percent by Brunswick Pulp & Paper Company (owned jointly by Mead and Scott); The Mead Corporation, 15 percent; Alberta Energy Company Limited, 18 percent; and 41 percent is controlled by Canadian Public.

In 1958 the pulp markets were very weak. Two years later a major fire destroyed the firm's head office and mill in False Creek. However, there were brighter spots ahead: The market recovered and the Crofton mill was expanded. BCFP pioneered and launched the first self-loading, self-dumping barge.

The corporation began an acquisitive look at the timber supply in the north-central interior of British Columbia. By 1966 its development was obviously feasible. The P.G.E. Railway reached Prince George and B.C. Hydro was building the huge Portage Dam on the Peace River. The company constructed a sawmill and began erecting a townsite in the wilderness. The town, officially opened in 1968, was named Mackenzie after the explorer Alexander Mackenzie who camped nearby en route to the Pacific in 1793.

Swiftsure Towing Company Ltd., which now operates a fleet of tugs and barges on the British Columbia Coast, was acquired in 1967. BCFP also acquired Pinette & Therrien, a family sawmill business near Mackenzie. A 45-percent interest was purchased in Donohue St.-Felicien Inc.—which operates a kraft pulp mill, four sawmills, and extensive woodlands in Quebec. Another sub-sidiary, the Blandin Paper Company, in Grand Rapids, Michigan, produces lightweight coated paper; its subsidiary operation produces aspen waferboard. BCFP also holds minority interests in Finlay Forest Industries Ltd. and Western Forest Products Limited.

In British Columbia alone the corporation operates twenty-four logging divisions, nine sawmills, one plywood plant, two kraft pulp mills, and a newsprint mill. Company assets have grown from the original nine million dollars to exceed one billion dollars. The work force numbers 7,200 and sales are approximately one billion dollars. The first forty years have indeed been years of growth!

The company's operations at Mackenzie on Williston Lake in north-central British Columbia. Current facilities include three sawmills and a kraft pulp mill on one industrial site.

WOODWARD'S LIMITED

John William Woodward arrived from his native Lincolnshire in 1850 with two sovereigns in his pocket. He settled and married in Ontario. His first son, Charles, intensely interested in marketing, left school at fourteen. The young man's enthusiasm and talent led him to several retailing ventures in Ontario before he moved to Vancouver in 1892.

The city of some 14,000 people encouraged Charles. He opened a store selling groceries and footwear at Georgia and Main. Charles' earlier experiences in Ontario had convinced him that he should always sell quality goods as reasonably as possi-

Charles Woodward, founder.

ble—and for cash!

But Vancouver's boom collapsed and Charles was forced into bankruptcy. Later, his creditors paid off, Charles outfitted many of the prospectors heading north for the Klondike in 1897. In 1903 Woodward Department Stores Ltd. opened its new store on the northwest corner of Hastings and Abbott streets. Over the years this $25,000 investment has expanded upward and outward, but the original building still remains.

In those early days the Woodwards fought hard to maintain the principle

of free trading and to fight retail price fixing. At times Woodward's has been considered a maverick store but many of its innovative marketing techniques and ideas have been subsequently copied.

In 1910 Charles organized the store's first "one-price" (twenty-five cents) sale and later introduced a mail-order department. A profit-sharing policy was instituted in 1915 for senior employees. Charles' theories were followed by his two sons, William Charles "Billy" and Percival "Puggy," who both devoted their lives to the company. In 1920 Puggy introduced a self-service groceteria—another wild success. Other "firsts" over the years have included the installation of electronic-opening doors, the emphasis on parking, shopping for the handicapped, and the introduction of lower-priced "bargain" stores.

Woodward's enjoys good employee and community relations. Charles served as an M.L.A. for Vancouver. Billy, president of The Vancouver Board of Trade in 1929, became lieutenant-governor of British Columbia in 1941. When Puggy retired, he and his wife devoted considerable time, thought, and money to the

P.A. Woodward Foundation. The university and many people in Vancouver have benefitted from his generosity.

Since World War II, and under the leadership of William's son Charles "Chunky," Woodward's has aggressively expanded. It now has a total of twenty-four department stores, one book store, and a separate grocery store in British Columbia and Alberta. Some stores, like Park Royal, were leased; others, like Oakridge, the company developed. In 1985, however, Woodward's Limited sold its real estate assets while retaining the retail department store chain.

In 1947 William's son Charles, only thirty-two years of age, became the president and chief executive officer of the fourth-largest department store chain in Canada. Charles' sons John and Kip joined the family enterprise in 1974 and 1977, respectively. Four generations of service and tradition are bound up in Woodward's— the Western Canadian department store that started in Vancouver.

Newly opened in 1903, this is the Woodward's store at Hastings and Abbott streets, site of the Vancouver downtown store today.

EBCO INDUSTRIES LTD.

A 3.25-metre water turbine used for generating electricity for hydroelectric power plants.

They make it all seem so simple—like a game of chess. According to Hugo Eppich, "You inspect all the possibilities, use your judgment to discard dangerous plays, and arrive at the logical and correct move to make. That, and the joy of doing what we're doing."

For Helmut and Hugo Eppich, chairman and president, respectively, of EBCO, joy has been blended with some difficult times, hard work, and long hours. Between 1956 and 1985 the firm grew from a staff of three and sales of $10,000 to 770 employees and sales of nearly fifty million dollars. The original 450-square-foot workshop is now an eighteen-acre site. The initial operation is now a conglomerate of fourteen, and its little local market has become an international one.

Helmut Eppich, a tool and die maker, and his twin brother, Hugo, an electroplater, arrived from Germany in the early 1950s. While touring Canada, an injury to Helmut's eye kept the brothers in Vancouver. They decided to open a bumper exchange shop but were checkmated by uncooperative bankers. After "reviewing the possibilities" they opened a tool and die business in 1956.

EBCO soon outgrew the first machine shop, a vacant garage, and in 1961 moved to more spacious premises at Fifth Avenue and Main. The firm continued machining, fabricating, and making custom chrome wheels. The wheel business was so successful that the Eppichs formed their first affiliate company, Keystone A&A Industries Ltd., to handle automotive products.

When more space was again needed in 1969, EBCO purchased eight acres in a new industrial park in Richmond. The dynamic growth of the company necessitated the later acquisition of another ten acres.

In the early 1970s two projects enhanced the organization's stature and international reputation. The first was a cyclotron for the Triumf centre for medical research and cancer treatment at the University of British Columbia. The $2.5-million cyclotron involved the fabrication of ninety-six resonators and an irregularly shaped tank fifty-six feet in diameter, inside which an absolute vacuum was created.

One other project was the tunnel borer built for a Seattle company. It was seventeen feet in diameter and designed, but never used, for a test tunnel under the English Channel. EBCO proceeded with other tunnel borers ranging from six to thirty-six

A man is dwarfed by the 26-foot tunnel-boring machine manufactured by EBCO Industries Ltd. for the Robbins Company of Seattle, Washington.

An 85-ton portal crane, installed at the Burrard Yarrows Dry Dock.

feet in diameter, including a 26-foot borer for a diversion tunnel in Yugoslavia.

While the two special projects were making headlines, the firm quietly continued expanding in other directions. Its subsidiary and affiliated companies include metalworking-related services such as chrome plating and anticorrosion coating. One produces wood stoves, and another manufactures construction machinery and special equipment—including a locally designed container crane for port terminal use.

E.I.F. Sales Ltd. has one of the largest compression-molding capacities in Canada. Originally a school furniture supplier, it has expanded to millwork, specialty metalwork, painting, and office furniture.

Richmond Industries Inc. provides custom furniture for commercial and institutional projects. It made the ritual chairs used by Pope John Paul II in the "Celebration of Life" event during his Vancouver visit.

The light metal stamping and fabrication division's production ranges from food display cases to sound barriers for aircraft testing and com-

ponents for satellites.

The machine division tradesmen work, very precisely, with lathes, planer mills, and large-capacity boring mills. The heavy fabricating division utilizes semiautomatic welders, 150-ton cranes, large plate-bending rolls, and a 1,500-ton forming press to produce industrial machinery and equipment.

The plating division galvanizes or plates items like truck bumpers, wheel rims, and even twenty-six miles of material for Vancouver's rapid transit system.

Controlling all these different activities—and keeping track of production, inventory, and costs—is a major project in itself. Manual systems were too slow, and Helmut searched in vain for a small, durable, relatively inexpensive, and simple computer terminal to use on the various shop floors for cost controls. He decided that it could be made and that EBCO would research and design it. A new subsidiary was born in 1976—Epic Data Industries Ltd.—to manufacture computer systems and terminals for customers. More than 400 Epic systems now operate in fifteen countries. Epic Data now employs 150 and had sales of thirteen million dollars in 1985.

The founders pay tribute to the hard work and dedication of their employees, but not with idle words. While the entrepreneurs hold over 70 percent of EBCO stock, employees—who are encouraged to participate—hold practically all the rest.

Helmut and Hugo Eppich endorse the system of apprenticeship rather like theirs in Germany. As many as five years are spent learning a variety of related tasks. EBCO has adopted the European style, teaching people

An Epic Data Industries factory data-collection system in operation.

on the job using both theory and practical experience. This enables workers to relocate between divisions as the demand in each fluctuates.

The Canadian Ironworkers organized the work force in EBCO's heavy construction operations in 1982, making the firm eligible to bid for projects requiring union labor.

The Eppichs' leadership is an "open door" style, encouraging suggestions or criticism. They see management's prime job as managing and problem-solving. Hugo Eppich adds, "We're here to help and guide, and we do just that." This philosophy spills over into training for employees, as well as recreational activities for them and their families.

The EBCO organization is built with care—care for quality of product and service, and for the people who produce it. In the company's thirty years of steady growth, this has not always been easy, but—as others have discovered—"Don't tell the Eppichs it can't be done—they will just go out and do it!"

One of three chairs specially made by Richmond Industries Inc., an EBCO subsidiary, for the visit of Pope John Paul II to B.C. Place Stadium.

THE BANK OF NOVA SCOTIA

The old—The Bank of Ottawa building, Scotiabank's West Coast headquarters from 1919 to 1977. Courtesy, The Bank of Nova Scotia Archives

Vancouver was described as being in an age d'or in the first decade of this century. One of the city's biographers, armed with a melange of metaphor, commented on the economy and the spirit of the time:

". . . in 1903 came another panic in New York and the ripples of it affected every city on the coast. But this time Vancouver was better buttressed, she had begun to hear the music of the deep-sea shanties, and the smell of the ocean was in the nostrils of her traders."

The aroma of success further buttressed Vancouver in 1904, when trade was opened up to the south by the linkage of the Great Northland Railroad. Good times had arrived.

That same year mill owner John Hendry took delivery of the first automobile in town to be powered by an internal-combustion engine. But it was another four years before the first gasoline station was built and Hendry fed his wondrous machine with a fuel used for cleaning ladies' shoulder-length gloves.

On July 25, 1904, The Bank of Nova Scotia, founded in 1832 in Halifax on the opposite shores of Canada, opened its first branch on Hastings Street, midway between Homer and Richards streets on the south side.

While the first decade of the century was a feast of plenty for Vancouver, it was something less for the banks. In fact, Vancouver was to become known as "the graveyard of bankers," and in those early days banks were little more than repositories for small deposits by children.

Nevertheless, Scotiabank, as The Bank of Nova Scotia is commonly known today, persevered. Meanwhile, Vancouver boomed. H.D. Burns, the Vancouver branch manager at the time, later to become president of the bank, caught the flavor of the day in writing an article for the bank's staff magazine in 1907.

"In 1886," he wrote, "Vancouver, then little more than a village, was visited by a fire which left but one building standing; in 1907, twenty-one years later, it has a population of upwards of 70,000, and so great is the monthly influx that there is no reason to believe ere the close of the present decade there will be 100,000 souls within its confines."

Burns was correct, and the bank did persevere. In 1919 Scotiabank amalgamated with the Bank of Ottawa and moved to a new location in The Bank of Ottawa building, erected in 1911, at the southwest corner of Hastings and Seymour streets.

Over the years Scotiabank's rate of growth in Vancouver and British Columbia was steady through two world wars and a depression. By 1956, when the old Bank of Ottawa building was significantly redesigned and

And the new—Scotiabank's flagship office is now located in the towering Vancouver Centre. Courtesy, The Bank of Nova Scotia Archives

expanded, Scotiabank was operating fifty branches in the province, twenty of them in Vancouver.

As the bank grew, the old building on Hastings Street, while very much in use today, was no longer appropriate as the bank's flagship office in British Columbia. On Valentine's Day in 1977, therefore, the bank moved its main office operations to a 25,000-square-foot branch in the 34-floor octagonal-shaped Vancouver Centre, at the corner of West Georgia Street and Granville Mall.

In 1986—eighty-two years after The Bank of Nova Scotia opened its doors in Vancouver—operations had been expanded to 110 branches province-wide, 26 of them in Vancouver. From shore to shore, Scotiabank's part in the growth of Vancouver and British Columbia has been one of perseverance and confidence, service and opportunity. And that will continue.

GRAY BEVERAGE COMPANY LTD.

The Gray Beverage plant, at 1875 Boundary Road, with magnolia trees in full bloom. Approximately 225 employees produce 7Up, Pepsi, and Schweppes soft drinks.

This private company, which now has more than 500 employees, began in a small plant under the Burrard Street Bridge thirty-eight years ago. A.L. "Abe" Gray purchased the operations of the original Seven-Up bottler in British Columbia, George Irvine, and started business as Seven-Up Vancouver Ltd. on New Year's Day, 1948. It was an industry Gray knew: He had grown up in Winnipeg, where his father had been in the soft drink business since 1921.

The corporate name later changed to Gray Beverage Company Ltd. as Gray purchased other franchised trademark operations in Vancouver. In 1960 the purchase of the assets of Crush International Limited in Vancouver added the Crush and Hires Root Beer franchises. In 1968 the plant, assets, and employees of Pepsi-Cola Ltd. were acquired and this added the franchises for both Pepsi-Cola and Schweppes to Gray's operations.

The company fleet of 7Up trucks and their drivers under the Burrard Street Bridge in 1949.

tions.

These acquisitions soon made the original Burrard Street premises too small. Different plants and properties were acquired and the company operations are now spread through four various production and distribution locations in the Lower Mainland.

Throughout all this time the Gray Beverage Company was progressing with every marketing and technological change in the industry. The aggressive nature of the ownership and management led to 7Up achieving its largest share in the Canadian market. Throughout the 1960s and 1970s 7Up was the number one soft drink in Vancouver.

In 1972 a series of out-of-town acquisitions began with the assembly of the Pepsi-Cola/7Up/Crush franchises on Vancouver Island and in Edmonton and central Alberta.

By 1986 Gray Beverage Company

was Canada's largest privately owned soft drink operation and, thus, the largest independent bottler of 7Up, Pepsi-Cola, and Crush in Canada. Over the years other smaller beverage franchises have been added, including the distribution rights for Perrier, nonalcoholic beer, fruit juices, and juice drinks. The company also custom packs juices and juice drinks for private labels.

Gray Beverage is unique in that, while locally owned, it competes in all of its markets with branch plants of some of the world's large multinational food and beverage corporations: Beatrice Foods Limited, the Coca-Cola Company, and RJR-Nabisco.

Abe Gray continues to practise the management criteria and progressive management techniques he used to build the enterprise to the status it enjoys today. He stresses that the people employed in the enterprise are its most important asset. The strong loyalty of employees is demonstrated by their service records, many of which exceed twenty years.

The firm is proud of being locally owned—and of the fact that it is 38 years old while Vancouver is only 100 years old. The Gray Beverage Company exemplifies the spirit of entrepreneurship and pride in citizenship that has made Vancouver the great city it is.

The first 7Up plant purchased by Abe Gray in 1948 can be seen through the arches of the Burrard Street Bridge.

COOPERS & LYBRAND

Coopers & Lybrand traces its Canadian origin back to 1867 when John McDonald, from Tain, Scotland, established his accounting practice in Montreal. His son, George, founded the firm as it is today in 1910. The following year, when cousin George Currie joined him, the concern became McDonald, Currie & Co. The firm now has twenty-two offices across Canada and a total staff of 2,500.

In 1957 McDonald, Currie & Co. joined with the British firm, Cooper Brothers, and the American firm of Lybrand, Ross Bros. & Montgomery to form the international firm, Coopers & Lybrand. In 1973 related member firms throughout the world all agreed to practise under the Coopers & Lybrand name.

The autonomy and professional independence of these member firms is one of Coopers & Lybrand's great strengths. Each has a strong national presence and subscribes to the highest standards of professional service and practice. The Canadian firm played a prominent part in the development of the international organization.

One partner opened the Vancouver office in 1948, in the Rogers Building—one of the oldest downtown office facilities. Two years later the venture merged with the local firm, Andrew H. Rathie & Co. (established in 1912), and was joined by a partner from Montreal.

Coopers & Lybrand is now one of the largest accounting firms in Vancouver and occupies six floors in the Coopers & Lybrand Building on West Hastings Street. It has offices in Victoria and Langley, and correspondent relationships in the Okanagan and Cariboo regions.

Although many of the largest companies in British Columbia are its clients, Coopers & Lybrand has always been committed to providing service to smaller and fledgling enterprises. Many of these have grown into substantial businesses and continue to be clients.

The firm has steadily expanded its auditing and accounting practice. It now offers a wide range of special services ranging from taxation, insolvency, and receivership to business valuations, acquisitions, and mergers.

It has also added a broad range of consulting services—now provided under the name of The Coopers & Lybrand Consulting Group. It offers business advisory services, computer and information technology, executive recruitment, and other management consulting services. This group serves Canadian clients and development agencies and private-sector enterprises overseas.

Coopers & Lybrand member firms serve Canadian interests in many Pacific Rim countries and can advise foreign investors and businesses interested in Canada. The company's exchange program trains foreign staff

here and sends Vancouver staff overseas.

The firm's partners and staff contribute their time and energy to many charitable, educational, and cultural organizations, including the Canadian Red Cross, the Cancer Society, and local universities.

Coopers & Lybrand's roots are planted firmly in Vancouver and British Columbia. The firm looks forward to growing with the city and the province by continuing to provide its clients with the highest level of service.

David R. Sinclair, F.C.A., managing partner of the firm in British Columbia.

The Rogers Building, at Granville and Pender streets, where one partner opened the Vancouver office in 1948.

Today twenty-four partners and a staff of 250 people occupy six floors of the Coopers & Lybrand Building at 1111 West Hastings Street.

BC RAIL LTD.

Incorporated in 1912, the Pacific Great Eastern Railway—forerunner of BC Rail Ltd.—was originally envisaged as a conduit between the growing industrial and seaway centre of Vancouver, and the Grand Trunk Pacific (later CN Rail) line-point town of Prince George. The new railway would also provide access to the agriculture- and mineral-rich Peace River region. Although it was a private venture, Premier Sir Richard McBride's government guaranteed the interest and principal of the railway's 4.5-percent bonds, due in 1941.

Inauguration of train service was January 1, 1914, on a twelve-mile line from North Vancouver to Horseshoe Bay. Track was laid in different sectors along the proposed route to Prince George, but there were still many gaps when financial problems stopped the work in 1918. Premier John Oliver, in an effort to avoid hardship to settlers along the route, determined to complete the line to Prince George; as a result, the prov-ince acquired all the rights and stock of the railway.

Construction resumed, and by 1921 the line was operational from Squamish to Quesnel. Construction was halted until 1949, and in 1953 the line went to Prince George; by 1956 the southern portion—North Vancouver to Squamish—was completed. Two years later extensions reached the Peace River country; by 1971 the railway had reached Fort Nelson, close to the Yukon Territory border. In 1972 its name was changed to the British Columbia Railway Company.

In 1983 a new eighty-mile line was opened to carry coal from the mines at the northeast coal project, near Tumbler Ridge, to BC Rail's main line for transfer to Prince George and on to the coal port at Ridley Island. The railway electrified the line using a fifty-kilovolt system, reducing the costs of fuel and maintenance, and using locomotives with longer life potential. It is the first heavy-freight electrified line in Canada, and one of only four fifty-kilovolt systems in the world.

The financial and corporate structure of the company was reorganized in 1984, and the operating railway became BC Rail Ltd. The firm issued $200 million worth of nonvoting preferred shares. The common stock is held by the Crown corporation British Columbia Railway Company, and newly created BCR Properties Ltd.

Despite public ownership, BC Rail is not protected from competition. Its mandate allows management to make corporate decisions on an economic basis. BC Rail aggressively pursues new freight business, including using its fleet of tractors and trailers. In 1985 permission was granted by the Canadian Radio-Television and Telecommunications Commission to further market its microwave communications system for certain kinds of long-distance telephone users.

The original visions of a rail line linking Vancouver and Prince George, though fraught with problems, have become a reality.

Incorporated in 1912 as the Pacific Great Eastern Railway, the line became BC Rail Ltd. in 1984.

DAIRYLAND FOODS

In contrast, thirty-five years later B.C. Place Stadium dominates the skyline.

Dairyland Foods has been delivering dairy products to Vancouver-area consumers for nearly seventy years. It has grown from a horse-and-wagon operation, covering the unpaved streets of Vancouver, to a modern technologically advanced business serving every community in the province. While its head office is now part of the city's suburbs, the organization still prizes its roots within the heart of Vancouver.

In fact, it was only when a train line was built between Chilliwack and Vancouver in 1910 that the impetus to form the organization that owns Dairyland began. Prior to that time the milk supply for Vancouver came from the Delta area of the Lower Mainland.

After the construction of the Inter

The head office of Dairyland, or Fraser Valley Milk Producers Association as it was formerly called, was located at the corner of Eighth Avenue and Cambie in Vancouver from 1919 to 1963. This photograph was taken in the early 1950s, looking south from Vancouver City Hall.

Urban Railway in 1910 and the completion of the Canadian National Railway's transcontinental line to Vancouver shortly thereafter, fresh milk from Chilliwack was available in Vancouver within three hours time. Fluid milk dealers started to play off Delta producers against Chilliwack producers.

The Fraser Valley Milk Producers Association was formed in 1913 to offset the whipsawing that was occurring between producers and fluid

milk dealers. The first year of actual operation for the FVMPA was 1917. Two years later the Association purchased the Standard Milk Company Building at Eighth and Cambie in Vancouver. That became the organization's head office for the next four decades.

In 1920 the Association purchased the Delair evaporated milk plant in Abbotsford. Five years later it built a powdered milk plant in Sardis, outside Chilliwack. Though both of the buildings have undergone extensive renovation over the years, they stand today on their original sites. The Eighth Avenue plant, which included a barn and blacksmith shop for the horse-drawn carts, lasted forty-five years before the Association moved its head office to Burnaby in 1964.

The relocation of the head office was not the only reference point for Dairyland Foods in the 1960s. That

decade also marked the expansion of Dairyland to communities outside the Lower Mainland. The first development took place in 1965 with the purchase of depots in Prince Rupert and Terrace. Over the past two decades Dairyland has, through various amalgamations and purchases, added plants, branches, and even an extra word to its corporate name. Fraser Valley Milk Producers Co-operative Association now represents dairy farmers in every milk-producing area of the province. It also operates eight plants and twenty-eight branches throughout British Columbia.

Coincident with the geographic expansion has been the expansion of the product line. Dairyland Foods now markets much more than just milk. The new products include cheeses and "ultra high temperature" or long-life milk, juices, and drinks. The new product list grows as Dairyland's research and development laboratory staff continues to develop new products.

There are a number of brand names that also reflect the growth of the organization over the years. Two of the oldest are Fraser Valley butter and Pacific evaporated milk. These two names have been identifying products for Vancouver consumers since the beginning of the Association's operations. In 1986 that list of brand names, under what is now the Dairyland Foods logo, includes Armstrong cheese, Nature's Treat yogurt, Dairy Maid milk and juices, and Super Socco drinks.

One of Dairyland's product names recalls Vancouver's past. Dairyland 1886 ice cream is so named to evoke the ice cream parlors of another era. It is also, of course, a distinctly Vancouver name.

The total sales from all product groups reflect the growth of both Dairyland and, more generally, the population of the province. Annual sales are now nearly $400 million. Dairyland is one of the major employers in British Columbia with approximately 1,500 employees. The Association has 2,000 member owners of whom about 900 are active ship-

pers, and these, in turn, are another source of financial stability to the rural communities in which they operate.

As a corporate citizen, Dairyland Foods' contributions to the community take the form of scholarships, sports programs, and public service donations. Through the B.C. Dairy Foundation, an industry-wide organization, Dairyland also contributes to a nutrition education program that is available to schools throughout Vancouver and the rest of the province.

The growth of Vancouver to a major metropolis has been integral to the success that Dairyland has enjoyed over the years. As Vancouver moves into its second century Dairyland Foods will be a continuing partner and contributor to its development and prosperity.

Dairyland's head office for the past twenty-two years has been in Burnaby on the Lougheed Highway. Dairyland has also expanded outside the Lower Mainland since it moved to Burnaby. It now has branches in twenty-eight communities throughout the province.

MICROTEL

Microtel is a young company, but its roots go back to the early days of telecommunications in Canada.

Microtel's history began in the Yukon in 1906. That year, Automatic Electric (one of two companies that later would form Microtel) installed a telephone exchange to serve the growing population lured north by the Klondike Gold Rush.

This was Automatic Electric's first automatic switching installation in Canada. In 1907 the company inaugurated Canada's first large automatic telephone system in Edmonton.

These exchanges were installations of the electromechanical Strowger switch, which would keep the firm at the forefront of Canadian telecommunications for the next sixty years.

The Strowger switch was invented in 1889 when a Kansas City funeral parlor director, Almon Brown Strowger, suspected that telephone operators were diverting calls away from his business to a competitor's. Using a cardboard collar box, straight pins, and a pencil, Strowger devised a switch that would allow calls to reach him without going through the operator.

An entrepreneurial Chicago salesman heard of the switch and persuaded Strowger to develop it commercially. It dominated automatic switching technology until the 1960s.

In 1935 Automatic Electric began manufacturing the Strowger switch and other terminal equipment at Brockville, Ontario, as part of Phillips Electrical Works Limited. Phillips was owned by Automatic Electric International, a subsidiary of Theodore Gary and Company, the second-largest independent telephone company in the United States by the 1950s.

Gary sold all the assets of Phillips in 1953. Automatic Electric retained the telephone operation and set up AE Canada (1953) Ltd.

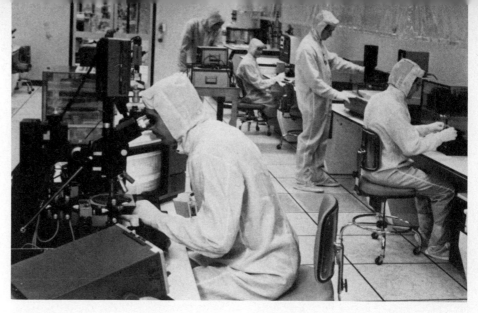

"Chip Centre." Designers at the Pacific Microelectronics Centre work on large-scale integrated chips in an ultraclean environment.

Microtel's other predecessor, Lenkurt Electric, was founded in 1944 by two electrical engineers, Lennart Erickson and Kurt Appert, who had developed an apparatus known as Telephone Carrier Equipment which allowed the simultaneous transmission of a number of messages along the same circuit—a great boon to telephone operating companies.

The firm soon grew from a storefront operation in San Francisco to one of the first high-tech tenants of California's Silicon Valley. Along the way, it also became a successful manufacturer of microwave transmission equipment for the international market.

In 1949 Lenkurt set up a subsidiary operation in Vancouver to assemble a limited line of telephone equipment. Lenkurt (Canada) expanded to larger premises in Burnaby in 1956, and continued to grow. By 1959 Lenkurt had begun to design and develop its own products. Within a few years the company had grown to be the largest secondary manufacturer in British Columbia.

In 1955 GTE took over control of Lenkurt and AE. In 1979 the British Columbia Telephone Company acquired AE (Canada) and Lenkurt (Canada), and the two companies were merged to form Microtel.

Since its formation, research and development have been a priority at Microtel. Microtel Pacific Research Limited (MPR), the research and de-velopment subsidiary, is located in a $10-million laboratory opened in 1982 in Simon Fraser University's Discovery Park. The lab employs over 325 scientists and support staff.

In 1984 MPR opened the Pacific Microelectronics Centre, an $8-million facility which designs, tests, and packages large-scale and very-large-scale integrated circuit chips.

The company took over Viscount Industries Limited, a Vancouver manufacturer of electronic products, in 1980.

In 1982 Microtel began a major restructuring to reflect changing technologies and markets. New products from MPR were opening up important opportunities for the firm. Microtel consolidated its operations and brought its product portfolio under more complete control.

It established U.S. headquarters in Atlanta in 1983. Learning Services, Microtel's education and training division, opened sales offices in Dallas and Chicago.

With this thrust, Microtel has emerged from the changes of recent years with a stronger, more efficient organization and with a sharpened sense of its goals. Senior management changes and strategic planning have helped to define new directions.

The year 1986 saw the relocation of corporate headquarters to downtown Vancouver, and the award of Microtel's largest contract in its history, the provision of satellite and monitoring communications equipment for the North Warning System, which will replace the existing DEW Line.

WILLIAMS MOVING & STORAGE (B.C.) LTD.

Those who purchased furniture at Love's auctions in 1929 often used Williams Transfer to transport it home. This was the modest start of the company now known as Williams Moving & Storage (B.C.) Ltd. Equally modest was its first truck, a Dodge touring van acquired with fifty dollars borrowed from the landlord of the firm's founder.

George James Williams, born in Ontario and schooled in Alberta, started work in 1922 with the Great Northern Railway. Seven years later he was operating Williams Transfer, with one truck and two helpers. The business grew steadily, and in 1945 the entrepreneur bought property on which to build a warehouse for his five trucks and staff of six.

When his son, George Stewart Williams, joined the firm in April 1949, it operated seven trucks and used one trailer for cross-Canada hauls. That year the company was incorporated under its present title.

In the early 1950s the corporation was operating ten trailer units across Canada. It had become affiliated with the fledgling United Van Lines (Canada) Ltd., which had been formed to reduce the amount of deadheading by the independent

One of the modern fleet of trucks owned and operated by the moving and storage firm.

truckers, with the senior Williams serving as an inaugural director. The company now works with United Van Lines when moving household goods in or out of British Columbia.

In 1953 Williams began building a provincial network of branches: first in Penticton, Cranbrook, and Prince George, and later in Kamloops, Kelowna, Terrace, Sparwood, Victoria, and Castlegar, all in British Columbia; Cold Lake, Edmonton, and Calgary, Alberta; and Regina, Saskatchewan. A new head office was established in Burnaby on Lougheed Highway, where it remained until 1964 when the company moved to 4285 Dawson Street. Today the head office is in Coquitlam, British Columbia. That move included the firm's sixty-seven trailer units, plus seventy permanent employees and thirty casual laborers. Williams then had fifteen acres of industrial property at six locations.

George Stewart Williams succeeded his father as president in 1971. He also served as president of United Van Lines (Canada) Ltd. and remained as a director until recently.

The organization has grown and expanded to fourteen branches in Western Canada, and has working affiliations with other Canadian companies and around the world. Its fleet of more than 500 trailer units is op-

This 1929 Dodge touring van was the first truck of Williams Moving & Storage (B.C.) Ltd.

erated by 250 employees whose average length of service is sixteen years—although many have accrued more than twenty-five years.

When asked what would surprise his father most about the operation today, the founder's son said it would be the extensive use of containers (something the firm pioneered) and the tremendous flexibility that this equipment gives.

Williams Moving & Storage remains a family business, with the third generation—three sons and a son-in-law—now involved. It is a business working co-operatively with its industry and with the community it has helped to build.

In its fifty-seven years the company has moved thousands of people to, from, and in British Columbia; and has hauled in many of the amenities the residents enjoy. It continues to look ahead and has plans for new locations as it strives for greater efficiency. However, the Williams "family" stresses that the firm's first priority is always the care of its customers.

REED STENHOUSE LIMITED

On a sunny August afternoon in 1985, a group of executives gathered in a vacant downtown Vancouver parking lot. The occasion was a special ground-breaking ceremony. With that simple ceremony, Reed Stenhouse Limited, the international insurance brokerage that helped shape the destinies of thousands of Vancouver firms, began to reshape its own future in Canada's major West Coast city.

Plans called for construction to transform the corner parking lot site into "900 Howe Street," a modern ten-storey office complex, the new Vancouver address of Reed Stenhouse. In contrast, the firm's West Coast origins were extremely modest.

Just after World War I, B.L. Johnson, a retired submarine commander, opened a Lloyd's agency on Vancouver's waterfront. The marine brokerage and insurance agency was housed in a cramped one-room office. The business flourished during the city's postwar "boom," and continued to prosper despite the disastrous worldwide financial decline that followed.

The company hired a $60-a-week office assistant, James "Judd" Whittall, at a time when the firm and its clients were struggling out of the Depression. By World War II Whittall and partner Arthur Law had assumed control of the firm, then called B.L. Johnson, Walton Company. The name change reflected a change in emphasis to insurance. Whittall's entrepreneurial spirit encouraged the creation of innovative coverages. Soon the firm was providing insurance services to major industrial firms and smaller manufacturing and supply businesses throughout Western Canada.

After the war larger clients of Johnson, Walton began to expand eastward. Their need for national insurance programs grew. Upon his return from active service in the Royal Canadian Navy, Whittall began to

visualize the possibilities of an expansion of his own company. British Columbia's growing mining, forestry, and service sectors gave the firm—by this time, the largest in the West—the solid foundation upon which to base its expansion plans. As senior partner, Judd Whittall was in a position to lead the firm in a new direction.

As B.L. Johnson, Walton executives looked eastward, the directors of a distinguished Toronto insurance brokerage firm, Reed Shaw McNaught, looked westward. The two firms joined to create a national entity in 1959. Then, in 1973, a merger with the renowned Scottish firm of A.R. Stenhouse & Partners created today's international concern, Reed Stenhouse Limited. By the mid-1970s Judd Whittall had become president of Reed Stenhouse Limited.

The desire for participation in the large American insurance market led to an additional merger between Reed Stenhouse and the major American firm, Alexander and Alexander. The

An architect's model of the new ten-storey office complex at 900 Howe Street, which is the new Vancouver address of Reed Stenhouse. Attending the ground-breaking ceremonies in August 1985 are (inset) Reed Stenhouse British Columbia regional director Don Gordon (left) and CN Real Estate president David Burstow.

operation of Alexander and Alexander, like that of Reed Stenhouse, was international in scope. The benefits derived from integration have been worldwide.

Today a Vancouver staff of over 200 co-ordinates the operations of Reed Stenhouse's regional offices in Victoria, Prince George, and Kelowna. Reed Stenhouse insures some of British Columbia's largest corporations against an ever-growing number of risks. Reed Stenhouse protects industries and services that are changing the lives of Vancouver residents, and the construction projects that are changing the skyline of their city. It is a skyline that, with "900 Howe Street," Reed Stenhouse itself has helped to change.

C.H. CATES & SONS LTD.

Charles Henry Cates was a seafarer from Maine who had sailed on a square-rigger as ship's boy. In 1885 he arrived in Vancouver, a settlement of wooden buildings. It burned down a year later, then was rebuilt more solidly. Cates bought a 240-foot steam scow, *Spratt's Ark,* and hauled stone from Gibsons and Squamish to Vancouver.

The next few years brought the railway and abundant opportunities for entrepreneurs. Captain Cates, a tugboat pioneer with one little steamer tug, the *Swan,* won the tug *Stella* from a rival skipper who wagered her in a race.

The captain built a wharf on the harbor's north shore, and, with his brothers, began shipbuilding and towboating. By the turn of the century the Cates family was a dominant force in the Vancouver Harbor. In 1913 the C.H. Cates Company was formed—the appendage "& Sons Ltd." was added in 1921. A new fleet was assembled around the *Charles H. Cates III,* formerly the *Gaviota,* which is still seaworthy.

By the 1930s the captain's three sons, John, Charles, and Jim, were at the helm and the major source of the

Charles Henry Cates, a seafarer from Maine, arrived in Vancouver in 1885, and by the turn of the century the Cates family was a dominant force in Vancouver Harbor.

firm's business was ship berthing/ship assistance. More, and bigger, vessels were coming to Vancouver, and Cates developed a fleet to handle them. Until the 1950s the company built wooden tugs with sturdy hulls and huge rudders. Power ranged from 160-BHP (brake horsepower) diesels to 630-BHP gas and 700-BHP Detroit diesels. This was power unheard of in the first days of the *Charles H. Cates III.*

Vancouver grew—and the port grew with it. The large vessels and the bulk carriers needed more powerful and manoeuvrable tugs for assistance. In 1968 Cates built three steel tugs, with power of 700-1,000 BHP.

As the ships using the Vancouver Harbor continued to get larger, the firm developed a still more powerful breed of tugs: "Supertugs" with two 900-BHP diesel engines. The four Supertugs have record horsepower-to-length ratios, and each can crab sideways and turn about its own axis.

Today John's son-in-law, Terry

Waghorn, is president and general manager, and Cates' fleet of fifteen tugs ranges from 510 to 2,400 BHP. The latest addition is the Z-Peller Supertug with the ultimate in ship-handling equipment. Its 2,400 BHP sets a new world record in horsepower-to-length ratio.

Cates recently built a new facility with modern offices, vessel-repair shops, and a transfer dock. It maintains tradition with a special display of antique fittings and equipment. However, tradition also means a century of service in the Port of Vancouver and a company record of integrity, ingenuity, flexibility, and safety—all reflected in the corporate maxim: "When you do something, do it right."

The Charles H. Cates VI *and the* Charles H. Cates VIII, *with the city of Vancouver in the background.*

VERSATILE PACIFIC SHIPYARDS INC.
FORMERLY BURRARD DRY DOCK COMPANY LIMITED

It has changed its name and it has grown, but for nine decades it has been Vancouver's foremost shipbuilder and ship repairer.

Alfred Wallace established Wallace Shipyards in False Creek in 1894. Later, in 1906, he moved to the company's current location in North Vancouver.

Until 1914 the largest ship built by the firm was a 145-foot ferry, but wartime production included nine steel cargo ships more than 400 feet long.

Although demand for new ships declined after the war, Wallace Shipyards built *Princess Louise* for CP Steamships, and *St. Roch* for the Royal Canadian Mounted Police. The 95-foot *St. Roch* was the first ship to circumnavigate the continent, sailing from Vancouver to Halifax via the NorthWest Passage, and returning home by way of Cape Horn.

In 1924, under Alfred Wallace's sons, Clarence and Hubert, the company installed a floating dry dock to serve the growth in merchant shipping, and changed its name to Burrard Dry Dock Company Limited.

World War II created a demand for ships. The firm expanded, and at one time its payroll numbered 13,000. Some 126 ships were built during the war years, and a similar number of conversions and completions of U.S.-built hulls took place as well.

In 1946 the company acquired Yarrows Limited of Victoria. Started in the 1890s as the Esquimalt Marine Railway Co., it was renamed when Alfred Yarrow took it over in the 1920s and developed shipbuilding and ship-repair yards.

The shipbuilding and ship-repair industry has experienced vicissitudes since 1946, but Burrard and Yarrows have been able to survive by building a wide variety of vessels and by carrying out a sizable volume of ship repairs.

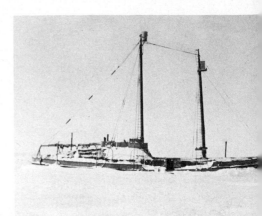

The R.C.M.P. St. Roch, *built by Burrard Dry Dock in 1926, was the first ship to circumnavigate the NorthWest Passage in both directions. Schooner rigged and diesel powered, the* St. Roch *is on permanent display at the Vancouver Maritime Museum.*

Cornat Industries Limited acquired control of the firm from the Wallaces in 1972. In 1978 Cornat was merged to form Versatile Corporation, and in 1985 the operation became Versatile Pacific Shipyards Inc.

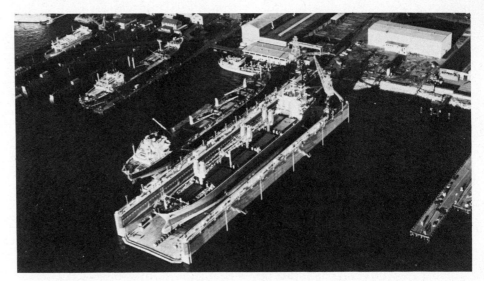

This aerial view of the facilities at Versatile Pacific Shipyards Inc. (formerly Burrard Dry Dock Company Limited) was taken in October 1981, and shows the new floating dock in the foreground.

The Vancouver and Victoria divisions operate as one organization with roughly equivalent work forces. Most technical and administrative staff work in the North Vancouver corporate headquarters.

The Victoria shipyard handles new construction and repairs but specializes in major conversions. It uses the adjacent government graving dock for dry-docking and major repair work.

The Vancouver operation can handle the needs of most of the 2,000-plus ships that arrive in Vancouver each year. A new floating dry dock and lifting equipment inaugurated in 1981 increased its capacity to accommodate ships weighing up to 75,000 tons.

Versatile is a world leader in building icebreakers for both the Coast Guard and commercial users. It expects to be a major player in the development of the Beaufort Sea and in the Canadian naval fleet replacement program.

The firm continues to implement modern shipbuilding technology and methods. It plans further investment to improve productivity and expand steel-fabricating capacity.

Many ships have gone "down the ways" since 1894. From Wallace to Versatile, there is a ninety-year tradition of pride in service.

EMPIRE STEVEDORING COMPANY LIMITED

Colonel Walter Roy Dockrill, C.I.E., founder.

A four-storey square building, where Dunlevy and Railway streets intersect, is the home of Empire Stevedoring Company Limited—but the firm began life in Chemainus on Vancouver Island.

Years after Captain Cook visited Nootka Cove in 1778, a lumber trade began to develop. Sawmills were built—including the Hastings Mill in Vancouver and the Thomas Askew Mill in Chemainus. By 1891 the latter mill had become the Victoria Lumber and Manufacturing Company, managed by E.J. Palmer. As exports grew, individual stevedores began to appear and the 1899 B.C. Directory listed nineteen.

Mining chemist Walter Dockrill worked for Victoria Lumber and later married Palmer's daughter. In October 1909 Certificate of Incorporation No. 2614 shows that he founded the enterprise still known as Empire Stevedoring Company.

For two years Empire was housed at 565 Water Street, Vancouver, in a combined warehouse and office building. In 1911 a third office was opened in Victoria. The following year the Vancouver office moved to CPR property near the railway tracks and changed its name to the Empire Stevedoring and Contracting Company.

The year 1925 was one of labor unrest and difficulty on the waterfront. The firm became Empire Stevedoring Company Limited, with its registered office at 325 Howe Street.

Many of Empire's current activities stem from long-standing break-bulk contracts like those made in the 1920s with CPR and CNR, and which expired in 1968 and 1983, respectively. The company handled both break bulk and passengers at the Terminal Dock (1968-1983), the Centennial Pier (1968-1975), and Ballantyne and Lapointe (1923-1957). In 1975 Empire was awarded the contract to provide handling services at the Vanterm Container Terminal.

Over the years Empire has built Vanterm into one of the most efficient and comprehensive terminal operations in North America today.

Through subsidiary companies (Empire Traffic Services Ltd. and Wallace Transfer Ltd.) Empire offers its customers a full range of services to include the movement and handling of freight between the port area and the customer's door anywhere within Canada.

Empire is the terminal contractor at Canada Place/Ballantyne Pier, Van-

The M.S. Jessie Norcross *anchored in Genoa Bay, British Columbia, awaiting its cargo of lumber. Photograph taken in July 1917*

couver's showcase cruise ship facility.

Empire provides "on-board" service for many export and shipping companies, and offers comprehensive stevedoring in B.C. ports. It is a major stevedore for bulk grain, handling about 40 percent of export volume through B.C. ports, including Ridley Island Terminal.

Empire's skill in maritime transportation is recognized in its selection as

local transport carrier for Expo 86. It is also consulted by firms or engineers involved in projects overseas. The Empire Group has a long tradition of service that began in Chemainus and now spreads throughout eighteen ports in British Columbia.

A crew takes a breather from loading lumber in the early days of Empire Stevedoring Company Limited.

237

CHEVRON CANADA LIMITED

From the ground up: This literally describes Chevron Canada's first fifty years.

When Standard Oil of California started its fledgling venture, Standard Oil Company of British Columbia, it was 1935, the middle of the Depression. The firm made a strong start with the purchase of three local oil distribution companies. The first bulk plant was established at Eburne on the Fraser River and work began on a refinery in Burnaby. The head office

The Standard service station at the corner of Georgia and Burrard in 1935. Note the clear view of the Marine Building.

The Stanovan refinery was still in Burnaby in March 1936, when this photo was taken.

was opened in the prestigious Marine Building on Burrard Street.

Sales were tough as other suppliers fought to retain the loyalty of the few customers that were buying. People who had jobs worked hard to keep them. At the first service stations Standard employees gave customers exceptional service using the "two-man service" procedure—along with courtesy, promptness, efficiency, and neatness.

By January 1936 the Stanovan refinery in Burnaby was processing 2,000 barrels per day. The following year the company expanded its area of service and tackled the atrocious roads around Vernon and Kamloops to sell bulk oil. On the coast, a small

tanker dubbed the *B.C. Standard* started supplying the isolated logging camps, pulp and paper mills, and fishing fleets with oil and gas fuels and other supplies.

Just as the firm was settling in, war was declared. The *B.C. Standard,* equipped with a machine gun and other defensive equipment, continued quietly about her business. Refinery production was doubled and aviation gasoline was introduced.

It was 1945 before the private sector started to move. Standard expanded its area of operations again, opening stations in the West Kootenays and the Cariboo and, once again, these were areas with little paved highway. The company's gasoline brand name was changed from Standard to Chevron. While Stan-

A modern gas station, 1985.

dard stations and marine dealers retained the red/white/blue color scheme, the Chevron stations burst out in cream, green, and burgundy.

Standard's introduction to servicing the airline industry started outside the airport limits. Later, when its reputation for service was firmly established, the firm was allowed inside the airport. Once there it obtained contracts to supply most of the major airlines.

The booming 1950s arrived. Premier W.A.C. Bennett transformed potholed and muddy back roads into highways, people spent money easily, car purchases soared, and the oil industry prospered.

But a new problem arose: keeping

up with demand. It was finally resolved in 1954 with a new 11,000-barrel-per-day refinery in Burnaby, and the new Trans Mountain Pipe Line started replacing the California crude with oil from Alberta. The next year a platformer installation at the refinery increased its capacity to 18,000 barrels per day.

Standard's province-wide network in 1963 included over 600 stations, 55 plants (53 agent-operated), and 72 marine agents. While the company made unsuccessful attempts to move into Alberta, everything else was going extremely well for Standard. Various technological improvements increased the capacity of the refinery to 24,000 barrels per day. The entire oil industry was doing so well that competition became very fierce and the 1960s were a time of "games, gimmicks, and giveaways."

But it was also a time of change—rapid and intense change. New, modern stations replaced the old 1935 stations. It was also the time when the name Chevron Canada Limited appeared for the first time.

In 1974 the two tankers, the *B.C. Standard* and the *Standard Service,* were sold, and from this time on the firm used barges exclusively.

Plans to expand the Burnaby refinery in 1971 met with considerable lo-

The supply ship B.C. Standard *plies the coastal waters of British Columbia.*

cal resistance. The public was very concerned about pollution and was reluctant to allow further refinery construction. For the next three years Chevron held innumerable public meetings with the citizens of Burnaby and their town council. Finally, the go-ahead was given and work started. When the refinery was completed in 1976, it was able to handle 35,000 barrels per day. During the whole process, Chevron gained a reputation for its co-operation in listening to public concerns and for its leadership in meeting pollution standards.

Support of, and involvement in, community welfare and cultural projects is a way of life for Chevron. Its activities range from the well-known United Way campaigns to its lesser-known support for Native Indian organizations and university scholarships. Chevron employees give an exceptional level of time and energy to public service and the firm is a valued corporate citizen.

Chevron won an Award of Distinc-

An aerial view of the refinery's processing facilities. The tank farm is visible in the upper right-hand corner.

tion for Sustained Support in the 1985 *Financial Post* Business in the Arts Awards. In 1986 the firm was a major sponsor of Vancouver's centennial celebration.

The company has a long history of research and development that has maintained, improved, and expanded the range and quality of its products. It continues to be an aggressive marketer, a talent acknowledged when the American Marketing Association of British Columbia chose Chevron as the 1984 Marketer of the Year. But nothing stands still, and the company continues its search for more imaginative and competitive ways of doing business.

In its first fifty years the refinery at Burnaby has grown in every sense. The original 15 tanks now number 110, while their total capacity has mushroomed from a modest 130,000 barrels to a mammoth 1,886,000 barrels. During this period the rated crude capacity has expanded from 2,000 to 36,000 barrels per day.

In its strenuous climb "from the ground up" Chevron has made a major contribution to the development and growth of Vancouver and British Columbia. Management is determined that, in its second fifty years, Chevron will be equally committed to quality and service, and the recognition of its most valuable asset, its people.

MOHAWK OIL CO. LTD.

Mohawk defines its basic philosophy as leading rather than following. Founded by Hugh Sutherland in 1960, the firm has attributed its growth to foreseeing business opportunities.

The company's operations started in 1961 with gas stations in British Columbia and Alberta. Now, much expansion and many acquisitions later, Mohawk celebrates its twenty-fifth anniversary with a marketing area stretching from the Lakehead to Vancouver Island.

One early acquisition was Centennial Transport Ltd., which Mohawk used to supply its various outlets with light petroleum products. In 1965 the expanding firm acquired its first oil and gas properties and began an active exploration program.

The 1970s were a time of growth and innovation. Mohawk Oil and Gas, Inc., was formed in 1973 and later became the company's United States exploration arm. It has numerous mining claims and a 100-ton-per-day custom mill in Alaska.

The corporation purchased an interest in Dominion Bulk Sales Ltd., another petroleum transport operation, in 1973. The gasoline marketing network in Alberta was enlarged in 1975 when Mohawk became a shareholder in Payless Oil Company Ltd. and Speedway Oil, the latter being completely absorbed by Mohawk in 1979.

Mohawk began to diversify in the mid-1970s. Tidewater Holding Company Ltd. was formed to look after the firm's real estate and to develop revenue-producing properties. Mohawk diversified into mining in 1975, and has a large nephrite jade mine in northern British Columbia.

The acquisition of four businesses in 1977 added propane to the company's product line. Mohawk has since acquired four more in British Columbia and central Alberta. Mohawk Propane sells propane, rents

One of Mohawk's first service stations in Vancouver was the Pay-Less Service Station at Grandview and Lakewood.

out tanks and construction heaters, and sells propane conversion kits.

Mohawk Lubricants, a subsidiary operation established in 1978, extracts high-grade lubricating oils from used oil. A plant was built in North Vancouver for this process with modern custom oil blending and packaging equipment.

In 1980 Mohawk Oil Canada Limited, the parent company of the Mohawk group, was federally chartered to facilitate the employee share-purchase program. Today Mohawk has more than 1,800 members.

In the early 1980s Mohawk began producing fuel alcohol for use in gasohol—using an old distillery in Manitoba. Current annual production is seven megalitres (1.6 million

gallons); however, demand is expected to justify expansion to twelve megalitres or more.

Mohawk continues to expand its product base. It is the only Canadian company offering three alternative fuels for cars: compressed natural gas (CNG) in Kamloops; gasohol, which it blends and markets in Western Canada; and propane, sold by most Mohawk stations.

The firm pioneered convenience stores in service stations, building more than a dozen Stop 'N' Shop units in 1984. In British Columbia, it introduced cash-dispensing machines at retail outlets early in 1985.

While expanding its gasoline business to a wide range of related products, Mohawk continues to look in Canada—and abroad—for yet more opportunities.

Today that same station sports a new look. Mohawk's Stop 'N' Shop locations sell gasoline, propane, oil, and other products, but offer as well a convenience store and a bakery operation.

H.Y. LOUIE CO. LIMITED

A young Chinese immigrant, H.Y. Louie, who came to Vancouver in 1896, would be very surprised to see the company that bears his name ninety years later. When he arrived, like many other newcomers, he took what work he could find—first as a truck gardener, and then later working for the Hastings Saw Mill—before setting up his own modest business in 1903. That business, known as Wah Jan and located near the corner of Pender and Carroll streets, was a small general store catering to the daily needs of the local population.

The Wah Jan Co. became the Kwong Chong Co. in 1907 and the Louieds Company in 1915; it was finally incorporated as H.Y Louie Co. Limited in 1927.

From 1928 through to the 1940s the firm acted as fertilizer dealer to the Chinese market gardeners, from the Indian reserve (present site of Shaughnessy Golf Course) and along Marine Drive all the way to Queensborough in New Westminster. Herbicides such as CIL's Blackleaf 40 and Paris Green were sold to the various truck gardeners during this period. Another popular item was Three Twins tobacco from Landau and Cormack of Toronto, and the company first introduced sesame seeds to the bakery industry in Canada. Also carried were supplies for the many hand laundries in Vancouver— starch, Klondike soap, and lye. In addition, restaurants and small grocery stores were many of the outlets supplied by H.Y. Louie Co. Limited.

The company continued to grow and eventually moved from 255 East Georgia Street to 615 Taylor Street in 1950. The first major expansionary move came in 1955 when Tong Louie, son of the founder, purchased the I.G.A. franchise for British Columbia and launched a provincial network of the grocery store.

In 1957 the Eastern Canada chain of Dominion Stores opened in the Vancouver area. When it decided to pull up stakes after a few disappointing years, the logical purchaser was the firm that had been supplying the outlets. Leases, equipment, and store inventories were sold to H.Y. Louie Co. Limited in 1968.

In 1970 the firm moved its headquarters and distribution centre to its present location in Lake City Industrial Park in Burnaby.

London Drugs, a chain of drugstores in the Vancouver area, was available for purchase in 1976. Tong Louie acquired these ten stores from

H.Y. Louie, founder.

the Daylin Corporation of Los Angeles and started an expansion program. There are now twenty-five stores: six in Alberta, one each in Victoria and Kelowna, and the remainder in the Lower Mainland.

Despite its tremendous growth, H.Y. Louie Co. Limited remains a private family enterprise, and the next generation is already active in both the grocery and drugstore aspects of its operation.

The corporation has expanded from its early days of a small family business with a total of five people to more than 2,000 employees in all its businesses. H.Y. Louie Co. Limited is an integral part of the Vancouver community.

OVERWAITEA FOODS
SAVE-ON-FOODS

In 1915 Robert Kidd, a blender of Irish tea and a coffee roaster, started a business venture in New Westminster with only $500 and his own unique philosophy of service to invest. He had extraordinarily high standards for the treatment of customers and staff, and he was dedicated to absolute integrity in merchandising.

The company name came from a bonus that the founder used to attract customers. Every pound of tea he sold was packaged with an extra two ounces. Therefore, it was overweight tea—hence the name Overwaitea.

Kidd's limited investment would only allow for the most inexpensive fixtures in his store, and he could not afford to carry extra stock. It was essential that he hire employees who believed in a day's work for a day's wages.

Determined to succeed, the entrepreneur used innovative ways to boost sales. He broke new ground by advertising products in the local newspapers and using special window displays to catch the eye of passersby. He is also credited with introducing

Overwaitea Foods and Drugs in Kelowna, a new-generation store with fresh fish, sausage factory, deli, full-service drug store, snack bar, and bulk pop.

odd-penny pricing, as previously all items had been sold in increments of a nickel.

Overwaitea did well in New Westminster; people liked Kidd's way of thinking and his way of doing things. Three years later, in 1918, a second store was opened in Nanaimo—and the Overwaitea chain was launched.

Kidd was well aware that any suc-cessful marketing techniques would be copied by his competitors. He determined that the one way in which his stores would be unique would be in the attitude of the people working there. As his wife, Anne, once said, "He was as keen on building people as he was in building Overwaitea because he knew Overwaitea *was* its people."

Unfortunately, Robert Kidd died fairly young, and the management of his enterprise passed first to members of his family and then to a succession of general managers. The founder had earlier introduced a corporate structure in which the employees owned all the common shares and the Kidd family the preferred shares. He wanted the employees to consider that the company was theirs, confident that they would then have a very real interest in its success.

However, that structure proved to be a disadvantage in the years following Kidd's death. The appointed managers presumed that they had to show a high rate of return on the employees' common shares. In order to achieve this goal, they set a policy of no company borrowing—which made it virtually impossible for the firm to grow.

As the years went by the world

Innovators in bulk-foods merchandising, Overwaitea was the first to introduce this concept in British Columbia.

Robert Kidd's philosophy of extraordinarily high standards of customer service has been carried on to the present by a new generation of Overwaitea and Save-On-Foods employees.

changed but Overwaitea stood still. Huge multinational corporations, with easy access to financing, became active in the retail food industry. Despite having second-rate stores and third-rate locations, Overwaitea was able to hold its own because of its peoples' entrepreneurial spirit and skill.

Clarence Heppell, current president of Overwaitea Foods, has spent four decades in the grocery trade. He began his career on a part-time basis while attending Lord Tweedsmuir High School, then moved into full-time employment with Overwaitea after graduation and began his rapid progress through the then employee-owned company. Heppell was promoted to head office in 1964 as district manager and in 1968 he became branch operations manager.

That same year Jimmy Pattison purchased the Overwaitea operation. Heppell says, "Suddenly we had a man who believed in us, believed in where we were trying to go, and was willing to invest in our dreams." Describing skilled and enterprising people who only needed stores and locations comparable to their competitors, Heppell notes that the merg-

er fulfilled those needs.

In the eighteen years it has been part of the Pattison group, Overwaitea has grown by some 300 percent. It used the capability to acquire new sites to company advantage, but the people-oriented philosophy and style established by Robert Kidd did not change. Every person in the organization is encouraged to make recommendations, implement ideas, and comment on company programs. Heppell credits this team spirit with the concept for a new generation of stores that was begun in 1982—the

A full-service drug store and pharmacy, another first for "British Columbia's Very Own Food People."

Save-On-Foods stores.

These markets, designed with a central core for bulk foods surrounded by packaged foods, were built in response to what was perceived as a new trend in British Columbia—a trend toward a combination of health consciousness and a "back-to-the-basics" life-style. It called for less red meat and whole milk, fewer cigarettes, and more fruit, vegetables, fish, and yogurt. Consumers seemed to distrust fancy packaging, looking instead for freshness, quality, and value. Save-On-Foods intended to meet those needs.

Heppell points out that Save-On-Foods is also responding to customer needs with longer hours and economies achieved through less labor, lower bag costs, and shopping cart control—savings that are passed on to the customers.

Overwaitea and Save-On-Foods have each, in turn, brought a distinctive style of food merchandising to British Columbia. The company emphasis on the value of its people was undoubtedly its greatest strength during the slower years. This policy is also the key to the firm's successful new growth and its development into British Columbia's second-largest food-store chain.

THE LAURENTIAN GROUP

"Partners in Progress" is a fitting description of The Laurentian Group of companies' involvement with Vancouver. Although the group's activity in the city has intensified in the past decade, the history of its affiliates and subsidiaries in Vancouver dates back over 100 years.

IMPERIAL LIFE ASSURANCE COMPANY OF CANADA

In 1897, when Vancouver was only eleven years old and the city's population a mere 20,000, Imperial Life Assurance Company of Canada appointed Ceperley, McKenzie and Rounsefell of Vancouver to represent it in British Columbia. Two years later J.W.W. Stewart became manager for mainland British Columbia and opened the city's first Imperial Life office in a building known as the Fairfield Block.

By the end of that year the firm had more than seven million dollars of life insurance in force in the province. In 1913 a separate Vancouver branch was opened with Stanley Henderson as branch manager, a position he held until 1932.

By 1933 the city's population had grown to 243,000, and the Vancouver branch alone had more than twelve million dollars of life insurance in force. Eleven years later branches were organized in Victoria and southern British Columbia.

In August 1984 the company opened its Central Vancouver branch at 1285 West Broadway. It places special emphasis on serving the area's Chinese population, which numbers about 60,000. The Central Vancouver branch, with twenty-eight full-time agents and eight administrative employees, is managed by Nelson Tsang.

In addition to its sales operations, Imperial Life Assurance Company of Canada has $73.3 million on loan for commercial, industrial, residential, and apartment mortgages.

LAURENTIAN PACIFIC INSURANCE COMPANY

Laurentian Pacific Insurance Company (formerly the Paragon Insurance Company of Canada), headquartered in Vancouver, was incorporated October 25, 1979. The chief operating officer at that time was Simon Farrow. The new company's major attraction to agents and brokers was its Western Canadian base in Vancouver.

In 1981 The Laurentian Group purchased five insurance firms from the Prenor Group including the Paragon Insurance Company. The firm had a staff of thirty-four, and in 1983 total premium writings were $9.9 million.

In the fall of 1983 a conscious decision was made to expand the operations of the company. R.P. Vickerstaff, who had thirty years' experience with another insurer in Vancouver and whose father is a native of Vancouver, was hired as executive vice-president and chief operating officer. At the same time four million dollars in additional capital was injected into the business.

During 1984 the base of the com-

The Laurentian Pacific Building was officially opened by Jean Marie Poitras in 1984.

pany's operations was expanded from commercial property, livestock, and marine to include liability, personal lines, boiler and machinery, and contract surety. In June 1984 the firm changed its name to Laurentian Pacific Insurance Company and moved into the Laurentian Pacific Place Building.

By 1985 the firm had proven to be one of the top three general insurers in the province, with premium income of thirty-two million dollars. It

The Imbrook Properties 885 West Georgia Building was nearing completion when this photo was taken in 1986.

is the leader in the casualty and contract surety fields in British Columbia. Today the Laurentian Pacific Insurance Company has eighty-eight employees and, in addition to its attractive headquarters in Vancouver, has offices in Victoria, Kelowna, and Prince George, British Columbia, and in Edmonton, Alberta.

The Vancouver skyline. In good company.

IMBROOK PROPERTIES LIMITED

Imbrook Properties Limited is the property development and property management arm of the Imperial Life Assurance Company of Canada Ltd. The firm has been active in Vancouver since 1982, when it invested in offices and commercial property in the Lower Mainland. Today under the direction of regional manager Les Lawther, the company is aggressively pursuing exciting opportunities in the gateway to the Pacific Rim.

Two major Imbrook office properties in the heart of Vancouver, Westar Place, and Laurentian Pacific Place, provide first-class accommodations to many leading businesses. Tower 885, to be known as the Bank of British Columbia Building, will be ready for occupancy in the fall of 1986 and is destined to be Vancouver's most outstanding corporate address.

In less than five years Imbrook Properties Limited has become one of the largest landlords in Vancouver, and intends to maintain and expand its commitment to the city.

IMPCO HEALTH SERVICES

Impco Health Services is a subsidiary of Imperial Life Assurance Company and a member of The Laurentian Group. Founded in 1980, the firm operates its facilities under the name of Harbourside Executive Health Club at 999 West Hastings Street.

Today the company is one of the leaders in the field of preventive medicine for the corporate world. Led by Jim Miller and Dr. Peter Bell-Irving, Impco Health Services has brought together a highly qualified group representing the fields of medicine, physiology, kinesiology, psychology, and nutrition.

In summation, The Laurentian Group of companies (including its most recent acquisition, Yorkshire Trust Company), under the leadership of Claude Castonguay, president and chief executive officer, has established itself as a leader in the provision of financial services. The corporation is truly a Partner in Progress with Vancouver and looks forward to assisting the city in establishing itself as Western Canada's financial centre of the future.

YORKSHIRE TRUST COMPANY

"Solid, steady, and sterling," was Colonel George Norton's opinion of British Columbians when he first met them in the 1880s. After a tour of the United States and Canada, he chose Vancouver as the most promising location for a new venture. In 1888 he founded the Yorkshire Guarantee and Securities Corporation Ltd.

He named his new company after his home county in England, a region inhabited by people renowned for their thriftiness and caution. Those values guided Yorkshire and its subsidiaries through three generations of Nortons and the first seventy-five years of its existence.

While others rushed to the goldfields, George Norton realized that there was a more reliable fortune to be made in real estate and mortgages. The company's holdings at one time included land that is now home to two of Canada's largest retail and office developments, Vancouver's Pacific Centre and Bentall Centre.

Other men found gold—the Nortons made money out of brokerage and securities, establishing an early and lasting relationship with the Vancouver Stock Exchange. The company's early leaders went on to play a major role in the development of such British Columbian commercial pillars as B.C. Telephone, B.C. Hydro, and the Bank of British Columbia.

In 1965 Yorkshire underwent a fundamental change when it was sold to a Canadian company, Power Corporation. It entered an era of innovation and aggressive marketing that continued through several changes of ownership, culminating with its acquisition by The Laurentian Group in 1985.

Its first major move was to enter a field dominated by powerful eastern financial institutions—multi-branch trust services. The Yorkshire Trust Company, as it is known today, was formed in 1965. By 1972 there were

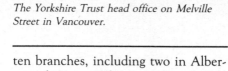

The Yorkshire Trust head office on Melville Street in Vancouver.

The Victoria branch has played an important role in the firm's growth.

five branches, nine by 1975. Today it is still one of only two British Columbia-chartered trust companies. Gerald McGavin, who joined Yorkshire as general manager in 1972, has been president since 1975.

Since then Yorkshire has led the field in innovative and personalized financial services. In 1968 it was the first western institution to introduce what is now a mainstay of personal financial services—the daily interest savings account. The company has

ten branches, including two in Alberta and one at Kelowna in British Columbia's interior.

Yorkshire led the way again in tax deferral services in 1968 with the introduction and aggressive marketing of Self-Directed Registered Retirement Savings Plans. This continued with a stream of new RRSP product introductions, such as the exclusive Tight Money RRSP, designed to meet the changing needs of local investors.

Retirement planning has been another area of growth as the firm has designed services to suit the needs of the mature individual. Yorkshire has also been active in the field of commercial mortgages, specializing in flexible financing for smaller developments.

A new era has begun with the acquisition of Yorkshire by The Laurentian Group, a leader in the financial-services industry. The company intends to take maximum advantage of the opportunities offered by the fast-evolving financial-services industry to present its clients with a wide range of quality financial services.

CP RAIL

On November 7, 1985, Canadian Pacific Railway celebrated the 100th anniversary of the completion of the railway line from Montreal to the West Coast.

Construction of a railway to connect British Columbia to the rest of Canada was an important prerequisite to the province's entering Confederation in 1871. The House of Commons passed an act incorporating the Canadian Pacific Railway in 1881, and construction began the following year.

There had been much criticism, and even ridicule, of the viability and cost of bridging Canada with steel rail, and justifiable concern about the problems of laying rail across some of the most difficult terrain in the world.

Despite the tremendous challenges he faced, general manager William Cornelius Van Horne completed the railway in fifty-four months, six years ahead of schedule, and at a cost of $107 million.

On November 7, 1885, the last spike in the transcontinental railway was driven at Craigellachie, British Columbia. The next day the first train to traverse Canada arrived at Port Moody carrying Van Horne, Donald Smith (later Lord Strathcona and Mount Royal), Thomas Shaughnessy (later Lord Shaughnessy), and other officials.

The *Pacific Express*, the first scheduled passenger train from Montreal, arrived at its West Coast destination of Port Moody on July 4, 1886. It took 139 hours and was then running the longest scheduled train ride in the world.

The rail line was extended twelve miles to Coal Harbour, and Vancouver became the official western terminus of the CPR. The City of Vancouver was incorporated on April 6, 1886—its birth coinciding with the arrival of transcontinental train service.

The railway has had to adapt to handle ever-increasing traffic and today is engaged in its largest construction project since the original undertaking. A 14.7-kilometre tunnel is being burrowed through Mount Macdonald in the Rogers Pass. When completed in 1988, it will be the longest railway tunnel in North America.

This project will remove the last of four main line bottlenecks between Calgary and Vancouver and will increase freight-handling capacity in this important corridor. The $600-million project, which is thirty-four kilometres in length, includes seventeen kilometres of surface routes, six bridges, and two tunnels.

At Expo 86 in Vancouver, Canadian Pacific has a 2,500-square-metre pavilion featuring a pre-show area and two theatres, one with a multi-screen production and the other with a seventy-millimetre show.

In 100 years Canadian Pacific has grown into a diverse corporation with interests not only in land, sea, and air transportation, but also in mining, real estate, oil and gas, iron and steel, forest products, and hotels. The centennial of the *Pacific Express'* arrival in Vancouver will be the culmination of a series of milestones marking Canadian Pacific's growth

Preliminary work at the west portal of CP Rail's Rogers Pass tunnel project, west of Glacier, British Columbia, includes construction of a 270-metre reinforced concrete box under the Trans-Canada Highway and into Mount Cheops.

The driving of the last spike at Craigellachie, November 7, 1885. The Honorable Donald A. Smith, later to become Lord Strathcona and Mount Royal, drove home the spike that completed the transcontinental link between the Atlantic and Pacific oceans. Smith is flanked by Sanford Fleming (left, top hat and white beard) and W.C. Van Horne (right, hand in pocket, black beard).

and development into one of the country's major corporations.

The railway played a vital role in the settlement of the Prairies, the Rockies, and British Columbia. To echo what Van Horne said at Craigellachie: "Well done in every way."

WHITE SPOT LIMITED

For virtually any current or past resident of this city, a visit to White Spot is part of life in Vancouver. Ask any Vancouverite about dining out with one's parents, meeting school-mates on a Saturday night, or simply having a casual meal during the week, and "Hitting the Spot" is sure to be mentioned.

For its first forty years the story of White Spot is the story of Nat Bailey. It begins in the 1920s when young Nat Bailey purchased a 1918 Ford Truck for eighty dollars. He used it bile hot dog stand, selling to people on beaches and in parks. At the same time, the aggressive young Bailey was hawking peanuts at base-ball games and using his magnificent voice as an announcer at baseball, boxing, and wrestling events. His experience with his mobile hot dog truck suggested to Bailey that people on the move outdoors would enjoy having food brought to them in their cars. Bailey planned to do just that.

On June 16, 1928, Bailey opened his hot dog barbeque stand on Gran-ville Street at Sixty-seventh Avenue. The site was literally "out in the country" and once the lot was lev-elled (for eleven dollars, which caused him a seven-dollar overdraft), twenty-five cars could be serviced by Bailey and his staff of two.

The stand, an imitation log cabin, cost $1,400. It had a large white spot painted on the roof and was called "White Spot No. 1." Hamburgers were added to the menu a year or so later. Word gradually spread about the cabin in the country, but the ear-ly 1930s were difficult times for Nat Bailey and his wife, Eva. To keep White Spot going, Bailey continued to work with his truck and kept his baseball park concessions operating. In 1933 the first of Bailey's new buildings was put up at the Granville location. By this time the line-up of cars often went around the block. Gradually times improved, and peo-

ple could once again afford cars and eating out. The new building was en-larged, and then enlarged again as the rear section housed the food preparation area.

Bailey's recipe, "quality, consis-tency, and service," was successful. He built more White Spot outlets, and by 1955 brought a group of key employees in as part owners of the company. In 1959 Industrial Catering Limited was purchased and it became necessary to move the food prepara-tion area to a new commissary on Southeast Marine Drive in Vancou-ver. Such was the growth of White Spot that by 1968 the commissary needed to be increased to 66,000 square feet.

Nat Bailey gradually became a leg-end in the restaurant industry and eventually met another legend—Col-onel Harland Sanders. As a result, in in 1961 White Spot acquired Ernie's Kentucky Fried Chicken outlets in British Columbia. In addition to the Kentucky Fried Chicken outlets, rec-ords show that by that time White Spot was serving 18,000 people daily at its eleven drive-ins and coffee

shops and the Industrial Catering division was delivering a variety of meals to thirty-five industrial and of-fice locations. The company had its own warehouses, commissary, and laundry, and continued to train its own personnel.

In 1968 Bailey sold the White Spot operation to General Foods Limited, although he remained as general manager. By now, the firm included many White Spot, Kentucky Fried Chicken, and Industrial Ca-tering outlets, as well as "Newton Farms," where chickens were raised to company specifications. It took thirty-five people at the Fraser Valley farm alone to raise the 14,000 chick-ens for the famous White Spot chicken dishes.

Bailey went on to become presi-dent of the Canadian Restaurant As-sociation and actively supported local businesses. He was president of the Vancouver Mounties baseball team and his love of sports was evident in the company sponsorship of young people's activities in baseball, hockey, and lacrosse. He took an interest in the car hops White Spot employed,

The White Spot Number One was built to replace the imitation log cabin that served as Nat Bailey's first take-out stand. The site, on Granville Street and Sixty-seventh Avenue, was later developed into the White Spot Restaurant.

making sure that their schoolwork did not suffer and setting up bursaries for the most needy.

In 1983 ownership of White Spot Limited passed from General Foods Inc. to a B.C. native, Peter C. Toigo, through his family company, Shato Holdings. After a fifteen-year hiatus, ownership of White Spot Limited was once again in the hands of a B.C. resident. That change signalled the return of Peter T. Main (a former General Foods manager) as president of White Spot Limited and the start of the most aggressive expansion program in the company's history. By 1986 a hotel operation had been added, the Industrial Catering Division had grown, and the Kentucky Fried Chicken operation was expanded to virtually every community throughout the province. And White Spot has become a neighborhood presence not only in greater Vancouver but in Kelowna, Abbotsford, Nanaimo, and Victoria. The commissary alone is one of the largest food-manufacturing operations in Western Canada, operating its own dedicated bakery, meat-processing, and food-production facilities.

While customers appear to have had a long-term love affair with White Spot, the same seems true for its employees. During 1985, 52 employees received recognition for 10 years of service, 15 for 15 years, 3 for 20 years, 3 for 25 years, 2 for 30 years, and one, Bob Stout, celebrated 50 years with the company. The record continues in 1986; White Spot reported that 241 employees have logged more than 10 years of service and that 32 of them have more than 20 years with the company.

A sign of Vancouver's relationship with its beloved White Spot occurred in early 1986, with the tragic fire that completely gutted the well-loved and familiar White Spot No. 1 restaurant on Granville Street. Rush-hour traffic in south Vancouver came to a halt, and for a month afterwards, a procession of cars passed through the parking lot, its silent passengers recalling the high points of earlier times spent with friends devouring the famous White Spot "triple O" burger on that very site.

While White Spot has yet to announce the specifics of its new restaurant at that location, the company looks forward to a landmark project in 1986, its appointment as the host restaurant at the B.C. Pavilion, Expo 86. The 350-seat restaurant will be called "Nat Bailey's on the Plaza," in honor of its founder, and will remain as one of the few permanent legacies of the fair.

Today, with all of its operations in British Columbia, and most of that in Vancouver, White Spot Limited ranks among the fifteen largest food-service companies in all of Canada.

Some part of its operation has direct, face-to-face contact with a third of all British Columbian families each and every week. That unique relationship reflects the firm's continued commitment to Nat Bailey's original philosophy of "quality, consistency, and service." The number of parties, business deals, and even marriages discussed over a triple-O at "The Spot" will never be known. But the love affair continues for residents of British Columbia, and White Spot frequently "air-freights" its unique menu items to expatriates all over the world. Whether they are trying to recapture a specific taste or a general B.C. feeling depends on the customer. One thing is certain, however; White Spot plays a unique role in that arena and Nat Bailey's favorite quote perhaps said it best: "Smile! Life is beautiful in British Columbia."

White Spot continually upgrades its buildings. This remodelled version brings a new, modern feel to the North Road location in Burnaby.

THE ALUMINUM SHOP

It all started almost fifty years ago when Kathleen Bradshaw needed something to keep flies out of her West Thirtieth bungalow. Using snap-on fasteners, metal screen cloth, and her sewing machine, she made a perfect fly screen and a true cottage industry was born.

Demand from friends and neighbors was immediate. The Bradshaws made up some samples and Laurie Bradshaw, Kathleen's husband, went door to door with them. Sales were tremendous and soon production was moved to their neighbor's basement. The Bradshaws patented the window screen for Canada and the United States in June 1941 and during World War II also produced blackout blinds.

After the war Laurie left his job at the Burrard Shipyard, and the Bradshaws launched their own business in the basement of the home they built at Forty-eighth and Dunbar. Business was good in the 1950s and 1960s, and the Bradshaws created a proprietorship called The Aluminum Shop. Screen and storm doors joined the production line and, for a time, were sold through department stores. The Bradshaws have two sons: Barrie, who joined his father in 1959, and Peter, who became associated two years later.

In the spring of 1960 the growing firm constructed Phase One (2,000 square feet) of its 15,000-square-foot plant on Vanguard Road in Richmond. The Bradshaws began manufacturing and installing windows in 1963, and annual sales passed the million-dollar mark in 1969. Sales continued climbing as the firm introduced the innovative continuous aluminum-guttering machines in 1970. The Aluminum Shop represents the U.S. gutter machine manufacturer and introduced this equipment to Australia in 1974 with great success.

The 1970s saw the start of The Aluminum Shop's most aggressive advertising campaign. The company logo, "Gumper," the cartoon tradesman, has been incorporated into all the corporate advertising and is now a well-recognized figure to greater Vancouver home owners. Radio and television advertising featured Peter Bradshaw and coined the now well-known phrase, "It's the dead air space that insulates." Growing business necessitated installing a computer system with custom software, which was very innovative in the early 1970s.

The energy crisis in 1973 focussed attention on energy-saving products, and The Aluminum Shop began to manufacture and install cellulose fibre insulation. Barrie participated in the government programs and standards boards that were created during this period to protect the home owner. In August 1978 the insulation plant containing raw insulation products for fall production caught fire and burned for three days. Production was moved to another facility and a replacement plant was purchased in June 1979.

The company and its partners have, over the decades, been involved as directors, officers, or volunteers of the Better Business Bureau, American Marketing Association, Richmond Chamber of Commerce, sheltered workshops for the mentally handicapped, Richmond Youth Agency, Variety Club International, Children's

The Bradshaw family lineup at The Aluminum Shop. From left to right: Laurie Bradshaw, founder of the company, and his sons, Barrie and Peter.

Hospital, Richmond Hamper Fund, and the BC Institute of Technology.

Nearly 2,000 households in the Lower Mainland enjoy the services, products, and security of The Aluminum Shop each year. Today the firm's product line includes the manufacture and installation of custom windows, siding, roofing, gutters, entrance doors, patio covers, and garage doors. Contemporary life-styles of the 1980s added the very popular "solarooms."

Ownership is still a family affair although Laurie Bradshaw is now attempting retirement and Peter is pursuing a career in the venture capital market. Under Barrie's guidance the company continues to grow by following the philosophy of delivering craftsmanship and service it has practised since 1941.

"Gumper," the company logo, appears on its publications. He represents the skilled workers who are part of the Bradshaw service team.

PEMBERTON HOUSTON WILLOUGHBY

Joseph Despard Pemberton arrived in Victoria from his native Ireland in 1851. He was colonial surveyor and engineer for the Hudson Bay Company, charged with laying out the townsite and surveying the surrounding area.

Not content with this career—nor his impressive record of elected office—Pemberton went into business in 1887 with his son, 22-year-old Frederick Bernard. They opened Pemberton & Son—as "surveyors,

Joseph Despard Pemberton, first surveyor general of Vancouver Island and founder of Pemberton & Son.

civil engineers, real estate and financial agents." The senior partner, active in the business only long enough to see his son firmly established, died in 1893.

Frederick Pemberton opened a branch at 314 Homer Street, Vancouver, in 1910. The firm reported that, through clients, over thirteen million dollars of mortgage funds was contributing to the development of property in Vancouver and Victoria.

During World War I the organization sold war bonds and, for the first time, dealt with individuals rather than institutions. F.B. Pemberton's daughter married Lieutenant H. Cuthbert Holmes, and later the corporate name changed to Pemberton & Holmes Ltd.

The years between 1927 and World War II saw Pemberton's underwriting business expand by providing capital for industrial developments and the accompanying housing. Company activities had widened, and Pemberton was offering a complete and integrated financial service.

F.B. Pemberton retired in 1933 and was succeeded by L.P. Smith. A subsequent president—W.J. Borrie, elected in 1939—was still a member of the firm in 1986.

Starting in 1929 the different departments of the original firm became separate organizations. In 1943 the

investment venture became Pemberton Securities Corporation Ltd.—a name it kept for forty years. Pemberton continued to develop its investment business under various leaders. Vice-chairman John Chaston became a director in 1952; chairman Bob Wyman joined the company in 1962; and president Fred Wright began his association in 1970.

Branch offices were opened in British Columbia and Alberta during the 1960s and 1970s as the corporation shifted to a retail business. Pemberton became recognized as the leading Western Canadian broker. The firm's growth is not one of acquisitions and mergers—with two key exceptions. In 1974 a Vancouver investment company, Ryan Investments, merged with Pemberton.

In February 1983 Pemberton's merger with Houston Willoughby of Saskatchewan made it the largest brokerage firm west of Toronto.

Almost a century after J.D. Pemberton founded his small enterprise in Victoria, Pemberton Houston Willoughby is one of Canada's major investment firms. It offers personal and institutional investment services, and has become a major force in the underwriting and distribution of securities for both governments and corporations. The company has over twenty-five offices and over 650 employees in Western Canada, and Bob Wyman stresses that "our real strength is in our people."

Pemberton Houston Willoughby's growth has been directly linked to the development of the West. It looks forward, with pride, to celebrating a century of service to western investors.

Taken outside 418 Howe Street in July 1925, this photo shows the entire staff complement of forty-nine. The Pemberton company at that time comprised four divisions: securities, real estate, insurance, and finance.

KEEFER LAUNDRY LTD.

Seventy-two years ago Wong Chow Yin and his brother, Wong Shek Yin, started a small laundry on Keefer Street in Vancouver's Chinatown. Wong Shek Yin later sold his interest to his brother and returned to China. How the laundry grew and became the most modern laundry in Canada is the story of Wong Chow Yin's life.

At the beginning Wong's laundry specialized in garments. They were collected from depots by horse-drawn carts and washed by hand and by using secondhand equipment. Clothes were pressed with coal-heated irons.

When the White Lunch opened on Hastings Street, Keefer Laundry Ltd. started laundering commercial uniforms. In time, it looked after many of the city's hotels.

The original plant was 3,750 square feet and processed about 200 garments a day. In the late 1930s it was expanded to 6,000 square feet and new equipment increased its capacity to an astounding 120 shirts an hour. Men usually looked after the washing, the deliveries, and the technical side of the laundry while women performed the finishing work.

Starting in the 1960s Keefer Laundry Ltd. began to concentrate on commercial service: restaurants and hotels. In 1970 the laundry moved to East Georgia Street, and again upgraded its equipment. Turnaround time, always a matter of twenty-four hours, was reduced to two and one-half hours for some downtown customers. Of course, the horse-drawn carts had long given way to a fleet of trucks covering the Lower Mainland.

New shirt and uniform presses were added in 1939, and over the years Keefer Laundry Ltd. has become the most automated in Canada.

Wong Chow Yin established Keefer Laundry seventy-two years ago.

For many years Wong's wife, Mee Fong, and son Paul had worked together with him and in 1972 the younger son, Howard, joined the firm. Wong had not retired. He was active in the company until his death in August 1983 at the venerable age of eighty-eight.

A major renovation program began that same year. The new generation of washing equipment, imported from the United States, is literally all controlled by computers. This is the first such installation in Canada.

Gone are the people on the wash floor; gone are the steam-filled environment and wet floors. Linen is washed according to the composition of the fabric—not solely according to how dirty it is. Formulas have been devised, and computerized, for each different material, and the laundry now uses fewer chemicals and utilities to produce the same amount of work as before.

From a tiny staff Keefer Laundry Ltd. grew until by 1981 it employed the equivalent of sixty full-time people. By 1985 there were seventy, many of whom have been with the firm for over twenty years.

The first phase of the renovation program is now complete. The next move, to the second floor of the building, was accomplished in early 1986, two years ahead of schedule.

It took tremendous faith and courage for a Chinese immigrant in the 1900s to start a business. He spoke no English, had little money, and was beset by regulations and prejudice. His success came from hard work and a willingness to make changes. One must, with his family, share the regret that Wong Chow Yin did not live to see Keefer Laundry Ltd. become the most automated laundry in Canada.

AMES BROS. DISTRIBUTORS LTD.

Ames Bros. is the oldest and one of the largest distributors of ceramic tiles in Western Canada. Its founder, Cyril Ames, was born in St. Helens, Lancashire, England, in 1885. St. Helens is the home of Pilkington Glass, and it was as its representative that he came to Canada in 1908. Shortly after Ames arrived he decided there was a better future for him as an agent for British manufacturers. With his older brother, who followed him from England, he formed Ames Bros. An office was opened on Alexander Street, now part of Vancouver's Gastown. The partnership lasted a mere two weeks, as the brothers found their interests were not compatible. Cyril Ames carried on alone and retained the name of Ames Bros., remaining on Alexander Street until 1930. At that time he moved to the Canadian Fairbanks Morse Building, now the site of B.C. Place, where he stayed for the next thirty years.

After the war Cyril's son, Jack, who had returned from overseas, decided to join his father's agency business. The time was opportune; the economy was beginning to recover in the early postwar era. The 1950s were active and prosperous years. However, by the end of the decade customers were becoming increasingly impatient waiting for materials from Europe. New sources of supply had to be found, and the company decided it must maintain stocks in order to service the market more efficiently. During this period the Japanese tile industry was gaining prominence, and Ames Bros. began a gradual transition of its tile purchases to the smaller and popular mosaics. A small warehouse of 5,000 square feet was built in 1960 at 1385 Odlum Drive, in Vancouver's Grandview District, and the company began importing tiles exclusively from Britain and Japan on a stocking basis. Also in 1960 Cyril Ames, after forty-eight years with his company, retired to his home

Cyril Ames, founder.

on Vancouver Island and the business was incorporated as Ames Bros. Distributors Ltd., with a staff of four.

The 1960s and 1970s were prosperous years. The company expanded to the Prairie provinces, opening warehouses in Edmonton (1964), Winnipeg (1966), Regina (1971), and Calgary (1974). In Vancouver it moved twice during this period, each time doubling warehouse capacity. In 1978 the firm moved to its present location in Burnaby, where it occupies over 45,000 square feet of office, showroom, and warehouse space. Also at this time, Jack's son, John, joined the company, bringing a third

John Ames, vice-president.

generation of the family into the business. The mid-1970s and 1980s brought the southern European and underdeveloped countries into focus as major sources of supply, and today Ames Bros. imports from four continents and twelve countries around

Jack Ames, son of the founder and current president.

the world. On May 1, 1985, a new phase in the growth of the company occurred when Ames Bros. expanded into floor coverings and became a distributor for Armstrong Resilient Floors, opening a second warehouse in South Vancouver.

From the modest start made by Cyril Ames in 1912 as a small agency business, the company has become a leader in the ceramic tile and floor coverings market in Western Canada, employing over eighty persons, some of whom are approaching twenty years' service with the firm.

John Ames, the founder's grandson and vice-president of Ames Bros., is looking forward to an exciting future. He believes growth will continue at an accelerated rate as consumers become increasingly aware of the beauty and practicality of ceramic tiles in the home and industry.

SEABOARD LUMBER SALES COMPANY LIMITED
SEABOARD SHIPPING COMPANY LIMITED

In 1985 Seaboard celebrated fifty years of serving customers worldwide with B.C.-produced lumber, plywood, and shingles and shakes.

The corporation consists of two companies. Seaboard Lumber Sales Company Limited handles the export marketing of its wood-product members to overseas markets. Seaboard Shipping Company Limited provides shipping and distribution services to transport those products from B.C. coastal ports to destinations around the world.

While the firms as they are known today were formed in 1935, their story actually begins much earlier. Even before the turn of the century, local mill owners talked of forming a co-operative export marketing venture. They were aware of the potential benefits, but—being fierce competitors—their individualism and lack of trust held them back.

The catalyst for a successful start was B.C.'s lumber commissioner in the United Kingdom, L.B. Beale. The Panama Canal, which would open in 1920, offered better access to the U.K. markets. Beale convinced the lumbermen of the logic of organizing themselves to meet the volume and range of products required in that area. A mammoth order for 70 million feet of Douglas fir and 1.77 million feet of western hemlock spurred them to organize.

So, on March 27, 1919, in Victoria, a diverse collection of lumber manufacturers formed the Associated Timber Exporters of British Columbia Limited. Astexo, as it became known, was the organization through which members' lumber would be sold on an FAS (free alongside ship) basis to existing export brokers for shipment abroad. At the same time, the Canadian government—supported by the B.C. industry—set out to sell Britons on the idea of wood construction and the superiority of Canadian lumber.

The company was successful from its beginning; and as its members prospered, the membership expanded. Shipments were made to markets around the world, including Japan, China, India, Australia, and the United Kingdom.

Astexo members soon realized that, by selling FAS, export brokers had the opportunity to profit on both sales and shipping arrangements. Some members considered forming an exporting organization to sell their lumber for export on a CIF (cost, insurance, freight) basis so that any opportunity to profit would accrue to the mill. The arrival of an experienced U.S. lumber broker, Charles Grinnell, led to the formation in 1928 of Seaboard Lumber Sales, which sold the members' lumber to the U.S. Atlantic Coast market on a CIF basis.

One of Seaboard's modern charter vessels, Skaubord, a ro/ro vessel carrying Seaboard products to Japan and returning with autos and general cargo. At 42,000 deadweight tons, these vessels carry twenty million fbm of lumber and plywood, sufficient to construct 2,000 timber-frame houses. Photo by Allen Aerial Photos, Vancouver

Sailing ships loading lumber at Hastings Sawmill around 1900. B.C. Lumber has always been highly dependent on overseas customers. This led to the formation of Astexo, Seaboard's predecessor company in 1919. Courtesy, Vancouver Public Library

Packages of Seaboard lumber, well marked and with sticker attached for efficient handling, ready for shipment.

The Marine Shipping Company Ltd. was incorporated in 1931 to handle Seaboard's freight arrangements. Both firms were successful until 1932, at which time the Smoot-Hawley tariff on imported lumber effectively killed the export of B.C. lumber to the United States. The operations of both Seaboard and Marine Shipping were suspended.

Sales to the United Kingdom and the U.S. Atlantic Coast had recovered sufficiently by 1935 for the Astexo shareholders to try again, and Seaboard Lumber Sales Company Limited was organized in its present form. The Marine Shipping Company

Seaboard House, the companies' head office (1948-1978) at the corner of Burrard and Hastings in Vancouver.

was revived and became Seaboard Shipping Company Limited.

The organizations were very successful, building and expanding on the success of Astexo, which was phased out in 1938. By 1939 there were thirty-nine shareholder mills and shipments were 843 million fbm (1.98 million cubic feet), virtually all sold CIF by Seaboard to export markets. Commission refunds, freight savings, and other surpluses totalled one million dollars over and above the individual mill results—a return of 7 percent on an FAS sales value of $14 million.

From 1935 to the present, the Sea-

board Companies have served their shareholders well in their main purpose of maximizing the mill return. The firms' first step was to establish a network of reputable sales and shipping agents along with representation offices in major markets. Later this network evolved into wholly owned sales and shipping subsidiaries in selected areas to ensure that Seaboard products received priority attention, not only in sales but in distribution as well. As ships became larger and cost control more critical, terminals were acquired to underwrite efficient operation of the organization's charter vessels.

Seaboard is well known for the quality of its products and the reliability of its service. The corporation has pioneered in opening new mar-

kets in contemporary times, such as China and North Africa. In the past it pioneered in developing the demand for new wood products such as western hemlock and waterproof-bonded softwood plywood. In recent times promotion of CLS softwood lumber has resulted in growing shipment volume.

On the shipping company side, Seaboard participated in the development of packaged lumber to reduce handling costs. With the advent of larger, more expensive ships, fast loading and discharge became important in order to keep freight costs economical. Terminals have been ac-

quired in North Vancouver, which is Seaboard's main loading point; in Tilbury; London; and in San Juan, Puerto Rico. In addition, ships have been built to company specifications in order to ensure that Seaboard products are loaded and discharged efficiently, with a minimum of damage, so that products arrive in the best possible condition.

Seaboard has always been a Vancouver-based operation, and its export supply has been from B.C. mills. The company first opened its doors in the Marine Building. In 1938 the two-storey structure on the northwest corner of Burrard and Hastings was purchased. The firm's head office operated its worldwide sales and shipping network from there until 1977, when the building was sold for redevelopment, and the corporate offices were moved to the Oceanic Plaza at 1066 West Hastings Street.

The company has overcome wartime shortages, extreme competition, and the excessive demands of a volatile lumber market worldwide. Today annual sales are in excess of $400 million, which places Seaboard among the top 500 corporations in Canada. It is evident that change has been the constant factor and the greatest challenge. The lumber industry today is stronger and better organized, and much of the credit for its development lies with the men who joined forces and worked together to promote its growth and success through Seaboard.

FARWEST SYSTEMS CORPORATION

Gordon Flack and Gary McPhee shared a total of thirty-six years with NCR. But more than that, they shared the desire to be a major supplier in British Columbia of cash register and P.O.S. systems using new micro-processor technology.

In 1977 Flack left N.C.R. with an option to buy part of an organization then called D.T.S. Sales Ltd. The company was originally formed in 1975 as the distributor for Data Terminal Systems. A year later McPhee followed Flack and along with an existing partner, Tony Muskett, proceeded to take the business from a 1976 volume of $304,000 to nine million dollars by 1981. In 1981 Flack and McPhee purchased Muskett's shares and began to operate a 50/50 relationship with Gordon Flack as president and general manager.

During the years 1980 to 1982 the company opened sales and service offices in Prince George, Kamloops, Kelowna, Cranbrook, Nanaimo, and Victoria, and increased its staff to eighty-four. In 1982 the company purchased its own home at 125 East Fourth Avenue and changed its name to Farwest Systems Corporation.

For the first few years Farwest concentrated on the sale of D.T.S. products and systems. Its ongoing program of technical and market research made it a retail systems specialist able to assemble customized systems for any retail business. It literally serviced the retail business from front to back—from cash registers in front to the support systems (accounting and inventory control) behind.

The year 1984 began a period of expansion: In October Farwest acquired City Office Equipment (1976) Ltd. in Victoria. This operation, now known as Farwest Retail Systems (1976) Ltd., facilitates better sales and service to businesses in that area. An office was opened in Terrace, and

in December 1984 Farwest became an IBM VAD PC dealer. On July 1, 1985, it acquired the assets of Pacific Coast Systems Inc., the exclusive Remanco dealer in British Columbia. Later that month it purchased the assets of the Vancouver Software Store Ltd., giving it nine additional staff and greater expertise in the microcomputer software field.

In August 1985 Farwest became the twenty-first corporate sponsor to Expo 86 in Vancouver. Even more impressive is the fact that it was one of a handful of British Columbia-based companies, as well as the smallest company to be honored with this sponsorship status. Farwest would provide 800 cash registers to be used for the five and a half months of the exposition from May 2 to October 13, 1986. These systems would perform many functions: gate ticketing, controlling sales in all the restaurants, bars, and buffeterias on site, as well as ringing up millions of dollars in souvenirs and purchases of exotic merchandise from pavilions of countries throughout the world.

Gordon Flack describes Farwest's business as 30-percent supermarkets and 40-percent hospitality industry, with the balance in general retail business where the company continually seeks new opportunities. Farwest's 3,700 clients in British Columbia account for more than 7,500 machine installations, and it maintains cash registers in about half of the retail stores or services in British Columbia. This is accomplished with a sales and technical staff of 115 (including 38 technicians) in eight offices.

Farwest is determined to maintain an "electronic edge" over its competitors and invests considerable time and money to ensure this. It seeks out state-of-the-art developments, and is perpetually training and upgrading its programs in computer technology and advances. Farwest

Gordon Flack, president of Farwest Systems Corporation. Photo by David ROBERTS, ARPS-VANCOUVER

believes that its service policy has contributed much to its success. It promises—and delivers—maintenance and repair service anywhere in the province. Corporate growth is proven by sales of $10 million in 1985, and president Gordon Flack projects a budget volume of $11.5 million for 1986.

Flack says his organization is comprised of people who want to provide services that make a difference to the retail businesses of British Columbia. This is reflected in the company's mission statement, as follows:

As a supplier to the retail industry, Farwest Systems Corporation has, as its primary goal, the achievement of excellence in its business practices. We are committed to recognizing the individual contributions of our staff; to making available the most beneficial products; and to creating honest, forthright, and professional relationships with our customers.

THORNE RIDDELL

It was in September 1869 in Montreal that James Riddell began his career in the accounting field, signalling the start of what would grow over the ensuing 117 years into Canada's largest firm of chartered accountants. At that time he had completed five years of service as an inspector with the Bank of British North America, having left Aberdeen, Scotland, to pursue his love of accounting in what was then the Dominion of Canada.

The firm had its origin in British Columbia in 1897, under the direction of John F. Helliwell, who quickly became part of an exciting and fast-growing province. A short five years after he founded the business, the Dominion Association of Chartered Accountants was formed, and he became the sole representative from the City of Vancouver.

Over the years there were many persons who contributed to the growth of the company within the Province of British Columbia. In fact, the present-day Thorne Riddell represents an amalgamation of many of the principal firms within the province, including E.A. Campbell and Company; Cowan and Cowan;

J.H. Gordon; Griffiths and Griffiths; Helliwell, Maclachlan and Company; and Ismay Boiston and Dunn.

There are also many individuals from within the firm that is now Thorne Riddell who have played a crucial role in its growth and development. Those who are considered founding fathers of the company include John L. Helliwell, Frank A. Griffiths, Denham J. Kelsey, Lionel P. Kent, William R.C. Patrick, and George S. Winter.

To provide for the needs of an ever-expanding client base, Thorne Riddell became one of the founding partners in the international firm of KMG Klynveld Main Goerdeler, the fourth-largest accounting firm in the world. Consulting services are provided in Canada through its affiliated company, Thorne, Stevenson & Kellogg.

Currently Thorne Riddell operates fifty-two offices throughout Canada under the direction of chairman William E. Goodlet and executive partner John R.V. Palmer. In addition the firm operates in nine cities in the Province of British Columbia.

G. Edward Moul serves as regional

G. Edward Moul (center) serves as regional executive partner of Thorne Riddell. Members of the regional council include (left to right) John J. Zaytsoff, John R. Brodie, Bruce P. Flexman, and James C. Cosh. Missing from the photo are E. Frank Estergaard and Brian J. Lamb.

executive partner. Members of the regional council include John R. Brodie, James C. Cosh, E. Frank Estergaard, Brian J. Lamb, and John J. Zaytsoff. Office managing partners include Gene McDonald (Cranbrook), Ray H. Sewell (Kamloops), E. Frank Estergaard (Vernon), John N. Morrison (Kelowna), Bruce P. Flexman (New Westminster and Surrey), Malcolm F. Clay (Richmond), James C. Cosh (Vancouver), and Brian J. Lamb (Victoria).

Today the firm offers a broad range of services including audit, accounting, income tax, microcomputer technology, and receivership. Because of its strong national and provincial presence, and its substantial international affiliations, Thorne Riddell has earned a superior reputation among the Canadian public and private sectors, and in the commercial, industrial, and financial communities.

TRANS CANADA GLASS GROUP

A "putty bench" in Lethbridge where two young brothers picked up the window glass trade is a far cry from Trans Canada Glass Group, an international concern based in Vancouver.

The story began when Arthur and Herbert Skidmore worked alongside their father, Ernest, at Lethbridge Sash and Door in Alberta. Arthur served overseas during World War II but the brothers determined that, when it was over, they would start a business of their own.

Herbert and his wife, Annie, remained in Lethbridge during the war but were ready, when Art returned from England, to move to Vancouver—the home of Art's bride-to-be, Elsie. Vancouver had the population and number of automobile dealerships to support a specialist auto and flat glass service store.

In 1946 Art and Elsie were married and, with Herb and Annie, moved to Vancouver. Their enterprise had begun. The first store, Central Auto and Window Glass Ltd., occupied a tiny building at 26 McGinnis Street in New Westminster. Rental space was extremely scarce at the end of the war. The brothers still recall with gratitude that it was Bill Hill, then manager of Fogg Motors Ltd., who provided them with the needed space.

Getting the business off the ground seemed almost impossible. The brothers' savings amounted to less than $1,000 and in the postwar depression there were no government assistance or small business loans. In March 1946 the brothers opened their doors. Their first sale was to McLennan Motors—a piece of tape for fifteen cents, cash.

For the next four years Art and Herb worked alone. Art took care of the paperwork but admits that the ledgers were kept in his pockets. A local Chrysler official told them they were too young to be in business. (They were under twenty-six years old.) But Chrysler opened an account with them within the year.

Financial difficulties were compounded by high demand and low supplies of glass. Stock was always limited to just a few sheets, and precision cutting was absolutely essential. For five years Art and Herb, with their father, Ernest, and brother, Ernie, worked in the evenings for Trufit Millwork Ltd. This extra work provided forty-five dollars weekly to help fund the company, which the brothers say continued to run mainly on the strength of their faith in God and each other, and a seemingly un-

The present retail operation in New Westminster at the 823 Carnarvon Street location was formerly Central Auto and Window Glass Ltd.

Arthur and Herbert Skidmore in front of their second shop at 827 Carnarvon Street. The firm's name was up but the building still bore someone else's markings.

Mr. and Mrs. Ernest Skidmore outside their sons' first workshop on McGinnis Street, New Westminster.

cating automotive windshields in Niagara Falls. It wanted two distributors for its own and other windshields. A & H Sales Ltd., an automotive wholesale division of Central Auto, became the western distributor and had warehouses in New Westminster, Calgary, and Edmonton. The eastern distributor, Faucher & Fils Ltée, was later taken over by the firm.

Through contacts made in the wholesale area, several retail stores were acquired during the 1960s. The basic premise was that the clientele, built by the previous owners, could be maintained by the same managers under the new owners.

When the company went public in 1969, it was incorporated as Trans Canada Glass Group and listed in Vancouver and Toronto. It had eight retail automotive and/or flat glass branches and six automotive wholesale outlets.

More retail stores were purchased during the 1970s in Nova Scotia, Manitoba, Saskatchewan, and Ontario. Speedy Auto Glass Ltd., established in 1932 in Ontario, is the oldest auto glass company in Canada.

Trans Canada Glass doubled in size when it bought the G. Lebeau Groupe in 1980. Lebeau is the largest auto glass, trim, and upholstery replacement company in the province of Quebec. The firm includes a division called Monsieur Silencieux Limitée—better known elsewhere as Mr. Muffler.

The latest Canadian acquisition, in 1985, was P & R Auto Glass Ltd. of Newfoundland. Trans Canada Glass became the only truly nationwide glass business represented across the entire country.

Trans Canada Glass looked abroad and purchased Bridgewater Windscreens Ltd., an old, established firm with some thirty-six stores in Great Britain. In the United States, Trans Canada Glass has created a growing chain of wholesale outlets and retail

stores. While the company is formally known as Trans Canada Glass, all the retail stores in English-speaking North America operate under the name of Speedy Auto Glass.

Forty years after the firm's establishment, Arthur Skidmore is its chairman and Herbert Skidmore is vice-chairman. In keeping with family tradition, the second generation has joined Trans Canada Glass. Art's two sons, Allan and Thomas, are both executive vice-presidents. Herb Skidmore's son, John, directs the newest division of the company, Speedy Celtel, which markets the new cellular telephone system.

Trans Canada Glass is one of the few national concerns that grew up in Vancouver and is still controlled there. The struggling partnership has become an organization with 1,500 employees in Canada. "To an outsider," Allan Skidmore suggests, "the idea that a company of this size can be such a fraternity would be astounding. But it is."

While pride in their firm's growth would be natural, the Skidmores point instead to their trained personnel and the quality of their work. Their service is thoroughly reliable, Art and Herb believe, because the corporate adherence to honest professionalism is reflected at all levels of the business. The Skidmores stress that the main reason for the success of Trans Canada Glass is the loyalty of its staff.

limited supply of energy. By 1950 Central Auto and Window Glass Ltd. moved to 827 Carnarvon Street. Later, forced into buying the premises, the brothers found it actually a blessing in disguise. Sales were beginning to mushroom and the first employee, Hammy Chapman, was hired. By 1953 Art and Herb could afford a 1952 Ford truck. In 1957 they were able to build a new shop next door, at 823 Carnarvon.

Corporate growth has been phenomenal since the early 1950s. It started with the acquisition of two B & A Auto Glass Ltd. stores in Vancouver and Prince George. This was the catalyst for other expansionary moves.

The market for curved windshields was developing. The Ford Motor Company started bending and fabri-

CENTURY 21 REAL ESTATE CANADA LTD.

It was an idea born in California, but when British Columbians Peter Thomas and Gary Charlwood discovered it, they saw its potential and quickly moved to secure its ownership for Canada.

Two California real estate veterans, Art Bartlett and Marsh Fisher, had established the first Century 21 office in 1971. By the end of the following year they had organized five regions and recruited 150 franchise offices.

Thomas was a Victoria-based real estate entrepreneur, and Charlwood was a Vancouver real estate broker. Beginning in mid-1975 the pair carefully laid the groundwork for a Canadian national operation. Their first offices, located on the West Coast, opened for business in January 1976.

Each Century 21 office uses the familiar brown and gold logo, and each operates under a contract with the master franchise. However, every Century 21 real estate office is independently owned and operated: It identifies and works with its own community although it is supported by the cooperative advertising of the total system. Other benefits include the economies of bulk buying and shared overhead of sophisticated management and administrative expense. Century 21 offices can attract good people through the firm's reputation for good service, and the public, recognizing the logo, knows what to expect.

So thorough was the planning of Thomas and Charlwood that Century 21 quickly became firmly established. Later, in 1976, the first franchises were set up in Alberta. Systematically it was expanded across the western provinces, arriving in Ontario in 1978.

Century 21 Real Estate Canada Ltd. continued to expand until by the fall of 1982 it extended from Victoria to St. John's, Newfoundland, with representation in every province. When it reached its tenth anniversary

Peter H. Thomas (left) and U. Gary Charlwood (above), the entrepreneurs who brought Century 21 Real Estate to Canada.

in early 1986, the firm had more than 300 offices serviced by some 4,800 trained and enthusiastic sales people. With total sales exceeding three billion dollars, Century 21 is one of Canada's largest real estate organizations.

In the United States, Century 21 also was growing and attracting attention. It became a public company in 1977. Trans-World Corporation, better known for its airline activity, purchased a majority of Century 21 stock for ninety million dollars. The new owners reorganized and started to repatriate many of the Century 21 regions across the United States that were originally sold to the enterprising pioneers who backed the concept in its infancy. In 1985 Trans-World Corporation sold its interest in Century 21 to Metropolitan Life for $122 million.

Century 21 Real Estate Canada Ltd. is a totally Canadian-owned corporation which holds the rights to the system for Canada. Its head office is in Richmond and all decisions affect-

ing its offices in Canada are made there. The company continues under the leadership of Thomas, Charlwood, and executive vice-presidents Blair Jackson and Donald Lawby. The head office has a national and divisional staff of thirty-five and, using experienced field personnel, provides direct communication links between Century 21 and its franchised members.

Jackson describes the real estate industry in Canada as being in a major rationalization process. The market, while not returning to the heady days of 1980 and 1981, is still volatile, and he calls for stabilization and a return to reasonable value for money. Century 21 Real Estate Canada Ltd. offers perhaps the only opportunity for new entrants into the business and could be one solution to continued growth and survival in a highly competitive industry.

MDI MOBILE DATA INTERNATIONAL INC.

In 1975 the federal government, in conjunction with the Department of Communications, awarded a research contract to a Vancouver company for the development of state-of-the-art radio communications technology. A key element of the resultant product emerged in the form of a radio modem, which was clearly a breakthrough, having established new standards in the speed of transmission of digital data over radio frequencies.

Two Vancouver entrepreneurs, Bill Thompson and Tom Purdy, recognized the possibilities for the commercial application of this technology. Together they purchased the rights and incorporated Mobile Data International Inc. in 1978.

The first few years were difficult for the new company due to slow market acceptance of the technology. In 1979 MDI sold its first system to the Vancouver Police Department, an installation of sixty mobile data terminals. Then in 1980 Federal Express, the international courier service, purchased a twelve-terminal pilot system. Today Federal Express has over 10,000 terminals installed across the United States.

The year 1981 was MDI's first profitable one, and 1982 proved to be even better due to market acceptance, growing awareness, and a strong management team headed by president Barclay Isherwood.

Isherwood built a solid management structure and launched a major program of product development. That year the first U.S. police system was installed in California, and a mobile data communications system was provided for the Hong Kong Joint Maritime Commission.

MDI expanded quickly into new markets. The Phoenix Fire Department purchased a 164-terminal system; Federal Express expanded its pilot system; and North York Hydro, an Ontario electric utility, signed on for ninety terminals.

Over the following few years considerable effort was placed on product development and marketing. To complement MDI's existing product (the full-size mobile terminal), a scaled-down version was designed, to be directed toward taxi fleet operators. In addition, MDI worked with Federal Express to develop a portable handheld terminal that would allow communication for personnel in the field—without a hardwire link. This brought MDI's product offering to three types of mobile terminals.

Numerous contracts were awarded to MDI during this time, including an Australian automobile association; the police forces of New York City, Toronto, and Ottawa; and utility companies in New Jersey, Oklahoma, and North Carolina. Distribution agreements were arranged in Canada, the United States, the United Kingdom, Europe, and Australia; and the first service center was established in Memphis.

MDI outgrew its sprawling leased complex and moved into its own architecturally designed high-tech building early in 1985, and the number of staff employed was almost 250 by the end of the year. A major step for MDI in 1986 was to open a manufacturing facility in Puerto Rico and sales presence in Southern California.

The year 1986 has brought further expansion for MDI, including another service center in New Jersey, a growing client list, and an increase in the number of staff to 340.

In the years since its inception, the corporation has quietly emerged as a pace-setter in the development and marketing of mobile data communications systems. MDI has built its reputation on market solutions, systems reliability, and close customer support. This dedication, together with exciting new areas of research, will ensure MDI's position on the leading edge of the industry.

The MDI mobile terminal is used by police departments, utility companies, taxis, automobile clubs, and various other applications in Canada, the United States, the United Kingdom, Europe, and Australia.

Federal Express, the international courier service, utilizes a handheld MDI terminal, which allows communication for personnel in the field without a hardware link.

BELKIN INC.

Morris Belkin's business career began in 1940 while he was managing the student newspaper at the University of British Columbia. What was left after paying the paper's printing costs helped him to meet tuition fees.

When the printing shop failed, Belkin bought it. He eventually developed the enterprise into what is now College Printers, a multimillion-dollar operation that he owned until 1979.

However, Belkin was not convinced that his future lay in printing. In 1945 he decided that packaging had a great potential in servicing the developing supermarket industry. The entrepreneur entered the market making cake boxes by converting the print shop's presses to die-cutting.

In 1949 Belkin Paper Box leased a warehouse on Kingsway, but by 1956 the forty employees and the growing business were straining its capacity. After a fire and unsuccessful efforts to rebuild, in January 1957 the firm opened a $500,000 plant on a nine-acre site in Richmond. Financing came from the Industrial Development Bank, whose initiative Belkin still commends.

Belkin Paper Box became MacMillan Bloedel's key customer for paperboard, and in 1968 purchased the latter firm's Burnaby mill. A $10-million investment from BC Sugar financed the purchase of the recycling plant, which makes paperboard and roofing material. By 1974 this facility had expanded into one of the largest recycling plants in North America.

Morris Belkin still sought a public company, and in 1975 he acquired Keystone Business Forms. That same year he purchased Somerville Industries from the Weston Group. Through Somerville's three factories and a plastics-packaging operation, Belkin had an entree into the eastern market and a national presence.

Numerous smaller acquisitions were made during the 1970s, plant capacities were increased, and Belkin subsidiaries expanded in every direction. In 1980 the founder purchased the packaging division and paperboard mill of Continental Can Co. Four years later he acquired a corrugated paper-board plant in South Carolina and established a similar facility in Toronto.

Belkin Inc. has twenty-three operating divisions across Canada. It is the country's largest supplier of boxboard and folding cartons, and also manufactures medium, linerboard, construction, and other industrial grades of paperboard. The company's folding carton plants use boxboard produced in Belkin's mills. Flexible plastic packaging is produced in Surrey, plastic products in Bramalea, automobile components in Windsor, and business forms and envelopes in Richmond.

The Belkin corporation has become the country's largest integrated supplier of paperboard packaging with over 2,600 employees. It is a tribute to Morris Belkin's perception in 1945 of packaging as a growth industry, and to his tremendous drive and leadership, that his company has grown from a modest printing shop to the national organization that supplies so many of Canada's packaging needs.

Belkin Inc.'s Vancouver plant.

SPEISER FURS LTD.

The name of Speiser Furs has been associated with fine furs and fashion in Vancouver since 1949. But the Speiser connection with furs started years earlier in Europe during the 1930s. Karl Speiser, growing up in Vienna, attended a special school committed to preserving and improving the furrier's craft. With a degree from the Master Furriers Guild in Vienna, Karl Speiser completed his apprenticeship under the tutelage of some of the great European master furriers.

His skills acknowledged, the young Karl opened his own salon in Vienna. But times became unsettled and Speiser moved to Shanghai which, at that time, was known as the "Paris of the East." His new salon, in the French Quarter, was very successful. Later Speiser, still in his forties, came to Vancouver intending to retire.

It was not to be. Speiser was a dedicated furrier and within a year had opened his third salon, this time on South Granville Street. It was an area that served the so-called carriage

James Laurenson, president of Speiser Furs Ltd.

trade of Shaughnessy and surrounding areas, and was known as "Vancouver's Fashion Row"—a title that, despite some changes, is still applicable.

Speiser recruited skilled furriers, designers, and cutters—all immigrants to Canada who had learned their craft in Europe.

The workroom then, as it is today nearly forty years later, had a truly international flavor. Many of the core group of a dozen furriers have been with the company anywhere between fourteen and thirty years. Together they offer a new standard of personalized fur styling to the West Coast.

Among those who joined the firm in 1949 was a sixteen-year-old apprentice, James Laurenson. Today, a decade after Karl Speiser's death, Laurenson carries on the Speiser tradition of quality and fashion as owner and president of the company.

Speiser Furs offers services ranging from fashion design, alterations, storage, and even advice on purchase taxes and shipping. The firm's own master furriers make many garments right on the premises from skins that Speiser's brokers buy on world markets. The majority are Canadian

skins, and auctions take place in Western Canada, Toronto, and Seattle.

Laurenson describes the market as changing or evolving. No longer, he says, does a woman consider just one all-purpose garment. Fashion trends, and a more casual life-style, have broadened the range of furs made—from sporty vests and casual jackets to elegant evening wraps and exciting full-length coats. Styles change, and today's buyers are prepared to keep pace—buying new pieces or having furs restyled.

With the changing styles has come another change—more younger people in the market. And as fashions in design change so, to some extent, do the furs. Some, like mink, are always favorites because of their quality and durability; others have peaks and valleys of popularity. Speiser Furs Ltd. carries a broad selection of mink, chinchilla, lynx, swakara, Persian lamb, beaver, and fox.

Karl Speiser brought new skills and new ideas to Vancouver. From the same location, thirty-seven years later, James Laurenson continues the Speiser tradition of "quality in the furs, fashion in the craft."

CANADA SAFEWAY LIMITED

Canada Safeway Limited, one of the oldest and most successful retail grocery firms operating throughout Western Canada, was incorporated as Safeway Stores Limited in Winnipeg on January 14, 1929. The current name was adopted in 1947.

An active expansion program resulted in the company building or acquiring 130 stores between British Columbia and western Ontario during the first year of operation. A corporate merger in 1929 with Macdonalds Consolidated Limited, a long-established Western Canadian grocery wholesaler, provided a reliable source of merchandise for the new Safeway stores.

Safeway has always taken pride in providing consistently high-quality merchandise to shoppers. With this concern for quality control in mind, Safeway in 1936 acquired Empress Manufacturing Company, a well-known packer of jams and jellies headquartered in Vancouver. A coffee and tea plant, producing the pop-brand, was opened in Vancouver in 1937. By 1948 fruit and vegetable canneries were acquired in Summerland, British Columbia.

This early Vancouver store at Main and Twenty-fifth streets opened in 1930.

British Columbia has always been an important area of operation for Canada Safeway, and by 1932 the province contained forty-seven Safeway stores. The first Safeway store in Vancouver opened in January 1929, and the number grew as the city developed over the years. In 1936 Safeway acquired the Piggly Wiggly grocery chain and changed these stores to the Safeway name. There are now ninety-four Safeway stores in

British Columbia in 1986, seventeen of these located within the city of Vancouver.

The average size of a Safeway store has increased over the years, from 2,600 square feet of retail area in 1929, to 38,000 square feet in the 1980s. The newest Vancouver Safeway store, due to open at Broadway and MacDonald in 1986, will contain 51,000 square feet and stock 15,000 items compared to 2,000 items in the 1930s. This added space allows the addition of specialty departments such as delicatessens, fish counters, bulk foods, and pharmacies.

Canada Safeway remains committed to providing quality, value, and service to its customers. The cornerstone in providing that service continues to be Safeway's friendly, courteous employees. The firm has traditionally promoted from within. Current Safeway vice-president and Vancouver Division manager Bruce Nicoll is a good example of this policy in action, having started in Vancouver as a part-timer during High School in 1955. Canada Safeway is rightly proud of its people and the role they and the company have played in the history, and will play in the future, of the city of Vancouver.

Neatly arranged interior of the Safeway store at 5655 Victoria Drive, circa 1935. Note the new-fangled shopping carts at right.

MARATHON REALTY COMPANY LIMITED

Marathon Realty Company Limited salutes the City of Vancouver on its centennial and the progress achieved in its growth over the past 100 years. The firm looks forward to taking part in the challenges and opportunities of Vancouver's second century.

Established in 1963, Marathon is a member of the Canadian Pacific Limited group of companies. The firm is a wholly integrated real estate business engaged in the acquisition, development, and management of income-producing properties. Marathon's assets total some $1.5 billion, making it one of Canada's leading real estate companies.

Marathon has truly been a Partner in Progress in Vancouver. The firm has worked with the private sector and with federal, provincial, and municipal governments to bring about projects that have helped shape Vancouver. Marathon's ties to Vancouver, its growth and development as one of the great cities of the world, date back to 1886 when the Canadian Pacific Railway made Vancouver the western terminus of its transcontinental rail line.

The revitalization of the Canadian Pacific Railway station in 1978 was a major corporate initiative. The station—one of Vancouver's significant historic landmarks—now serves as a major transit centre with links to the SeaBus and SkyTrain, two of the world's leading rapid transit technologies.

B.C. Place, the largest urban redevelopment project in North America; Expo 86; and the B.C. Place Stadium, Canada's first domed stadium, are built on properties once controlled by Marathon.

The company was closely linked with the development of SkyTrain, Vancouver's rapid-transit system. The agreement to provide SkyTrain's right-of-way along the waterfront is an excellent example of government and the private sector working to-

Waterfront Centre, a flagship development of some 800,000 square feet, will connect downtown Vancouver to Canada Place and the waterfront.

gether to stimulate growth and enhance the quality of life for the people of greater Vancouver.

Marathon is also proud of its contribution to the Langara, Arbutus, and Gastown areas of Vancouver. With Woodward's and the city, Marathon was a catalyst in the transformation of Gastown into a leading tourist attraction and retail area.

In 1973 Marathon spearheaded the development of Granville Square, the first large-scale commercial development on Vancouver's waterfront. Marathon worked closely with the City of Vancouver to ensure that the project met the special criteria for the development of the community's most valuable real estate—the waterfront.

The future holds much for Vancouver and for Marathon. The company will be a leading participant in the city's future development. A second tower is planned for Granville Square; and, adjacent to Canada Place, Waterfront Centre will be a prestigious twin-tower office complex of some 800,000 square feet.

Waterfront Centre represents the

The Canadian Pacific Railway Station, a Vancouver landmark, opened in 1914. It now serves as a retail and office centre and is linked to two main components of greater Vancouver's rapid-transit system, SeaBus and SkyTrain.

first phase for the shaping of a new Vancouver. The development of the waterfront lands from Burrard to Cardero streets will be one of the great challenges of Vancouver's second century. Marathon looks forward to working with the people of Vancouver to achieve a major goal long sought by Vancouverites: public access to the waterfront.

Vancouver's growth has captured the natural beauty of the land and the values of its people. Marathon Realty Company Limited is ready to do its part to ensure that the community will be an even greater "City of the Century" in 2086.

WILLIAM M. MERCER LIMITED

William M. "Bill" Mercer was only twenty-six years old when he founded his enterprise on May 1, 1945. He had seen that many employers needed advice on establishing pension arrangements for their employees using government annuities. Forming a business to provide that service, he started with $25 and a loan of $1,000.

Mercer was the first president and director; Ralph M. Brown, the second director; and Douglas M. Brown, was named secretary. Space in the office of the National Film Board was a temporary home until, in late summer, the firm moved into the Toronto General Trust Building at 520 Seymour Street in Vancouver.

In 1946 Robert S. Whyte opened a second Mercer office in Montreal. A year later an office was opened in Toronto. All the original company people came from Vancouver and graduated from the University of British Columbia.

Also in 1946 the organization began a two-year association with a New York firm. This extended Mercer's activities across North America and allowed it to profit from a mutual exchange of advice on the design and servicing of pension plans.

Originally organized to provide pension consulting, the company soon found it necessary to include advice on group life and health insurance. It was steadily adding to its expertise and facilities in new "products."

In 1948, when the anticipated increased cost of government annuities finally came, the founder was forced to expand the firm's services even further. He diversified into other forms of pension arrangements and, in January 1949, hired English actuary Laurence E. Coward. Coward has since become the expert on pension matters in Canada and is consulted by all levels of government. He wrote *The Mercer Handbook,* the only

William M. "Bill" Mercer
September 2, 1918-August 30, 1961

comprehensive outline of Canadian pension and insurance plans.

The company became a subsidiary of Marsh & McLennan Incorporated in 1959. In 1975 the employee-benefits consultants in the U.S. Marsh & McLennan offices transferred to a newly formed U.S. venture, William M. Mercer Incorporated of New York. This firm was renamed William M. Mercer-Meidinger Incorporated after the acquisition of Meidinger, Inc.

In Canada, William M. Mercer Limited was providing advice on pension and group benefits as well as human resource management and compensation. When it merged with Hickling-Johnston Limited in January 1984, the services expanded to include business strategy, organization culture and structure, communications, and psychological services.

Over the years the corporation has grown steadily in size and revenue. Its 1985 revenue totalled $48.454 million. Mercer now employs 600 people who serve more than 2,500 clients from offices in twelve cities across Canada.

William M. Mercer died suddenly in 1961, and a scholarship was established in his memory at the University of British Columbia. The business he originated has evolved into the largest firm in its field in Canada and part of the largest employee benefits consulting organization in the world.

VAN WATERS & ROGERS LTD.

Van Waters & Rogers Ltd. commenced business in Vancouver in 1950, distributing scientific supplies, upholstery, home furnishings, and, to a lesser extent, industrial chemicals.

The firm's original emphasis on high gross profit warehouse sales had developed annual sales of two million dollars by 1958. However, that changed with the March 1958 acquisition of Commercial Chemicals, which concentrated on industrial chemicals in British Columbia and Alberta. Its five salesmen, in what became the chemical division, specialized by industries: mining, paint, forest products, agriculture, and laundry and dry cleaning.

Van Waters & Rogers Ltd.'s policy of concentrating on areas where success is possible and getting out of the unrewarding ones led to the sale of its scientific division in 1965.

By 1973 annual sales had grown to between fifteen and twenty million dollars—all in Western Canada. In October of that year the company expanded into Eastern Canada with the McArthur Chemical, thereby expanding its facilities to provide tank farms, warehouses, and offices in all major centres in Canada. In addition it offered the specialization usually associated with smaller organizations.

In 1980 and 1982 additional facilities were built in Edmonton and Calgary. A new 100,000-square-foot complex, opened in Toronto in early 1985, offered more warehouse space, a modern tank farm, acid-packaging facilities, and equipment for the blending and bagging of dry chemicals.

The liquid chemicals—acids, alkalis (caustic), or solvents—each require different equipment for handling. They are distributed in drums, in company-owned compartmentalized tank cars, or in bulk tankers. Dry chemicals are sold in bulk and bagged.

Many of these products are defined as hazardous, but the management of

Van Waters & Rogers Ltd. takes pride in its record that there has never been a major accident involving either people or the environment. When legislation for the handling and movement of dangerous goods was introduced in 1985, the company had already implemented all the provisions voluntarily and was acknowledged as a leader in what industry calls "product stewardship," a position it means to maintain.

Van Waters & Rogers Ltd. handles more than 3,000 items from 300 domestic and foreign suppliers and represents nearly 100 of the world's foremost chemical manufacturers. The firm has 300 employees across

Van Waters & Rogers Ltd. handles over half-a-million drums per year.

Canada, including 70 at its headquarters in Vancouver, and its 55 sales representatives still specialize by industry.

The firm began as a small British Columbia subsidiary of Seattle's Univar Corporation. In 1975, after eighteen years on Skeena Street in Vancouver, it moved to a 60,000-square-foot complex in Richmond. The firm, one of the largest chemical distributors in Canada, is ranked 20th among British Columbia's top 50 private companies and No. 362 in the *Financial Post's* Top 500.

Van Waters & Rogers Ltd. has declared policies and actions on conservation and safety, and it insists that each branch be a good corporate citizen of its own community. From Vancouver, the firm once served just provincial industries—it now serves all industry across Canada.

FOREST LAWN MEMORIAL PARK

Fifty years ago Albert F. Arnold conceived the idea of a cemetery that would be a place of beauty.

Arnold received support from the community and the total cost of the project, $300,000, was subscribed exclusively in Vancouver and New Westminster. While the Arnold family retained control, there was a limited number of other shareholders. Associated with Arnold was a small group of local directors, including his son, Gilbert Arnold, and his son-in-law, Malcom S. Fergusson, D.E. Buzza, Fred Dawson, C.S. Arnold, A.T. Robson, R.H. McDonald, and Paul Murphy.

He purchased 145 acres at Canada Way (then Grandview Highway) and Royal Oak Avenue, a site that had once been the best timber limits of the old Hastings Mill Timber & Trading Company. All but one of the huge twelve-foot stumps were removed as Arnold directed the cre-

ation of the park. He combined his knowledge of flowers, shrubs, and trees with an innate artistic sense to design an area of growth and everlasting beauty to remind the living that life in its essential is unending and eternal. In September 1936 Forest Lawn Memorial Park was opened.

When Albert Arnold retired in the mid-1960s, his son Gilbert assumed the presidency and Malcom Fergusson, the vice-presidency. In 1969 the shareholders, including the family, sold their interests to Service Corporation International of Houston, Texas, and became part of its Canadian subsidiary, SCI Canada Ltd. When Gilbert Arnold retired soon after, Malcom Fergusson stayed on to manage Forest Lawn until 1974.

Forest Lawn is associated with

The familiar entrance gates to Forest Lawn Memorial Park.

Ocean View Burial Park, Forest Lawn Funeral Home, and Mount Pleasant Funeral Home. Each operates independently of the other, but naturally cooperates when, as often happens, clients wish to use more than one facility.

Staff members at Forest Lawn have impressive records for longevity of service. The present general manager, Lenore Martin, joined the Arnolds in 1962; the superintendent has been with the company for thirty-eight years. Among the relatively small staff, between thirty and thirty-five, there are five others who have been part of the Forest Lawn family for more than twenty years.

While the needs of the families have changed over the years, the management of Forest Lawn has remained constant to its principles of serving the public. It started with Albert Arnold, and it is just as strong fifty years later.

McDONALD'S RESTAURANTS OF CANADA LIMITED

The first McDonald's restaurant in Vancouver was opened on South West Marine Drive in November 1967. Six months earlier the McDonald's of Canada story got its start with a store in suburban Richmond. These McDonald's in British Columbia marked the beginning of a story of meteoric growth in the food-service business and community involvement that in two decades has made an enormous impression on the area.

In Vancouver the outstanding example of that community involvement is Ronald McDonald House at 4116 Angus Drive, just a short bus ride from Childrens' Hospital. It serves as a temporary home for people from out of town so that they can visit and comfort their children who are in hospital undergoing treatment for cancer or life-threatening diseases. There are no golden arches on "the house that love built," but it stands, nonetheless, as a symbol of the emphasis McDonald's places on community service and public involvement.

The company's growth has been spurred by the dedication of McDonald's employees to what they call QSC&V (quality, service, cleanliness, and value), supported by marketing that has turned such expressions as "Big Mac Attack" and "You Deserve a Break Today" into household phrases.

Today McDonald's of Canada has nearly 500 restaurants in ten provinces and the Yukon. They employ 50,000 people, serve more than one million customers per day, and do more than one billion dollars a year in sales. Their economic impact is wide spread, purchasing more than $400 million per year in food supplies, paper products, and other goods and services, 98 percent of which comes from suppliers in Canada.

George A. Cohon, president and chief executive officer of McDonald's of Canada, unabashedly describes the

The Ronald McDonald House in Vancouver.

Canadians who own, manage, and operate these restaurants as "the best hamburger people and the best people people in the business." Much of McDonald's success can be traced to the fact that its restaurants are run locally by dedicated, well-trained people who tend to grow with the corporation.

Ronald L. Marcoux, executive vice-president responsible for McDonald's in Western Canada, was born and raised in greater Vancouver. He joined the company in 1968, less than two years after it was formed.

In 1986, as the City of Vancouver celebrated its centennial, Marcoux took the lead role in McDonald's plunge into Expo 86, where the company has opened its first floating restaurant in Canada. This unique

McDonald's Friendship, the restaurant chain's first floating restaurant in Canada.

facility, with two decks and seating for 390, was designed and built in British Columbia and is dressed in nautical splendor befitting its location on the main False Creek site of the world exposition in downtown Vancouver.

This flagship is one more of the firm's landmarks on the Vancouver scene where McDonald's Restaurants of Canada Limited has thirty-six facilities out of a total of seventy in British Columbia. Roughly half of these are operated by licensees and the others by the company itself. All are community-minded, as evidenced by the support they give to literally hundreds of neighborhood activities, and especially to the nonprofit society that operates Ronald McDonald House.

VANCOUVER PORT CORPORATION

Burrard Inlet, a natural harbour, has welcomed the ships of many nations since Captain Vancouver explored and named the inlet in 1792. But it was not until 1864 that the isolated inlet, with its magnificent forests, attracted the attention of shipping. Following nearly two months of loading 277,000 board feet of lumber and 16,000 pickets, the barque *Ellen Lewis* sailed through First Narrows bound for Australia. This modest shipment confirmed not only the future success of the inlet's sawmills but also established Burrard Inlet as a world port.

Twenty-three years after the first export, the inlet's residents welcomed a new arrival—the railroad. The completion of the transcontinental railway at Vancouver opened new opportunities for the western port, having connected it with the larger markets of Eastern Canada and the United States.

But the railway itself could not assure the future of the port. However, by incorporating it with regular and economic ocean service on the Atlantic and Pacific oceans, the shipping of valuable cargoes such as tea, silk, and mail from the Orient to the United Kingdom, via Vancouver, sliced two weeks off the time of the fastest clipper ship.

A prosperous trade with Pacific Rim countries, and the expansion of coastal trade, offered new opportunities for the operators of private waterfront facilities. And the pending completion of the Panama Canal renewed western interest in Burrard Inlet. Prairie farmers recognized the potential of exporting their products to the United Kingdom via a route that was 5,500 miles shorter than the long Cape Horn route.

In response to western pressure, the Vancouver Harbour Commission was established in 1914 by the Federal Department of Marine to plan, develop, and operate harbour facilities.

Spectacular Canada Place is the harbourfront site of the Canada pavilion at Expo 86 in Vancouver. The flagship of Expo will showcase Canada's finest technological and cultural achievements. The shiplike structure also houses a cruise ship terminal, a luxury hotel, an office complex, and a three-dimensional IMAX theatre. After Expo 86, the pavilion will become a world-class trade and convention centre, the largest facility of its kind in Western Canada.

The harbour commissioners were granted extensive powers over their jurisdiction, which included most of the navigable salt water in the Lower Mainland.

The commissioners' first project was the construction of the government grain elevator on the south shore of the inlet for cleaning, storing, and the transfer of bulk grain. The elevator remained inactive until 1917, when an experimental cargo of wheat to the United Kingdom proved the viability of the route. After World War I, commercial shipping returned to the North Pacific and the steamer *Effingham* sailed from Vancouver in 1921 with a cargo of 2,048 tons of wheat, launching Vancouver's shipping boom.

The growth and development of the port in the following decade was phenomenal. The construction of wharves and facilities, the expansion of shipping and related commerce, and the increasing number of firms engaged in the import and export business brought international recognition to the harbour. In just over ten years, the value of port facilities increased sixfold to $36 million.

To meet the demands for a general cargo wharf, Ballantyne Pier opened in 1923 as one of the largest and best-equipped harbour structures in North America. Its four warehouses, wharves, cranes, and grain galleries improved the efficiency of the port by handling a wide range of cargoes at one facility.

The global Depression of the

The *Effingham, which sailed from Vancouver in 1921, launched Vancouver's shipping boom.*

1930s, and consequent decline in shipping, led to an examination of port development in Canada. Sir Alexander Gibb, an engineer noted for his port experience, was invited by Ottawa to survey Canada's national ports and comment on plans to improve their efficiency and expansion to meet anticipated demands in the coming decades. Gibb's report reflected the importance of ports to the Canadian economy and stressed the need for public funding of new port facilities. Following the recom-

its new role as the largest port on the West Coast of the Americas. Bulk facilities increased substantially in 1970, when Roberts Bank opened to ship coal brought by unit train from the interior.

In 1975 the opening of Vanterm with its container gantries and related surface equipment permitted the efficient transfer of containerized cargo between marine and land transportation systems. On the north shore, the opening of Lynnterm in 1976 provided new facilities for the shipment of forest products, steel, general cargo, and petrochemicals.

February 24, 1983, and in July of the same year, the Port of Vancouver officially became the Vancouver Port Corporation with an appointed board of directors and increased responsibility for the day-to-day management of the port.

The celebration of Vancouver's centennial will debut an exciting new development on the city's waterfront—Canada Place. Built on the site of historic Pier B-C, where the great Pacific liners were once familiar sights, the Vancouver Port Corporation's Cruise Vessel Terminal boasts the most modern facilities in the

mendations of the report, the administration of the major Canadian ports was centralized in Ottawa under the National Harbours Board Act of 1936.

The effect of Gibb's recommendations on the Port of Vancouver was delayed by World War II and the concentration of Allied shipping on the North Atlantic route. This shipping depression affected Vancouver until the 1950s. The construction of new facilities was delayed, too, as capital funds were directed to the construction and repair of Canada's overworked Atlantic ports. Consequently, the Port of Vancouver did not enjoy any new facilities until the opening of Centennial Pier in 1959.

The increase of resource development in Western Canada has influenced the building of private wharf facilities in Vancouver. One of the pioneering innovations was the construction of the *Clifford J. Rogers,* the world's first containership which operated on the Vancouver-Skagway route. Specialized bulk transfer facilities were also constructed to service increasingly larger ships more efficiently. From these developments, the Port of Vancouver evolved into

Vanterm Container Terminal, Port of Vancouver.

The expansion of trade and the regional growth of ports in the 1960s and 1970s focussed attention on decentralization of port management in Canada. After a decade of negotiations, a new policy for Canada's national ports was developed. Legislation was passed in Parliament in 1982, repealing the National Harbours Board Act and replacing it with the Canada Ports Corporation Act. The Act was proclaimed on

world. Passengers will embark and disembark via walkways connecting the ship directly with spacious corridors offering spectacular views of the harbor's activities and scenery.

For over 120 years the port and its commerce have constituted a most important influence in the daily life of Vancouver. In 1985 one in ten jobs in the Lower Mainland relied directly on port activities or support services. With a vital role in Canada's expanding Pacific trade, the Vancouver Port Corporation is planning tomorrow's port—today.

KELLY, DOUGLAS & COMPANY, LIMITED

With capital of $14,500 and much determination, Robert Kelly and Frank Douglas opened their small grocery business on Water Street in Vancouver in 1896. Two years later Frank Douglas went to explore the possibilities of supplying food to the Yukon gold rush miners. Tragically, he never returned. His ship hit an iceberg on the way back.

In 1905 Robert Kelly asked Frank Douglas' younger brother Edward to join him, and the business was incorporated as a limited company in 1906. Needing more space, the firm moved to a new, nine-storey brick building at 367-377 Water Street. When Robert Kelly died in 1922, Edward Douglas became president and Robert's son, Fred, vice-president.

Management has changed many times since then and Kelly, Douglas is now a public venture with annual sales exceeding $1.8 billion. Robert Kelly's grandson, Victor McLean, was president during the 1960s and Mildred Douglas, daughter of Edward Douglas, is still a director. An enthusiastic traveller in her younger days, Miss Douglas was interested in the company's trade with tea and coffee plantations.

A new head office and warehouse was built on Kingsway in 1948. The 230,000-square-foot building could load or unload seventeen boxcars and twenty-eight trucks at one time. In 1950 Kelly, Douglas established the chain of Super Valu stores.

During the 1940s and 1950s Kelly, Douglas made several acquisitions: Squirrel peanut butter, Dickson's Blossom tea and coffee, and Murray jams. "Nabob" was Kelly, Douglas' brand name for quality products.

By 1962 Kelly, Douglas & Company, Limited, was a wholesale distributor with two subsidiary divisions: Nabob Foods (manufacturing at Lake City since 1958) and Super Valu (retail). It had 160 Red & White franchised stores, 175 Associated stores,

The original Kelly, Douglas warehouse on Water street in Gastown, Vancouver. Sharp eyes may discern that the sailing vessel tied at the wharf is the ill-fated Pamir.

10 wholesale distribution branches, and 6 Cash and Carry stores.

One continuing competitor over the years was W.H. Malkin Ltd., a company founded in 1892. Kelly,

The head office and warehouse complex built in 1948 on the Kingsway in Burnaby. This view, from the Kingsway side, shows where the firm's head office was until the recent move to downtown Vancouver.

Douglas acquired Malkin in the early 1970s and many of its employees have remained with the firm.

Nabob Foods was sold in 1976. The diversification program begun earlier was reversed and the company now concentrates on its special expertise—food distribution. It has warehouses throughout Western Canada to service retail grocers: its own Super Valu chain, the ShopEasy and Econo-Mart stores, the Red & White and the Lucky Dollar stores, and many other independent retailers. The Foremost Dairy plant at Burnaby supplies dairy products.

In the prairie provinces, the company operates the O.K. Economy, EconoMart, and Pik n' Pak stores. In 1979 Kelly, Douglas developed a new concept, the Real Canadian Superstores. There are ten of these combination stores trading throughout the Prairies. Another is planned for the new Metrotown when the Kingsway site is redeveloped. The head office was moved to downtown Vancouver.

Kelly, Douglas is continually revising its distribution system to provide better service to retail grocers in Western Canada. The firm's principals say that it, in turn, has been extremely well served by its loyal and dedicated staff for ninety years. There are about 250 people in its 25-Year Club, which is open to present and previous employees with twenty-five years' service in Kelly, Douglas.

VANCOUVER AUTO LTD.

In 1961 Adolf Laepple and his partner, Kurt Neumann, opened a small specialized independent workshop to service Mercedes-Benz automobiles. They called it the German Auto Company.

Three years later the two men acquired a Mercedes-Benz dealership. In addition to selling the cars, their firm offered service and parts. This business was conducted in what had formerly been a Texaco station on Sixteenth Avenue at Macdonald in Vancouver.

The operation, now Vancouver German Auto, in 1968 became the Western Canadian dealer for the relatively unknown BMW cars imported by BMW Distributors (Western) Ltd. This was the first commercial import of the vehicles; those in the city previously had been privately imported by the Bentleys of Canadian Forest Products. A new building was constructed at the corner of Fourth Avenue and Fir to accommodate this new business.

Obtaining the Mazda line of cars in September 1969, the company changed its name to Vancouver Auto

Vancouver Auto Ltd.'s showroom, 2040 Burrard Street.

Ltd. Again space became a problem, so the current showroom and workshop was built at 2040 Burrard Street. It became the showplace of the Mazda and BMW cars, while the Mercedes operations stayed at the Fir Street address.

The Mazda line was dropped in 1971, enabling the firm to transfer the Mercedes cars to the Burrard location. Two years later another change took place when the Mercedes-Benz company decided to do its own retailing in Vancouver. Since that time, Vancouver Auto has concentrated on the BMW operation.

In 1980 BMW gave the distribution rights for its motorcycles to BMW Distributors (Western) Ltd. Vancouver Auto began selling the vehicles, and another building, fronting Fourth Avenue, was constructed to sell and service them. Motorcycle sales have climbed in Canada, and in 1985 Vancouver Auto sold 31 of the 430 BMW's sold in Canada.

Meanwhile, through pursuing its original concept—specialized service—the company prospered and grew. Some clients have been bringing their cars to Vancouver Auto for service for years, so much so that a second generation of clients is beginning to appear. The emphasis by BMW on quality and service, strongly reinforced by Vancouver Auto, is reflected in the growth of both sales and service operation. In 1968, 65 BMW cars were sold; the accumulated total by the end of 1985 was 4,600—this despite the fact that some cars run until they are well into their teen years, and that significant model changes are only made every few years.

The year 1986 was one of change at BMW AG headquarters in Munich, whose wholly owned subsidiary, BMW Canada Inc., now imports and wholesales BMW cars in Canada. However, there will not be any change for Vancouver Auto. Adolf Laepple and Kurt's son, Heino, will continue to uphold the tradition of a high standard of service that was developed by the original partnership.

BRITISH COLUMBIA TELEPHONE COMPANY

The British Columbia Telephone Company, which has the technological heart of its province-wide telecommunications system on Seymour Street in downtown Vancouver, will celebrate the centennial of its founding in 1991. But it traces its history back even further than the beginnings of the city of Vancouver—back to 1884, in fact.

Today, from the B.C. Tel headquarters building on a high point of land at the western edge of the District of Burnaby, it is possible to see the Gastown area where the city began. There, a switchboard was in use for two years before Vancouver was incorporated in 1886, a switchboard that survived the great fire that wiped out Vancouver that very year.

The head office of British Columbia Telephone Company, Vancouver.

In the century since then, Vancouver has grown to become Canada's third-largest city, situated in one of the most beautiful settings in the world. In that same period, B.C. Tel has become the second-largest telecommunications company in Canada. Its business has expanded to include telephone operations and the provision of the full range of sophisticated telecommunications services, as well as research, development, manufacturing, and marketing of telecommunications products and equipment.

Today, with an employee force of more than 15,800 B.C. Tel serves 99 percent of the population of British Columbia with a modern, electronic switching and transmission system that provides communications links within the province and with the rest of Canada and the world. The network moves, stores, and processes information in virtually any form,

Gordon F. MacFarlane, chairman and chief executive officer.

whether voice, data, television picture, or facsimile.

B.C. Tel traces its direct corporate history to 1891, but it can claim links all the way back to 1884 when the first phone services began in the mainland area that now encompasses Vancouver. That early operation included the switchboard that survived the 1886 fire.

The present name—British Columbia Telephone Company—was established in 1923 under a federal charter obtained in 1916. The firm is shareholder-owned and, because it is incorporated federally, it is regulated by the Canadian Radio-television and Telecommunications Commission (CRTC).

Its early growth came under the leadership of William Farrell and Dr. John Lefevre. Farrell—whose name was given to the Seymour Street building which for many years was B.C. Tel's head office and which continues as the home of the major network switching and control centre—received the first long-distance phone call to Vancouver from Montreal in 1916.

As the telephone was transformed

The first switchboard in Vancouver.

from a scientific curiosity to a potent instrument for change in business, personal life, and society as a whole, B.C. Tel and its people played the leading role in applying its capabilities in British Columbia.

It built the telephone systems to transmit person-to-person messages— in local communities and over long distances—and it developed those systems for the technologies that eventually brought radio, television,

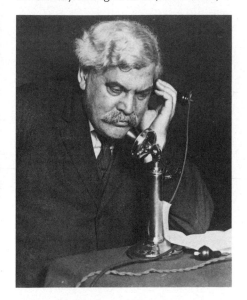

William Farrell receives the first call from Montreal.

and data communications into business and personal lives.

B.C. Tel and its predecessor companies did pioneer work in ship-to-shore radio-telephone and created one of the world's largest marine radio-telephone systems. B.C. Tel became a founding member of the TransCanada Telephone System when it was formed in 1931 to create an all-Canadian telephone network. Until then, many long-distance calls between Canadian cities were being routed through the United States. Today B.C. Tel is the West Coast anchor of Canada's national telecommunications system, now called Telecom Canada.

With other members of Telecom Canada, B.C. Tel also pioneered the development of provincial and national microwave radio transmission systems, then satellite communication and electronic and digital technology, which play such important roles in the movement and processing of information.

Through much of its life, B.C. Tel's headquarters was situated at 768 Seymour Street in downtown Vancouver. The William Farrell Building also houses the major switching, operating, and network facilities and, as the space demands for equipment increased there, the administrative headquarters was moved.

Since 1977 B.C. Tel's headquarters has been located at 3777 Kingsway, at the corner of Boundary Road, which separates Vancouver from the District of Burnaby.

Gordon F. MacFarlane has been the company's chairman and chief executive officer since 1977. Under his leadership, B.C. Tel has expanded directly into research, manufacturing, and a variety of other business activities flowing from technological and social change.

Through several divisions and subsidiaries, B.C. Tel competes successfully in the marketing of various products and services and in the research, development, and manufacture of telecommunications products and equipment.

Telephone Operations provides phone services to 97 percent of the telephones in British Columbia and links all of the province's phones to the long-distance network. Business Telecom Equipment (BTE) markets voice and data terminal equipment and new microchip-based technologies. Telecommunications Services International (TSI) markets products and expertise, including telecommunications training, on an international basis. B.C. Cellular, established in 1985, offers the most modern por-

table phone service, called "cellular" telephone service.

Microtel is a manufacturing subsidiary and, with its research development arm, Microtel Pacific Research, it offers B.C. Tel customers advanced technology and an ever-expanding product line. The technology includes the GTD-5 digital switch that handles telephone and other telecommunications traffic through exchange offices. It also includes an expanding network of fibre-optic transmission facilities and sophisticated microwave and network supervisory control systems. Microtel also has developed a unique "thin route" satellite communications sytem called Spacetel, which uses portable earth station components and the Anik series of communications satellites to create voice and data links from remote sites to the entire network.

The key to the success of all these parts of the organization is people. B.C. Tel's more than 15,800 employees bring a wide variety of skills to the company, ranging from the highly technical to human resource management. They develop their skills further through extensive training programs at the B.C. Tel Education Centre, one of the most advanced telecommunications training facilities in North America. They live in communities throughout the province and they provide leadership and service in both their business and their community lives.

BCE DEVELOPMENT CORPORATION

Some companies show progress in their balance sheets. BCE Development Corporation writes it also in steel and glass, concrete and wood—across the North American landscape.

Beginning in the mid-1960s, BCED, then Daon Development Corporation, rode a North American real estate boom through the 1970s and became one of the continent's most successful real estate investment and development companies.

The driving force behind BCED is Jack Poole, an engineer from Saskatchewan who founded the Vancouver-based company in partnership with Graham Dawson in 1964. Dawson, who heads a leading British Columbia construction company, recognized in the young Jack Poole the imagination, intelligence, and drive required for success in the highly competitive housing industry.

It was housing—first in resource towns and later in urban centres such as Vancouver, Calgary, and Edmonton—that launched the company into the forefront of real estate development in Western Canada.

Since then, the company has developed and marketed a myriad of housing projects, from immense subdivisions and apartment complexes to the more modest town houses and garden apartments. In the commercial and industrial field, the firm has produced an endless variety of office towers, shopping centres, and industrial parks.

Until the mid-1970s BCED concentrated most of its attention on British Columbia and Alberta, two provinces whose booming economies created a ready real estate market.

In 1976 the company looked southward, especially to California, where housing demand far exceeded supply. In the following five years the company's success in British Columbia and Alberta was repeated in California and to a lesser extent in Washington and Oregon.

Within two years more than half of the company's profits was being generated from south of the border. It was an era marked by the success of many Canadian real estate development companies operating in the United States. BCED was in the forefront, gaining a wide reputation for quality design and construction and for innovative financing of its projects.

No place has the company left a more lasting mark than in Vancouver, however. Among the most notable landmarks are Daon Centre and Park Place, two of the city's most prestigious downtown office towers.

And Woodcroft Place and Langara Estates, as examples, rank high among the region's finest residential complexes.

The firm has developed numerous shopping centres, most notably in Alberta, and has been a leading builder of industrial parks in various locations.

BCED survived the recession period of the early 1980s when many development companies fell victim to high interest rates and waning demand for real estate.

In 1985 Bell Canada Enterprises Inc. acquired almost 70 percent of the company's outstanding shares in a "friendly" offer to its shareholders. A name change from Daon to BCE Development Corporation followed, with the expectation that the company will continue to have a profound influence on Vancouver's landscape and economic well-being.

Park Place, Vancouver's largest and most impressive office building, was completed by BCED in 1984.

Woodcroft Place, six buildings with more than 1,200 residential units, built by BCED on the Capilano River in North Vancouver.

SANDMAN HOTELS & INNS

Sandman Hotels & Inns was founded in 1967 when Bob Gaglardi and Ralph Beck built a motel in Smithers. From that modest beginning, they have developed a chain of twenty-one hotel properties across Western Canada, in addition to other holdings in the United States.

Gaglardi's private corporation, Northland Properties Ltd., was both a holding and a development company. In 1973 it began construction of the Sandman Inn opposite B.C. Stadium at Cambie and Georgia. That event marked the first step in a master plan to change the company's thrust from rural motels to urban hotels. The next step, in 1978, was the construction of the Sandman Hotel in Calgary. That was followed by the purchase of the Sandman Hotel in Lethbridge.

The chain was growing rapidly and spreading east, and in 1981 a hotel was acquired in Regina. At the same time the company was involved in other developments—primarily office buildings.

All but three of Sandman's twenty-one hotels have been constructed by Northland Properties Ltd. In each case, the company carried the project through from site selection and hotel design, to the construction and eventual operation of the hotel. The firm, with its corporate base in Vancouver, is one of the larger real estate development and leasing companies in Canada.

Sandman Hotels & Inns has a direct association with the Charter House in Winnipeg. The firm also has an informal marketing arrangement with three other major hotel chains—the Vagabond Inns, Nendels Hotels, and Sheffield Hotels. As a result of those arrangements, Sandman has created a network of over 100 locations on the Pacific West Coast, stretching from Alaska and the Yukon, throughout Western Canada, into the coastal states of Washington, Oregon, and California, and inland through Idaho, Nevada, Arizona, and Utah. This network enables its participants to service clients with reciprocal bookings through a shared reservation system. In both the direct association and the informal marketing arrangement, there are varying degrees of sharing in the reciprocal reservation systems and marketing functions.

In spring 1986 an arrangement was concluded with various small hotel chains in Austria, Australia, Switzerland, and Spain. Negotiations with other European feeder markets are currently under way.

These arrangements form a solid base for the company's development plans for the future. They start with an aggressive five-year plan for the development of a chain of ten roadside hotels along the Eastern Seaboard of the United States. The first of these facilities is scheduled to open in fall 1986.

Sandman Hotels & Inns has made a quantum leap from one roadside motel to a chain of twenty-one hotels with over 2,000 full- and part-time employees. Its ambitious plans may yet see this Vancouver-based company make significant strides into international markets.

Sandman Inn on Georgia Street, Vancouver.

Revelstoke Sandman Inn.

RENT-A-WRECK

The story of Ed Alfke renting a used car in Hawaii, and how that incident led to Rent-A-Wreck, has been told many times. However, it overlooks the effort that converted an idea into an international business. North Americans had to forget that "new is beautiful" and be encouraged to be practical.

In 1976 Alfke set up a corner-lot operation back home in Prince George. He started with five used cars, and two months later his fleet numbered twenty-six. Within a year he had a franchised outlet in Kamloops and had established the company in Vancouver.

Renting used cars, was a new idea and it brought problems. Alfke instituted a system of management to determine which makes, models, and years were most reliable. He compiled profiles of acceptable cars—and of acceptable customers.

Alfke called the company "Rent-A-Wreck"—a whimsical, attention-getting name but one that the company does not live up to. All rental cars are mechanically sound and between three and five years old. Experience had convinced Alfke to upgrade the cars over the years and they now compare well with those that customers drive at home. Rent-A-Wreck's customer is paying his own bill and therefore wants economy both in price and operation. This has led the company to specialize in mid-size and smaller cars.

Ed Alfke chose the franchise route as a means of expanding company's operations with restricted capital outlay—and expand it did! By 1980 there were forty Rent-A-Wreck offices across Canada and contemporary accounts say "Alfke had shifted the gears of the traditional auto rental industry and perhaps created a new one." The company was seen to be tackling the problem of inflation and the public considered the "Rent-A-Wreck" concept a bargain. Business,

which desperately needed to cut expenses as the recession deepened, became supportive.

As franchises spread across Canada from Vancouver, a national maintenance program was developed with Esso for the rare emergency use by customers. By 1983 Rent-A-Wreck operated more than eighty-six outlets. A toll-free computerized reservation system facilitates advance arrangements for rentals.

Rent-A-Wreck opened its first United States branch in Florida in 1981 and is now represented in nine states. Because Rent-A-Wreck no longer described its services, the company chose the name "Practical" to develop its network in other countries around the world. Practical began establishing outlets in the United Kingdom in 1985, and its success in England has already been recorded in Britain's leading publications.

In addition to expanding its locations, the company's services have broadened to include light-duty and moving trucks as well as all types and shapes of passenger vehicles, some equipped for a family of twelve or for a specific use like a skiing vacation.

In May 1985 Rent-A-Wreck inaugurated its $10-million Practical Rent-A-Car System. It purchased 1,000 new cars from Ford Canada for distribution to 100 Practical franchisees who were chosen exclusively

Ed Alfke, president and founder.

from existing Rent-A-Wreck franchisees. Such was the success of this Practical new car program that Alfke is already planning its expansion.

In ten years Rent-A-Wreck has become an international operation with almost 200 outlets in Canada, the United States, and Britain. Ed Alfke attributes its growth to attention to detail, service orientation, and careful quality control. It is certainly his "system" for success.

The company intends to develop its original system around the world as well as diversify within the fields of its expertise and experience. The diversification will include the making of a public offering in the near future in order for it to capitalize on some of its major opportunities.

Ed Alfke in front of one of the Rent-A-Wreck outlets.

WILKINSON COMPANY LIMITED

An artist's rendering of Wilkinson Company Limited activity in 1910. The painting was commissioned by the firm in 1985 to celebrate its seventy-fifth anniversary.

Most of the steel used to build Vancouver at the beginning of this century was imported from the United States. When Frank Wilkinson came here in 1909 he decided that Western Canada would be a good market for the distribution of steel products.

Wilkinson left his steel-importing employer in Montreal and, with his family, moved west to Vancouver. His first warehouse was a corrugated iron building on Beach Avenue at False Creek and most of his product was imported from the United States—initially on consignment.

Frank Wilkinson was an aggressive manager. In his first nine years the staff increased from five to twelve and annual sales multiplied from $20,000 to $300,000. That growth, however, necessitated larger facilities and the company moved to West Second Avenue.

Frank was succeeded as president by his son, Joseph, in 1949. Grandson Cameron (currently chairman and chief executive officer) joined the firm at that time. Archie St. Louis, who is now president and chief operating officer, had been hired by Cam's father the previous year.

Joseph took advantage of the postwar boom and expanded into Alberta in 1950, opening a modest plant in Edmonton. In 1968 the company moved into a new 40,000-square-foot distribution complex. A sales office was established in Calgary in 1955. A plant opened there in 1961 and was doubled in size five years later.

Cameron Wilkinson assumed the presidency upon the death of his father in 1964. During his tenure growth and change have characterized the company. Customers sought raw materials in semifinished or processed conditions. Significant investments were made in slitting, leveling, sawing, burning, and edge conditioning equipment. He also fostered an enlarged product offering to include aluminum and stainless steel.

In the late 1960s Wilkinson initiated large-scale restructuring of its operations. At that same time it increased its services and customer base. To this day, Wilkinson continues its policy of offering an extensive range of steel and metals to provide "one-stop shopping" for its customers.

Product diversification was accompanied by geographic expansion—into Saskatchewan in 1966, and into Toronto with the 1975 acquisition of Concept Metals Ltd. Plant capacity has been increased in other British Columbia locations, in the Prairies, and in Ontario. A number of corporate acquisitions have been made in the company's 75-year history.

Wilkinson's Vancouver headquarters sits on a seven-acre site on Marine Drive. After two major plant expansions, it now covers 175,000 square feet.

From the strong leadership of St. Louis and Wilkinson to the long-term service of many employees, there is a declared dedication to progress. This commitment and teamwork has helped the firm emerge, leaner and keener, from the recent recession. It explains Wilkinson's comment, "We're a company on the move, with the bad news behind us and the future, ripe with opportunities, ahead of us."

It's 1908 and the automobile has yet to make much of an impact on the city's traffic, even at the corner of Hastings and Granville streets, Vancouver's busiest thoroughfares. (VPL)

PATRONS

The following individuals, companies, and organizations have made a valuable commitment to the quality of this publication. Windsor Publications and the Vancouver Board of Trade gratefully acknowledge their participation in *Vancouver: An Illustrated Chronology.*

Allendale Insurance
The Aluminum Shop*
Ames Bros. Distributors Ltd.*
Andersen Bentley Securities Ltd.
David J. Armstrong
John N. Babcock Insurance Agencies Ltd.
Bank of British Columbia*
The Bank of Nova Scotia*
BCE Development Corporation*
BC Rail Ltd.*
BC Sugar*
Belkin Inc.*
Bow-Wow Parts of B.C. Ltd.
Jack and Doreen Braverman
British Columbia Forest Products Limited*
British Columbia Insurance Company
British Columbia Telephone Company*
Tony A. Bura
Canada Safeway Limited*
Canada Trust
Canadian Home Builders' Association of British Columbia
Canlan Investment Corporation
CAPCO Realty Services Inc.
Capilano Shipping Co. Ltd.
C.H. Cates & Sons Ltd.*
Cavendish Financial Corporation
Century 21 Real Estate Canada Ltd.*
Chevron Canada Limited*
CIBC Mortgage Corporation
Colliers Macaulay Nicolls Inc.
Coopers & Lybrand*
CP Rail*
Dairyland Foods*
Dexter Associates Realty Ltd.
EBCO Industries Ltd.*
elan Data Makers
Empire Stevedoring Company Limited*

Farwest Systems Corporation*
First Generation Capital Corporation
Fleetham Storage & Services Ltd.
Forest Lawn Memorial Park*
A.J. Forsyth & Company Limited
Four Seasons Hotels Limited*
Dr. Eric G. Gable
Gama Construction Ltd.
Gamble Foods Ltd.
Gray Beverage Company Ltd.*
The Great-West Life Assurance Company
Guaranty Trust Company of Canada
Hotel Vancouver
Jones Tent & Awning Ltd.*
Keefer Laundry Ltd.*
Kelly, Douglas & Company, Limited*
The Laurentian Group*
Lavalin Inc.
H.Y. Louie Co. Limited*
McDonald's Restaurants of Canada Limited*
Marathon Realty Company Limited*
Mascot Gold Mines Limited
William M. Mercer Limited*
Metro Canada International Limited
Microtel*
Miloni Food Importers Ltd.*
Ming Court Hotel, Vancouver
Mobile Data International Inc.*
Mohawk Oil Co. Ltd.*
Mointra Services Inc.
Montreal Shipping Inc.
The North American Group*
Overwaitea Foods Save-On-Foods*
Pacific Coast Mutual Marine Insurance Co.
Park Royal Hotel
Pemberton Houston Willoughby*
Reed Stenhouse Limited*
Reliance Insurance Agencies Ltd.
Rent-A-Wreck System of Canada Ltd.*
Sandman Hotels & Inns*
Seaboard Lumber Sales Company Limited Seaboard Shipping Company Limited*
Showa Maritime Canada Ltd.
H.A. Simons (Overseas) Ltd.
Speiser Furs Ltd.*
Star Shipping (Canada) Ltd.

John J. Sutherland, Jr.
Swedish Consulate
Synertech Systems Corporation
Joan E. Taylor
Teck Corporation
Teleconsult Limited
Texada Lime
Thorne Riddell*
Titan Steel & Co. Ltd.
Trans Canada Glass Group*
Van Waters & Rogers Ltd.*
Vancouver Auto Ltd.*
Vancouver Centennial Commission
Vancouver Port Corporation*
Versatile Pacific Shipyards Inc.*
Waisman Dewar Grout Carter Architects & Planners
Western Airlines
Western Canadian Land Corp.
Western Management Consultants
Westminster Management Corporation
White Spot Limited*
Wilkinson Company Limited*
Williams Moving & Storage (B.C.) Ltd.*
Woodward's Limited*
The Wyatt Company
Yada Tompkins Humphries Palmer & Co. Chartered Accountants
Yorkshire Trust Company*

*Partners in Progress of *Vancouver: An Illustrated Chronology.* The histories of these companies and organizations appear in Chapter VII, beginning on page 208.

The centre field bleachers at Athletic Park were packed August 23, 1924, for the game between Hammond and the Young Liberals. These were the cheap seats, and every kid there dreamed of catching a home run ball. Courtesy, City of Vancouver Archives

Advisory Committee

Windsor Publications and The Vancouver Board of Trade wish to thank the following people for their valuable assistance in the preparation of this book:

Robert G. Bentall
The Hon. John V. Clyne
Graham R. Dawson
Frank A. Griffiths CA
Arthur S. Hara
Gerald P. Haslam
Dr. Walter Koerner
Gordon F. MacFarlane
James A. Pattison
Gordon A. Thom
W. Robert Wyman

INDEX